MURMURINGS OF
A LICENSED
HERETIC

CHAIM BERMANT

MURMURINGS OF
A LICENSED
HERETIC

PETER HALBAN
LONDON

FIRST PUBLISHED IN GREAT BRITAIN BY
PETER HALBAN PUBLISHERS LTD
42 South Molton Street
London W1Y 1HB
1990

British Library Cataloguing in Publication Data

Bermant, Chaim 1929–
Murmurings of a licensed heretic.
I. Title
828.91407
ISBN 1-870015-34-7

Phototypeset by Computape (Pickering) Ltd, North Yorkshire
Printed in Great Britain by
WBC Ltd, Bridgend

Acknowledgements

The articles in this collection have all enjoyed an earlier incarnation in a number of publications, including *The Daily Telegraph*, *The Guardian*, *The Independent*, *The Israel Economist*, the *Jewish Chronicle*, the *London Daily News*, the *Observer*, *Present Tense*, *The Spectator* and *The Times* and I am grateful to their respective editors for permission to use them.

The *London Daily News* and *Present Tense* are now, alas, no more. I hope my contribution did nothing to hasten their demise.

Contents

Of People

Of Places

Of Zion and Zionism

Of Politics and Politicians

Of This and That

Introduction

The spoken word dies the moment is it uttered, the written word lives, but not if it's confined to newspapers, and journalists are often tempted to disinter their work and give it lasting form behind hard covers. It may suggest a certain vanity, but it answers to a perfectly natural craving for immortality.

Cynics might suggest that it answers to an even more natural craving for cash, for one is being paid and repaid for the same articles, or, as has been said in another context, "you got it, you sell it, you still got it", but no matter how highly journalists may regard their own work, few of them care to re-read it and the sort of royalties they might receive are totally unrelated to the effort involved. It is often less tiresome to write a new article than to re-read an old one. Almost every writer goes through the same stages; the agitation as he starts (wondering if he has anything to say); the cogitation as he continues (wondering how best to say it); the euphoria of the first reading; the despair at the next one. To re-read one's own work after a long interval is to suffer the despair without enjoying the euphoria.

I have been a journalist for thirty years but have rarely had to deal with hard news, or even soft news, and I have, so to speak, stood aside to comment on events after—sometimes three thousand years after—they occurred, which has sometimes helped me view them in perspective, but that alone does not constitute a claim to permanence.

In an average week I contribute about 3,000 words to one paper or another, or about 150,000 words a year, or nearly 5,000,000 words in thirty years. (I also write a book a year, but that is beside the point.) In compiling this anthology I have had to read through them all, and in doing so I began to marvel not only at my own industry, but at the indulgence of my editors.

Chaim Bermant

In writing a book—at least for a British publisher—one is master of one's own work. It may be accepted or rejected, but one has the last word. Writing for newspapers is quite another matter. Whatever happens the editor, sometimes buttressed by libel lawyers, has the last word. As a result some of my pieces were mauled, and some were spiked, but as I waded through the rest I occasionally wondered if the editors had not spiked the wrong ones, for I blushed at some of the articles which got through.

I cannot even claim in mitigation that they were produced at short notice and had to be rushed, for journalism necessarily is rushed, and in any case the quality of written work rarely corresponds to the time spent on it.

The value of journalism to the professional writer—apart from the fact that it is comparatively lucrative—is the discipline. One has to say as much as possible in as few words as possible, in as short a time as possible, not infrequently, under trying conditions. One of the best stories I ever filed was not so much written as shouted over a bad line, while shells shrieked overhead and the ground quaked under my feet.

The prospect of a deadline concentrates the mind wonderfully. The time one needs to write an article expands with the time one has to write it and like most journalists I leave everything to the last minute.

I am not sure if it's true that everyone has a good book in him, or even a bad one, but I do believe that anyone who has written 5,000,000 words should be able to extract two or three good books from it, otherwise he should never have started.

One likes to think that one improves with age and one of the depressing things about re-reading old work is to discover that one can also deteriorate. One loses the confident assertiveness and lively impudence of youth, observations become more qualified, one's language less shrill, but these are not necessarily improvements, yet one tends to favour one's later work much as one tends to favour one's younger children. Some of the pieces in this book go back to the early sixties, most of them were written in the past five or six years.

"Cassandra", the prince of newspaper columnists, once said to me, "never praise because you will almost certainly be proved wrong", and he was right, but I like to praise where possible because I like to be liked, and even where one is proved wrong, it is better to give unfounded praise than unfounded censure, if only because one is less likely to be sued for libel.

The trouble is that occasions for praise are rare, while those for censure are frequent. There is also the temptation to be clever, for one can have more fun, and be infinitely more amusing, in demolishing a reputation, especially a spurious one, than in enhancing it, and after a time criticism becomes a habit of mind.

And not only among journalists. My late father was a Rabbi and, but for the grace of God, I might have been one myself, for I received something of a rabbinical training. There is among Jews a tradition of reproof going back to the Prophets, and beyond them, to Moses and a congregation which has not been roundly berated in the course of a sermon can sometimes feel short-changed, and to the habits of the journalist I have added those of the Rabbi.

Of the many pieces in this book, most derive from a column I have been writing in the *Jewish Chronicle* for the past thirty years. I have in some respects used my column as a pulpit, except that where a Rabbi may claim the mantle of the Prophets and draw on the authority of Heaven, a Rabbi-manqué cannot. My comments have not always made me popular and I have even been denounced from the pulpit of my own synagogue, but then a journalist, or, indeed, a Rabbi, who has never made an enemy has not done an honest job.

I am usually forgiven my comments on domestic issues and my troubles have arisen mainly from my reservations about Israel. It is not that every Jew is happy with what is going on in Israel, but most seem to feel that Jewish commentators have no right to criticise her publicly, especially when she is under attack from other quarters, which is almost another way of saying that Jews shouldn't be journalists.

My own feeling is that Jewish commentators not only have the right, but the duty to do so, especially where they are personally involved in the fortunes of Israel.

I am not sure if Israel is central to the life of the Jewish people, but she has always been central to mine. I have studied there, worked there, and—as the contents of this book may show—lived there at various times. My married daughter has made her home there, and it is likely that my other three children will follow her example, so that my observations on Israel and my reservations about its policies, if strongly put, arise out of acute personal concern.

I also think that the sort of sacrifices, the dreams, the prayers, the hopes which went into making Israel could never be justified if she was to be merely a state like any other. She came into being in unique circumstances, survived against unique odds and has, for better or worse, established a unique claim upon the attention of the world, and if she has received more than her share of censure, it is partly because she has, so far, fallen short of the expectations she aroused. To draw attention to her shortcomings is not to question her achievements, but one has a right to expect more of her because she expects more of herself.

I have always felt that a good journalist should, given a certain modicum of notice, be able to turn his hand to any topic, drawing, where necessary, on the expertise of others, and the process of writing is, in some respects, a prolonged process of learning. It doesn't make one an oracle, but one can become a repository of stray facts knowing something about everything and everything about nothing, and it is therefore useful to acquire certain areas of expertise oneself.

The danger—especially to a freelance—of acquiring an expertise in a particular field is that one is thought of almost exclusively in that context and editors turn to me mainly when Israel or Jews are in the news—as they often are—and the two tend to dominate these pages. It does not, however, mean that I'm presenting a succession of weighty religious and political tracts.

J.B. Morton (the immortal "Beachcomber" of the *Daily Express*) once observed: "The English are a good-natured people. They like their humour to be pleasant, easy-going, innocuous. For this reason it is an advantage to a humorist who aims at a wide public to conceal any strong convictions he may have, and a greater advantage to have no strong convictions at all." He did not, however, suggest that where one has strong convictions it is an advantage to conceal one's sense of humour. There is a light side to Jewish life and a hilarious side to Israeli life, and even the gravest issues can be, and perhaps should be, touched on lightly.

I have few rare experiences to describe, but one can have rare responses to commonplace events.

I was born in a part of Lithuania which was then Poland, later became Russia and is now again Lithuania. When I was three we moved to Latvia (which is now Russia); when I was seven I went to live with my grandmother in Poland; when I was nine we moved to Scotland; I settled for a time in Israel, and now live in England. In Latvia I was a Pole, in Poland a Latvian, in Scotland a foreigner and in Israel a Scot. I don't even have a defined place in Jewish society, for I combine liberal sentiments with a conservative disposition, so that, for example, while I can see no reason on earth, or, indeed, in heaven, why one shouldn't have women rabbis, I would run a mile at the sight of one. I may be critical of Orthodox ideas, but would oppose any serious abrogation of Orthodox usage and I found myself defending not only the Jewish Sabbath, but the Christian one. Habit is the better part of faith, or at least the better part of my faith. If I can't hang my coat on my usual coat-peg in synagogue, my day is half ruined.

In other words, whatever I am, and wherever I've been, I have remained an outsider even among outsiders, which has possibly given me a slant denied to others and which may be evident in these pages.

I spent the most formative years of my life in Glasgow and keep returning to it on every pretext like a criminal to the scene of his crimes. I like travel, and so include the occasional excursion to far away places. I am interested in archaeology and was one of the first journalists to describe the epoch-making excavations at Ebla in any detail. I write rather a lot about money and greed and lust. I am extremely fond of food and wine, especially when it is paid for by others, and I therefore include some essays on gluttony, and, as I have suggested earlier, the very attempt to fob off the reader with articles that have already been published might look like an essay in sloth. In fact all the deadly sins are here, though I hope I have avoided most of the deadly virtues.

Not every act of writing is creative, but it is almost inevitably presumptuous, for one sets out with the notion that one has something new to say, or a new way of saying it. One doesn't always succeed, but I hope I have done so with sufficient frequency to justify this book.

Of Family
and Self

Time of Arrival

"I HEARD YOU were on one of the children's transports fifty years ago," began the woman, and even before she could finish, all the familiar resentments came flooding back.

"No," I could almost hear myself saying, "I didn't come on the children's transports. I came with Thomas Cook."

I owed my good fortune to a misfortune. My father, who was Russian, fell out with the authorities of the Latvian shtetl where we lived, and they cancelled his labour permit—which, for a man with a wife and four children, was a calamity.

He turned in all directions for help and eventually found work as a shochet in Glasgow. He went out in 1937 and a year later he sent us tickets to follow him.

I remember the tickets to this day. Each had a yellow cover, like a small book, with the name Thos Cook & Sons printed on the outside.

I approached Glasgow with some apprehension. In the course of my young life I had already attended the village school in Latvia and a Jewish school in Poland. In Latvia, I was persecuted because I was Jewish; in Poland, I was persecuted because I was Latvian.

Once in Glasgow, I glumly resigned myself to persecution on both counts—and perhaps also as a Pole. Instead, I became a star.

I spoke only Yiddish and was taken under the perfumed wing of a tall, elegant woman whom the boys called Big Aggie. She knew German, so that we were able to communicate after a fashion.

There was a large map on the wall and, with a long pointer, she showed the class where I came from. It was right at the other end of Europe.

Thirty tousled heads turned in my direction, eyes large with awe,

3

and I did my best to look nonchalant.

I was pointed out in the playground, and in the street. I was invited to parties. I became a local celebrity.

Then, one morning, a strange new figure appeared in the playground and, even before I knew who he was, I sensed that my status was under threat.

He was not so much a boy as a compact little man, with neatly brushed hair, a stern expression, rimless glasses, and the sort of scrubbed, polished look one didn't associate with school playgrounds.

His name was Heini and he was from Vienna. Possibly because his German was a good deal more intelligible than my Yiddish, he immediately displaced me in Big Aggie's affections.

Worse was to follow. In the next week or two, other Heinis appeared, all of them well scrubbed and neatly attired. Big Aggie announced that she was forming a special class for "the refugees".

By then I knew enough English to understand the word and had enough *amour propre* to take offence. "I am not a refugee," I protested, half in English, half in Yiddish, and half tearfully. "I came with Thomas Cook . . ."

It didn't help, and I had to troop along to a small room, where we were given special lessons. The Heinis picked up English in a matter of days; I took rather longer.

They soon shot to the top of the class; I hovered near the bottom, which made my status as a non-refugee and as a fully paid-up client of Messrs Thos Cook & Sons all the more precious.

Early in the new year, our synagogue organised a special treat for the newcomers to which all the youngsters in the neighbourhood were invited. I thought I had turned native by then and took my seat in the body of the hall with the rest of the boys, until a plump, harassed figure with goitrous eyes and breathless voice poked me in the ribs and ordered me to join "the refugees".

"But I'm not a refugee . . . Thomas Cook."

It all fell on deaf ears and I eventually gave up.

About thirty years later, after I had written a book set in Glasgow, I was invited for an interview on Scottish Television. I was picked up at the airport in a large car, lodged in a first-class hotel, treated to a first-class meal, and made to feel like a Very Important Person.

I was a celebrity again, and when I was led into the television studio and settled under the arc lights in a comfortable chair, I could

4

almost sense the spirit of Big Aggie hovering over me.

I chatted amiably with the interviewer for a minute or two. A red light flashed—we were on the air..

"I believe," the interviewer began, "that you first came to Glasgow as a refugee . . ."

Jewish Chronicle, 6 January 1989

Thumper

STOPP, THE SOCIETY of Teachers Opposed to Physical Punishment, is alarmed by reports of cruelty in Muslim religious classes. "Many cases involving Muslim children suffering severe punishment do not come to light," said one of their spokesmen. "We have written to the Yorkshire police in relation to a case where six boys were reported to have been injured by priests using sticks." And, as if to confirm the allegations, a *Sunday Times* reporter who visited a Muslim school in Birmingham, saw "six religious teachers each brandishing a long stick made of hardened plastic. Several children were struck with the stick while others were slapped on the head and back."

Gevald! If I could claim a pound, or even a shekel, for every time I was beaten, thumped, walloped, whacked, tanned, leathered, clobbered or cuffed during my cheder days, I would be a rich man by now, or at least solvent—and I was one of the good boys, a rabbi's son, no less.

My first teacher was Moishe Yudeh, a silent man with a long, sad face, made sadder and longer with a grey beard which turned white 'ere I was out of his class, and who hated teaching almost as much as we hated being taught. He was not, however, a cruel man and administered blows not by way of punishment, but as a study-aid in the belief that a fact was best driven home with a clout round the ears or a thump between the shoulder blades, and we would go through the weekly sidra, thus: "In the beginning" (thump!), "God" (thump!), "created" (thump!), "the heavens" (thump!), "and the earth" (thump, larrup, whack!), so by the time God rested and was satisfied, we were all black and blue. Many years later when I saw a pile-driver at work on a London bomb-site, I was reminded of Moishe Yudeh.

His successor, a stocky figure with bulging eyes, was, I suspect, a closet liberal, for he was clean shaven and did not believe in physical punishment. He would send any miscreant out of the room, so that by the end of the lesson there would be more boys out of the room than in it, and not infrequently he was left on his own.

In spite of his principles, he could, if sufficiently needled (and we made it our business to needle him sufficiently), fly into rages and would change from a waxen yellow, to a reddish pink, and finally to a deep purple, at which point we would dive for cover, for he could wade in at us with both his fists and sometimes his boots. A kindly man at the end of his tether is a dangerous thing.

It would never have occurred to us to complain, for suffering was the badge of our tribe, and had we exposed our bruises to our parents, the chances are they would have added to them, though I have no reason to believe that they loved us any less than we love our children. Moreover, our punishment was often richly deserved.

One often hears of the cruelties suffered by pupils, but never of the torments inflicted on teachers, though the cruelties are inherent in the situation. One attends cheder (and the same is, of course, true of Muslim religious classes) after a day at school, by which time few boys are on their best behaviour, and they seek moments of relief in baiting their teachers.

In my time in Glasgow there was an elderly rabbi who could never get a job as a minister because his English was inadequate for the kingmakers of the city (whose English, needless to say, was even more inadequate), though as a man and a scholar he was head and shoulders above those of his contemporaries who did speak "a gutten Englis", and, to eke out a livelihood, he turned to cheder teaching, where he suffered a daily martyrdom. His main tormentor, now a distinguished professor at the Hadassah Hospital, Jerusalem, had a giggling habit, which annoyed the rabbi, and to make him stop he would twist his ear. But the tighter the rabbi turned the ear, the more the boy giggled until, finally, it began to come away in his hand and we nearly had a Van Gogh in our class.

One does not, of course, condone the rabbi, but if there is anyone to be condemned it was the elders of the community for exposing such a man to the tender mercies of small boys. I suspect that the mullahs complained of in the *Sunday Times* are suffering the same sort of martyrdom as that rabbi.

Jewish Chronicle, 15 August 1986

Absent Without Leave

I RECENTLY MET up with some old friends and, as old friends will, we began talking about old times and I mentioned that I was expelled from school, to which one of them said: "But how could you have been? You were never there"—which is exactly why I was expelled.

The school was Queen's Park, Glasgow, a vast establishment with over a thousand pupils—the then equivalent of a comprehensive—founded in 1871 and housed in four huge, workhouse-type buildings.

At first I was one of the good boys, but it wasn't all that difficult to be good, for the war was on (World War II, that is), all the younger, abler and stricter masters were in the forces, and the school was largely in the hands of elderly dames, or old crocks with nodding heads who had been brought out of retirement. So the regime was fairly relaxed.

It was a mixed school, but I have only the vaguest recollection of female contemporaries, for my tastes ran to older, more mature women. In particular I was obsessed with one of the teachers, Alison Kidd, a handsome, rather large, but well-proportioned woman with sleepy grey eyes and an uncommonly varied and elegant wardrobe; for, wartime or not, she never wore the same outfit two days running, whereas the other mistresses were frumpish old dears who looked as if they were clad in their mothers' cast-offs (and probably were).

She taught English, my favourite subject, though I'm still not sure whether my passion for English was due to my passion for Alison Kidd, or vice versa. I was a foreign boy and had only recently acquired the use of the language. My knowledge of English literature was woefully inadequate and she had given me a special reading list so that I might catch up on the rest of the class. I caught up mainly in class—whether the lesson was geography or maths, physics or chem-

8

istry, I would sit in the back row and work my way unobtrusively through the English classics.

Then came peace, and my tranquil existence was shattered. Tanned, brawny figures appeared, ex-Majors, Squadron-Leaders, Lt. Commanders, who were determined to impose a new order and, by God, they did. One was suddenly expected to know trigonometry, and Boyle's Law and explain the intricacies of Humboldt's current. One was given homework, and lots of it, which had to be prepared neatly, and handed in on time. And if it was not done, or not done neatly, or on time, there was the strap, a leather tawse, about half an inch thick and fringed at the end. Administered by a dame, it tickled: administered by an ex-Major, one was marked for life. There was no escaping the new order, except in escape from school.

I would have breakfast as usual, set off down the road as usual, but instead of crossing to the island site occupied by the school, I would jump on a bus to town. I was often accompanied by Julian, a friend, who, though a class below me, felt with every justification that school had nothing to teach him (he is now professor of physiology at Stanford University) and we spent our day in the Mitchell Library, which is the most pleasant and, with the possible exception of the London Library, the most helpful library I have ever used.

My absences, of course, did not go unnoticed. I was invariably caught and punished, until I learned an important lesson: if you are out to do something you shouldn't, do it on a large scale. And thus, instead of taking off a morning here, and an afternoon there, and getting caught and punished in the process, I did not register at all when the school resumed after Christmas, and for three glorious months I was free to continue my education in the Mitchell Library with impunity. I read, I wrote and met with Julian and other fellow truants in a nearby tea-room for a coffee and a smoke (as the Talmud hath it: "Sin begets sin").

Then one afternoon as I was hurrying home, I was knocked down by a bus. It did not go right over me, but knocked me sideways into the path of a motor-bike, which did. I was bleeding and bruised, and felt as if my skull was coming apart like the two sides of a walnut, which was substantially what had happened. All this occurred within sight of a hospital. I put one hand to my head, the other to my side and hobbled over to the casualty department, where they washed me down, painted my wounds with purple dye, patched me up, and sent me home.

Chaim Bermant

I had come home in such a state before, after a game of rugby. Mother took one look at me and assumed that the same had happened again. Before I could stop her, she stormed over to the school, confronted the headmaster and demanded to know how he could allow his pupils to be mutilated and maimed on the playing fields. Whereupon he woke up to the fact that I had not been in the school for the better part of a term.

My crime was announced at school assembly a few days later, and so was the inevitable penalty. A thousand heads turned in my direction and a murmur went up as my name was read out—for a passing moment I was snatched out of anonymity. Nothing in my school life became me like the leaving it, and even then I was upstaged by another boy who was expelled for passing betting slips.

Observer, 25 July 1982

L'Chaim

I THINK I'LL change my name.

The first name I answered to sounded something like Chaimyitze, which I soon recognised as Chaim Itze. When I learned to read, I discovered that my actual name, as written on my birth certificate, was Chaim Icyk, which was the local rendering of Chaim Isaac. All that was in Latvia.

When we settled in Scotland, we were hemmed in on all sides by well-meaning people who wanted to help us adapt to our new homeland.

Today, green is all the rage and it carries benign connotations as the very symbol of life, fertility, freshness. In those days, it represented a form of original sin.

To be green was to be foreign, alien, outlandish, a *shlepper*. I was advised that even if I couldn't help looking like a "greener", I didn't have to sound like one and that I couldn't go around calling myself Chaim Itze, or even Chaim.

"You've got to have a good Englisher name," I was told.

"Such as what?"

"Such as Hymie."

Who was I—or rather, who were my parents—to question the wisdom of old families who could trace their British roots back to 1920, or even 1912? And so Hymie I became, and Hymie I remained for the next 20 years.

If I didn't particularly love the name, at least I preferred it to the other alternatives suggested, such as Claude, or Cecil, or Clarence, or Vivian (which in any case sounded like a girl's name). But when I began to appear in print, I decided to revert to Chaim.

It is not, I will admit, a name which fits easily on the English

11

tongue, and on the odd occasions I have been interviewed on the radio or television, I have variously been called Chaim (to rhyme with claim), Shame, Hyam (which almost caused me to burst into song: "'Enery the eighth Hyam, Hyam, 'Enery the eighth Hyam"), Khaim and even Khayam, the last of which led me to contemplate the possibility of writing *The Rubáiyát of Omar Chaim*.

Yet I like the name and its festive associations and it's nice to think that one's name is evoked wherever two or three Jews forgather to celebrate. Moreover, coupled with Itze or Isaac it means "life" and "laughter", and I have done my best to live up to both.

It is also a fairly uncommon name, at least in England, and the only other Chaims I had heard of when I moved to London were Chaim Raphael the scribe and Chaim Pearl the rabbi, so that I was in select company.

Why, then, am I thinking of changing my name? Because I am often in Israel, and in Israel every Tom, Dick and Harry is called Chaim.

But worse than that. Chaim is the name they call people whose names they don't know but whose attention they want to attract, like Mac or Jimmy in Glasgow.

As a result, every time I set foot in Jerusalem or Tel Aviv, the streets ring with my name and I keep turning my face in every direction, and it's Chaim here, Chaim there, Chaim, Chaim everywhere, like Figaro in the "Barber of Seville".

There is, in fact, a perfectly sound Hebrew name for somebody nameless and it is Ploni Almoni, but it is possibly too much of a mouthful for contemporary tongues and I have never heard it used in public.

In Yiddish, the generic name for the Jew in the street is Chaim Yankel and I suppose the popularity of Chaim owes something to the resuscitation of Yiddish.

I suspect that the fact that the President of Israel is called Chaim may also have something to do with it (though in an earlier incarnation he was known as Vivian, which must have been awkward when he served in a kilted regiment during the war).

Yet, where almost everybody has, or is called by, the same name, one is left virtually nameless. One can see it at its worst among Arabs. Once, on an archaeological dig in Syria, I called out for someone named Mohammed, and at once two hundred dusky faces looked up from the trenches.

No one who writes for a living cares for anonymity and I have thought of changing my name to Habakuk, a prophet I much admire, or Zephania; but even there, given the common tendency to abbreviation, I would probably be called Hab, or Zeph, or even Fanny.

It would also mean printing new letterheads and visiting-cards, so on balance, I suppose, I had better stick to Chaim.

Jewish Chronicle, 21 April 1989

Pains and Penalties

I SUFFER FROM a small but painful complaint. I would not be so indelicate as to say where it hurts, but hurt it does and, as I'm a writer by profession, I sometimes have to use my word-processor standing up or lying on my stomach.

As various medications had no effect, my doctor sent me to a surgeon at a London teaching hospital to get to the bottom of it.

He gave me a brisk but thorough examination with something like a periscope, inviting his students to have a good look. "A very interesting condition," he said, "very interesting," and they all agreed.

I hoped he might whip out his cutlery and clear up the matter there and then, but that's not how they do things under the NHS and I was placed on his waiting list.

That was in February 1986. Spring and summer passed, autumn followed and I waited in growing discomfort and despair. Early in the new year, my doctor phoned the hospital to ask what was happening.

"Bermant?" they said, "what Bermant?"

They had lost my records. They were not particularly abashed about it for, apparently, it happens all the time and I dare say losing a record is not half as bad as losing a patient. But it is annoying.

We may have superb doctors and nurses, but the administration in some areas constitutes an immediate health hazard and I half suspect they tear up hospital records for confetti.

They were apologetic and, by way of compensation, I was placed near the top of the queue, and on February 16—a year since I first saw the consultant—I was asked to come in for the operation.

At last! I immediately cancelled all my engagements and celebrated

14

with a coming-out, or rather going-in, party. But comes the day and, just as I was packing, I was told that there was no bed available. There was a red alert, or perhaps only a pink one, but in any case the hospital had been overwhelmed by a sudden inrush of geriatric patients.

On April 13 I was summoned again. By then, however, I was down with my annual bout of flu and couldn't go in, though from what I gather there wouldn't have been a bed available in any case, for half of north London was down with the flu, while the other half was down with pneumonia and there was a further inrush of geriatric patients.

(From which you may infer that I've got something against the aged, but on the contrary: I wish them the best of health—at least until my operation is over.)

On 4 May I was summoned a third time. I had grown wiser by then and did not cancel my engagements. Nor did I pack for, as I anticipated, there was again an alert of some sort, this time of indeterminate colour. I suggested that I bring in a sleeping bag and camp out on the floor, but my offer was not taken up.

Fifteen months have now passed since my consultation. No one has died from my condition—as yet—so I'm not what might be called an urgent case and I've been given tablets to deaden the pain. They also deaden me, and I've hardly been able to work. Once self-employed, I am now, virtually, self-unemployed.

What do I do? Wait till I'm bankrupt, or bankrupt myself and have it done privately?

I am undecided but I have one hope to sustain me: if this goes on for much longer I should be able to claim a bed as a geriatric patient.

London Daily News, 1 June 1987

Muffed It!

I RECENTLY HAD a chance to play the hero, and muffed it.

I have the good fortune to live in what is perhaps the quietest and most charming suburb in London. Apart from occasional burglaries there is little to disturb the even tenor of life—or at least the even tenor of my life. My busy day is usually Thursday, when I summon sufficient energy to go to the local post office to buy stamps and send parcels, and it was there, of all places, that my chance came.

I had just joined a lengthy queue when a young man in a grubby boiler-suit pulled out a gun. He motioned to a postman who had brought in some mailbags to go outside. He didn't push the man or raise his voice; but for the gun in his hand, he might have been asking him out for a drink.

I am not sure if anyone else realized what was happening, for if they did, they were phlegmatic about it. Counter staff continued to serve customers, people continued to buy stamps and post letters, while the queue edged steadily forward. But I, moved more by curiosity than anything else, went outside, and saw three men lined up against the side of a mail van with their hands in the air.

The gunman, with pistol still in hand, was threatening the driver. The man was lean, about 5ft 10in., youngish, with ginger hair and a ginger moustache. He had his back half turned to me—I was about five yards behind him.

As far as I could see, the gunman had no accomplice. I am large and rather heavy. It would not have been difficult for me to jump on him and—with the help of the postmen—disarm him.

Why didn't I? It is not always easy for a man to know his own motives, but one reason, certainly, was that I couldn't quite believe it was happening. From what I could see, neither could the postmen, for they stood there grinning sheepishly, like badly rehearsed extras in an Ealing comedy. In fact I looked around half-expecting to see a film crew, and if I did nothing it was at least partly because I was afraid of making a fool of myself.

Wasn't I afraid of the gun? I don't think I was. Fear and intrepidity are contagious. I have only been under fire once in my life, and that in the company of hardened newsmen, and I wasn't nearly as nervous as I thought I would be.

To the postmen lined up against the van it was, apparently, all in a day's work, for although they did as they were told, there was nothing in their manner to suggest alarm or stress. Moreover, the gun was so small and toy-like that it did not seem lethal, and in so far as it did, it was difficult to imagine that the young man would pull the trigger. He looked like a mechanic from the garage next door. Yet I stood there gaping, silent, inert.

I like to think that if there had been shouting, violence, bloodshed I might have been galvanized into action (or flight), but the episode seemed so devoid of menace or noise and was over so quickly that there was little scope either for heroics or cowardice. Both call for a sense of occasion, and there was none.

The whole incident could not have lasted more than two to three minutes. The gunman grabbed some metal cash boxes and fled, and it was only when the postmen ran after him that I emerged from my stupor and joined the chase. I don't know what I would have done if we had actually caught up with him, but he turned out to have an accomplice waiting in a car, and disappeared.

When I returned breathless to the post office two young constables were questioning bystanders. A little later a police car pulled up, then a police van with dog handlers. Finally there arrived some plain-clothed men in a plain-clothed car, who questioned me at length, while people in the post office queue gave me dark looks, no doubt thinking that I was the culprit.

By the time I got home some helpful soul had already telephoned my wife to say I was having trouble with the police. It was all rather ignominious, but I dare say I should be able to dine out on it.

The Times, 30 July 1987

Snuffed it!

THERE'S A SNUFF-BOX exhibition at the Church Farm Museum, Hendon, until 2 August—not only boxes, but bottles, Toby jugs, horns, barrels and shoes, all quite exquisite and all designed to hold snuff, but with not a pinch among them. It's a little like a bottle exhibition without a drop to drink.

Happily, a good Samaritan, noting my disappointment, pulled a small box from his pocket and offered me a noseful. He was to regret his kindness, for, given the size of my nose, I inhaled most of the box. I had forgotten the first rule of snuff-taking, which is gently does it.

One taps the lid to let the snuff settle down. One then opens it gently, away from any draught, and takes the tiniest pinch between thumb and forefinger thus, and, with a graceful twirl of the wrist and the elbow fully extended, one applies it first to the left nostril and then to the right (or vice versa) and shuts one's eyes to take in the full force of the ecstasy.

Snuff to me is what the madeleine was to Proust. I only need to take one sniff and I'm wafted back to a small village in Latvia where my father was Rabbi.

On Yom Kippur we spent the entire day (as one still does) in synagogue in fasting and prayer. One is not allowed to eat or drink, but one is allowed to breathe. About three in the afternoon, when the going got heavy, father would extract a box of snuff—a delicate little thing, made of polished olive wood—from the voluminous folds of his prayer-shawl, take a pinch himself, then pass it round among the faithful almost as an act of communion. They would respond with a chorus of sneezes like a moist amen.

A good whiff clears the mind (too good a whiff can sometimes blow it), and father, who also functioned as an ecclesiastical judge, would reach for his snuff-box whenever he was faced with a tricky problem. He sometimes used it as a study aid and the pages of his Talmud, always open before him, were freckled with it.

There were three main varieties of snuff—coarse, medium and refined—and it came in about a dozen flavours—jasmine, sandal-wood, eucalyptus, menthol, lavender, lemon and, for all I know, chocolate, strawberry and vanilla.

The variety favoured by my father had a mild medicinal tang and was even said to be food for the lungs. Mother had her doubts on the matter but, as she said, even if it was good for the lungs, it was bad for the linen, and when we moved to Glasgow shortly before the war, he was persuaded to give up the habit. "Snuff is for foreigners," he was told.

When I became familiar with British history I discovered that snuff, which I had associated exclusively with synagogues and prayers and Jews, was all the rage in 18th-century England. But there was a snuff famine in 20th-century Scotland, and when I tried to buy some from our local tobacconist, he looked at me as if I had asked for hashish.

Later, when I moved to London, one could still find a few East End synagogues with decrepit figures scattered among the pews who might refresh themselves with the occasional pinch of snuff. But that was long ago. The synagogues are now mosques and I rather fear the last of the snuff-sniffers have sniffed their last.

London Daily News, 27 June 1987

All Present and Correct

WE HAVE A division of labour in our family. My wife picks wedding presents and I pick barmitzvah presents, so that we can approach every *simcha* with perfect equanimity and no crisis over what to give whom.

In recent years my own choice of present has been fairly standardised, for apart from anything else barmitzvah boys too are fairly standardised: they're all boys, all Jewish (or nearly all), all 13. When I was 13 the presents I most appreciated (apart from actual hard cash) were books, and so I have also sent books, or, to be more precise, a book, one of my own, a study of Israel with lavish illustrations, so that those barmitzvah boys who have not yet learned to read can at least have the pleasure of looking.

A gift, we are often told, should express something of the personality of the donor, and what is more expressive than his own creation, the sweat of his brow crystallised in print? I must have disposed of a goodly part of the edition in this way. And if you should happen to see a copy of my Israel book in a Jewish home, the chances are that I've been to their barmitzvah.

I did not mention any of this to my wife in case she should have reservations on the subject (like most women she has reservations about most things). But a few weeks ago we had coffee at a friend's house, and there on the coffee table, amid the silver milk jugs and the brown sugar, was a copy of my very own book staring at us, and almost winking at me. I tried unobtrusively to push it out of sight, but I was obtrusive in my unobtrusiveness. My wife picked it up, opened it, and there it was, on the fly leaf, in black and white: *To ——, on his barmitzvah, with best wishes from Chaim and Mrs. Bermant and family.*

"How could you?" she later remonstrated. "Your *own* book."

I thought there was something original in giving of one's own, and I reminded her of our wedding, and the drapery we received from the drapers, and the napkin rings from the jewellers, and the fancy-goods from the fancy-goods merchants, all of them perfectly acceptable presents. "And don't the Rothschilds sent money?" I added in a moment of inspiration. "Well I'm in the book business and I send books."

"Lord Sieff doesn't send St Michael's underwear," she said.

"Lord Sieff can afford not to," I said. "Besides, how do you know he doesn't?"

But she would not be convinced.

"How would you like it," she said, "if a rabbi had sent you a copy of his collected sermons as a barmitzvah present?"

Now she had a point there, for as a matter of fact a number of rabbis, perhaps believing that I too was destined for the cloth, had sent me their collected sermons, and though I remember that they had fine bindings I do not recall that they were among my most cherished possessions.

On the other hand, though I do not make extravagant claims for my work, I ventured to suggest that it was probably more interesting than a collection of sermons. Apart from anything else it had pictures, which sermons do not.

"But it's the principle of the thing," she insisted. "You can't send your *own* work, not even if you had written *Paradise Lost*, which you haven't. Books make perfectly fine presents, and they don't even have to be expensive books—as long as they are not your own."

As long as they are not my own. That gave me an idea. I would phone one of my friends, say Dannie Abse, and make a mutual barmitzvah pact with him. I would send copies of *his* collected poems if he would send copies of *my* book on Israel. A brilliant idea, I thought, and I was dialling his number when I recalled some of his poems, and it occurred to me that they might not be suitable for an innocent child on the brink of manhood:

> "Later, the dark is shabby with paste electric
> of peeporamas, brothels, clubs and pubs . . ."

I tried Bernard Kops and several other Jewish poets next but kept stumbling upon situations unbecoming a barmitzvah boy.

And then I remembered Dan Jacobson. I had read nearly every one

21

of his books, had enjoyed them all, and as far as I could recall there was not a passage in any of them which could not be read aloud at a mothers' meeting. He wrote as if Portnoy's complaint had never been diagnosed. As a matter of fact I used to send his books as presents before I began writing my own.

But then, as I reached for the phone, another thought struck me. Dan was an expatriate. Expatriates don't get invited to many bar-mitzvahs, and if they do they don't always go, and if they go they don't always send presents. Whereas I, in a bad year, get as many as forty invitations (they may not be quite so numerous, but they often seem like it). It would be a mutual pact with unmutual benefits.

I had a better idea. I would enter into partnership with Dayan Grunfeld. He, if anything, has to attend even more barmitzvahs than I do, and he has written an excellent translation with commentary of Samson Raphael Hirsch's magnum opus, *Horeb*. I could not imagine even the most precocious of barmitzvah boys curling up with the book in an arm-chair. But I recalled that for my barmitzvah I had received two versions of Maimonides' *Guide to the Perplexed*, each of which I found (and still find) more perplexing than the other, but they both looked immensely impressive on the shelves, flanked as they were by all those collected sermons.

The two massive volumes of *Horeb* would be even more impressive, but they too have their drawback. *Horeb* costs five guineas, which brings them into the wedding class, while my book on Israel costs only 35s. I would have to wait till the Dayan wrote a cheaper book or I a more expensive one.

In the meantime I have come upon another solution. I am writing a new book, large, glossy, illustrated, drawing upon all the right sources, Rabbi Akivah, Maimonides, Samson Raphael Hirsch, Chaim Bermant, Baden Powell, Kipling, Prince Philip, tailor-made for the barmitzvah trade—and writing it, moreover, under a pseudonym.

Jewish Chronicle, 28 November 1969

RSVP

IN DER HEIM it was easy.

The shammos banged the table two or three times to obtain silence and then announced that the entire congregation was invited to the barmitzvah or wedding, or whatever. It was all so simple and straightforward that I sometimes wonder how people made enemies in those days.

Here it is rather different, for we, of course, live in the land of the printed invitation.

I still remember the first invitation we received. It was in gold lettering on cream-coloured vellum and, but for the fact that it was printed in Hebrew as well as English, we might have taken it for a diploma and framed it.

In this country, by and large, invitations, if sometimes ornate, are fairly functional. In America, they have been getting out of hand. I have seen one barmitzvah invitation which came in the form of a slim volume, with photographs of the young man depicting the various stages en route to his reaching manhood.

First he was shown as a chubby infant on an alpaca rug, then as a plump youngster on the way to school and finally as an overblown barmitzvah boy, with a talit round his shoulders and a prayer-book in his hand—probably the first and last time he would be seen holding such an object.

Wedding invitations are even more elaborate, for, of course, they have two lives to depict and prospective guests are sometimes presented with a historical family album, with the young couple apart in the earliest photos, then together, each pose more intimate than the other.

In this country, as I have suggested, we are more reticent and more to the point, but even so I'm beginning to wonder whether we should not dispense with printed invitations altogether, for they are almost specifically designed to create enmities—and I speak as a veteran with many children who already has one barmitzvah and two barmitzvahs behind him and who is now about to celebrate another barmitzvah.

I must say right away that batmitzvahs are no problem, for although the girls look pretty enough, they are always processed *en masse* and one is reminded a little of the emperor who baptised his army with a hose.

It is quite otherwise when a boy celebrates his advance to manhood, and no matter how many lists one makes and consults, and no matter how one racks one's memory for everyone who should be invited, one inevitably forgets someone, like, say, one's father-in-law.

Moreover, if one has a large family and many friends, one cannot always remember what has befallen them. We can all fail to forget somebody living, but a far more serious offence is to invite somebody dead.

Another more contemporary hazard is to invite Mr and Mrs X when Mrs X is by now Mrs Y; or worse, when Mrs X is still Mrs X, but cohabiting with Mr Y. And there are even more complicated relationships which I daren't mention in a family paper. The whole thing, I tell you, is a minefield.

Then, added to the vagaries of one's memory are the vagaries of the Post Office, and one can be fairly certain that at least 5 per cent of the invitations will go astray. At my last simcha, I enclosed reply cards and was outraged at the number of people who lacked the courtesy to reply whether they were coming or not, only to discover that they were equally outraged because they had failed to receive an invitation at all.

This time round, being more experienced, I was much wiser, sent no reply cards, but added "RSVP" and my telephone number at the bottom of the invitation. Most people, needless to say, did not bother to reply and I phoned them instead (am I glad I've got British Telecom shares), only to find that nearly 10 per cent of them had not received an invitation at all. But I was at least able to avoid the misunderstandings of the earlier occasion.

It is, all things considered, unlikely that I shall have yet another barmitzvah to celebrate, but there is the possibility of other simchas and I hereby give notice that if and when they arise, I shall do as they did in *der heim*, bang the shul table (I shall have to do so myself because in our shul they can't afford a shammos), and issue the invitations by word of mouth.

Jewish Chronicle, 6 September 1985

A Wedding
Has Been Disarranged

I HAD JUST about finished paying for the barmitzvah of my second son, when I was suddenly faced with the prospect of paying for the wedding of my first daughter.

I had vague intimations that my daughter was growing up when I came home one evening and found a line of battered cars without, and a horde of scruffy youngsters within. Could one of those ghastly creatures, I kept wondering, end up as my son-in-law?

I need not have worried, for she left for Israel the moment she finished school and joined the army (my daughter the soldier!) and as she was frequently stationed in or near one kibbutz or another I toyed with the hope that she might marry into the landed gentry. Not out of snobbery, you understand. It was more crass than that. If you marry a kibbutznik they pay for the wedding. They even arrange for the band and the flowers, and you roll up half an hour before the event, a guest at your own daughter's nuptials. You don't even have to bring a present. Marvellous institution, the kibbutz.

Needless to say, it didn't work out like that. She is marrying a medical student (my son-in-law the doctor!).

I have at various times fulminated against the extravagance, size and vulgarity of Jewish weddings, and this I thought might be an opportunity to demonstrate what a Jewish wedding should be, small, tasteful, intimate, inexpensive, a quiet little gathering of family and friends.

But again it didn't work out like that (it never does, does it?). First of all I have married into a vast and fertile clan which grows by the hour—I used to add, *v'chen yirbu* (and so may they multiply) but I've stopped doing it because it only encourages them—and we had to advance the date of the wedding, because the longer the delay the

26

more relatives there would be to invite.

Secondly, my *mechutanim* (or the MacNaughtons, as one calls them in Scotland), have a vast circle of friends.

Thirdly, my daughter, in the course of her military service, made friends with half the army, while her young man made friends with the other half, to say nothing of the better part of the Hadassah Medical School. On top of which I have (or think I have) one or two friends myself, so that when we came together to consider lists I suggested it would be easier to get the census returns and score out the names of people we wouldn't invite.

We did eventually manage to boil down the numbers but, even so, the date of the wedding was a military secret because of the borders of Israel being denuded that night.

But first there was the matter of venue. My MacNaughtons (bless 'em) and most of my wife's relatives live in Israel, which seemed to me as good a reason as any for having the wedding in England, but the young couple settled the matter between them. They would have it in Haifa and, given the number of expected guests, there was only one place large enough to contain them, the Dan Carmel hotel.

They say it's a small world, but it's a very large one when you're living at one end and trying to arrange a wedding at the other, especially when phone calls to the other end are about £3 a minute— considering the length and the frequency of the exchanges between my wife and my daughter it would have been cheaper for them to commute, King David class.

My daughter's identity caused consternation. She still had her army ID card, which said she was Jewish. Her passport said she was Jewish. Lord Jakobovits phoned the Chief Rabbi of Haifa to say she was Jewish, and our local minister, Rabbi Eddy Jackson, wrote to confirm she was Jewish, but being tall, blonde and blue-eyed (when she lived at home visitors took her to be our Swedish au-pair) she doesn't look Jewish. The Haifa rabbinate wanted further and better particulars and the matter was not finally resolved until she arrived with numerous female relatives, some sheitled, some murmuring incantations, and all brandishing *ketubot*, who avowed on oath that she was the Jewish daughter of a Jewish mother—though they were a bit non-committal about the father.

Then there were the invitations, or rather the lack of them. The proof copy arrived full of misprints. The final copy—entrusted to the tender mercies of Israel's postal service—failed, for a time, to arrive at all, and we had to start phoning around.

We needed a vast open space for the reception, which the hotel was happy to provide, but it included the swimming pool, and I could see myself spending half the night fishing guests out of the water, and the rest of my life fending off damage suits.

Finally, there was the not inconsiderable matter of refreshments. "The wine", the banqueting manager assured us, "will flow like water," but my MacNaughton and I feared that it might also taste like water and arranged for a fully stocked bar, which I thought had more or less settled the issue. Our wives, however, insisted that guests might also want something to eat and so the problems continued, each of them magnified by distance.

It so happens that one of our closest friends, Naomi Greenwood, was having a wedding in Israel in the very same week.

She too has a vast family and many friends, except that where our daughter is marrying a native, hers is marrying a fellow Brit, which has, if anything, added to her difficulties and when my wife is not on the phone to my daughter, she is on the phone to Naomi—I wish I had held on to my British Telecom shares—for prolonged sessions of mutual commiseration:

"Why did we have to have the wedding in Israel? Why could we not have had it in London? Why . . . ?"

The question I keep asking myself is, why couldn't they have eloped?

Jewish Chronicle, 22 September 1989

Of Faith
and the Faithful

A Funny Thing Happened
on the Way to the Synagogue

FUNNY THINGS OFTEN happened in the synagogue, as well as on the way there, when Rabbi Clifford Cohen was about.

As eccentrics go, Rabbi Cohen, 36, was not a patch on the infamous vicar of Stiffkey, but he went too far for the tastes of his middle-class north London congregation and he was asked to leave.

His departure last week was in a style befitting the knockabout humour of the man himself: his stage, an industrial tribunal which upheld his dismissal, and his audience, numbered in millions, regaled daily by the accounts of his zany behaviour.

From its ancient beginnings a rabbi was required to be scholar, interpreter of the laws of Moses, and spiritual guide. More recently, he is not infrequently called on to act as teacher, preacher, psychologist, marriage councillor, arbitrator, health visitor, prison visitor, almoner, ambassador and entertainer.

Given the length and vigour of his training and the range and nature of his responsibilities, a rabbi's salary—most earn between £10,000–£15,000, though a few "stars" can name their fee—is not high.

Rabbi Cohen's troubles arose partly from the fact that he got his functions mixed up. A rabbi is expected to show a certain amount of levity at a wedding or barmitzvah celebration, but Rabbi Cohen could sound like a master of ceremonies at a stag night even from the *terra sancta* of the pulpit.

God and the Jews have been together for so long that a certain familiarity has developed between them and a joke or two is not out of place even in the pulpit, but not the sort of sexual innuendoes which were the Rabbi's speciality.

British Jewry, though small and compact (there are only about

31

400,000 Jews in this country), is not particularly homogeneous, and can be divided into two broad streams, the Orthodox and the Liberal. Orthodox rabbis are bound by all sorts of restraints, precedents, the authority of rabbinical courts, and finally that of the Chief Rabbi.

The Liberal rabbi, on the other hand, is free to do what is right in his own eyes. Clifford Cohen, needless to say, is a Liberal rabbi, but even so he has been far too Liberal for his own good.

Thus, he had a ham sandwich at a wedding. While the Liberal synagogue is indifferent to dietary laws many Liberal rabbis regard the actual eating of pork as a conscious act of dissociation from the Jewish faith (the ultimate act is to eat a ham sandwich on Yom Kippur and to challenge God to strike one dead).

The Liberal synagogue has always argued that what goes into one's mouth is less important than what comes out of it. But what came out of Rabbi Cohen's mouth, if sometimes entertaining, was not always elevating.

The garb may not always proclaim the man but it usually proclaims the rabbi. The orthodox wear black, the less orthodox may be seen in descending shades of grey, while Liberal rabbis not infrequently look as if they are about to play tennis.

Rabbi Cohen, however, brought informality even to the formal occasion by appearing in T-shirts when he was supposed to be acting as a sort of ambassador of his community.

He sinned even against the precepts of his own particular denomination. The Liberal synagogue, while abandoning many ancient rituals, takes justifiable pride in its loyalty to prophetic teaching and its concern for social welfare. In other words, it has made pastoral care rather than formal observance its speciality.

Yet Rabbi Cohen, while agreeing to work a 50-hour week, was not disposed to be on call beyond that. He left telephone messages unanswered, and when he moved house he would not divulge his telephone number even to the council of his own synagogue, because he did not wish to be disturbed.

A man who likes to sleep o'night or—as in the case of Rabbi Cohen—o'mornings, is not ideally suited to be a rabbi. "The sleep of a labouring man is sweet," said Solomon, but then he wasn't a rabbi.

Finally, any clergyman who takes four months' leave—as Rabbi Cohen did—especially when he is in dispute with his parishioners, is pushing his luck, for they may discover that they can do without him.

Observer, 13 January 1985

Lord's Day

AS A LITHUANIAN-BORN Scottish Jew, I should perhaps be the last person to lament the passing of the English Sunday, but lament it I do, and I'm surprised it hasn't found more defenders. The Shops Bill which threatens it comes before the Commons tomorrow.

We are all ecologists now, when it comes to our physical environment. Cut a road here, threaten a marsh there, and clamorous hordes will rise in protest, but a measure which is about to kill the English Sunday and transform our psychological environment, is being allowed through Parliament on the trot. The opposition it has encountered so far has come mainly from trade unions rather than churchmen, while professional ecologists have said not a word.

The trade unions are afraid that shop-assistants might have to work longer hours. The hours would, in fact, only be more varied, which is possibly an advantage in itself. There would be more opportunities for overtime and it should create more jobs. In that sense, the proposed legislation could bring actual benefits; in every other sense it would be a disaster.

The Christian Sabbath is derived from the Jewish one which, in turn, has its origins in the Fourth Commandment:

"Remember the Sabbath day to keep it holy; Six days shalt thou labour and do all thy work; But the seventh day is the Sabbath of the Lord thy God; in it thou shalt not do any work, thou, nor thy son, nor thy daughter, thy manservant, nor thy maidservant, nor thy cattle, nor the stranger that is within thy gates."

The Christians chose Sunday as their day of rest because it was the day of the Resurrection, though early Jewish converts to Christianity, to be on the safe side, observed both the Sabbath and Sunday.

The Jews have kept the Sabbath now for nearly 4,000 years,

33

though in a sense it has kept them, for it is so central to their way of life that they would have hardly remained Jewish without it, and I think the English Sunday, even if less rigorously observed, is almost equally essential to the character of England and the unhurried pensive quality of English life.

The English Sunday, as traditionally observed, is a day out of time, less trammelled, more relaxed, an occasion for rest and recreation, or, as Addison put it: "Sunday clears away the rust of the whole week." Without it the year would become an almost endless succession of weekdays.

Why then has the opposition to the change been so muted? England is, after all, not yet completely pagan, and if church attendance is declining, regular worshippers can still be measured in millions. Why have they not made fuller use of their numbers and faced up more actively to the threat of desecration.

The English respect religion in others but are not sure how to cope with it themselves, and while fairly open about most things, they will hesitate to confess to a confession, as if a show of faith suggests a want of reason. They may marry in church, and opt for Christian burial when they die, but at other times they are not so much indifferent to their faith, as shy of displaying loyalty to it.

The attitude possibly derives from the bad press given to the Pharisees in the New Testament, so that the abhorrence of false piety associated with pharisaism has given rise to an abhorrence of piety itself, and the fear of being "holier-than-thou" has given way to a fear of being-less-profane-than-thou.

If the English Sunday had been secular in origin, it would have been sacrosanct, but as it is religious in origin, people dare not rush to its defence for fear of being labelled sanctimonious, or pietistic, or pecksniffian, or pharisaic, or perhaps all four. Even those Bishops who have defended Sunday have done so on pragmatic rather than religious grounds, as if nervous of introducing a spiritual dimension to the debate.

I hope I will be forgiven my chutzpah for saying so, but one does not have to be a Christian, or even English, to cherish the English Sunday, and it seems to me that a Church which has, so to speak, given up the ghost, and sees its mission in purely secular terms, is not equipped to check the depredations of hucksters.

The Guardian, 14 April 1986

Dem Bones, Dem Bones . . .

JUDAISM PUTS SHORT shrift to the presumptions of the living with the expression: "From dust thou art taken, and unto dust thou shalt return." We also show proper veneration for the dead, but I think that veneration should diminish with the length of their demise and it would not be unreasonable to suggest that, after a reasonable length of time—say one thousand years—it should make way for the claims of the living.

Again one would not suggest that one should trample on anyone's grave, but if a town should be expanding and should need room for buildings and open spaces, it should not be impossible to transfer human remains (if any) to another place. Thus, for example, much of what is now known as Independence Park in the centre of Jerusalem has been laid out on what was a Muslim cemetery (the remains of which can still be seen in a fenced-off corner).

There are, of course, people who will argue that there are dead and dead and that Jewish dust must not be spoken of in the same breath as Muslim dust; but in fact, when Jerusalem began to expand after the Six-Day War, two of the new suburbs, Ramat Eshkol and Sanhedria, were built over areas known to have contained Jewish burial grounds.

One heard no complaints, however, possibly because Ramat Eshkol is predominantly occupied by the holy, and Sanhedria by the holy of holies, but from time to time a body which now calls itself Atara Kadisha, and whom we may refer to as the Tomb Team (not to be confused with the Tim Tum, who are brethren of another kidney), springs into life as defenders of the ancient dead and go wild every time a bone is uncovered.

They, or their equivalent, have been active for some time. In the

35

early 'fifties, when I was helping to build the Beersheba to Sodom highway, our foreman cautioned us, "If you find any bones, bury yourself with them—but don't make a fuss."

In those days the Tomb Teams were comparatively harmless, but since then they have become more militant and organised and have acquired more friends in high places, especially Rabbi Shlomo "Bones" Goren.

Most of the Tomb Team's activities are, for obvious reasons, in and around Jerusalem, but in recent months their northern branch sprang to life with the claim that ancient Jewish graves in Tiberias were being desecrated by a subsidiary of the Bank Leumi, which was building an annex to the Ganei Hamat Hotel.

The bank, rather unwisely, I thought, brought in the Sephardi Chief Rabbi, Mordechai Eliahu, to investigate the claim. He ruled that there was no definite evidence of Jewish tombs, which was the good news. The bad news—and I could have warned them of it—was a *chashash*, a "possibility", that there could have been a Jewish cemetery on the site.

Now, when it comes to the consideration of actual possibilities, one daren't turn up so much as a sod in Israel, for, given the size of the country, its antiquity and its blood-drenched history, there is more than a possibility that Mea Shearim, Bnei Brak and Chief Rabbi Mordechai Eliahu's own home are likewise built on Jewish cemeteries. But, having asked for his advice, the bank felt bound to act on it, and it made adjustments—at a cost of $1.5 million—to comply with his ruling.

And that, you might have thought, was the end of it. But if you did, you can't know much either about the temper of the Tomb Team or about the character of the Sephardi Chief Rabbi.

The former, which doesn't recognise the authority of Israel's Chief Rabbinate (except when it suits it), continued with its campaign, while the latter began to feel that he had perhaps been a little too amenable.

And thus the possibility he had spoken of became a probability, the probability became a certainty, and Rabbi Eliahu made further demands which would have involved the suspension of the building project altogether. By which point the bank had had enough and proceeded without his *hechsher* (which is, of course, what it should have done in the first place).

The Tomb Team, to do it justice, has proved one point. It has demonstrated that the contempt it has always shown for Israel's ecclesiastical establishment is well founded, but given its head, it could turn the whole of Israel into a graveyard.

As a start, it (and its supporters) has called for a boycott of Bank Leumi and, to date, they have withdrawn about $10 million—which, given the fact that they do not appear to be too active in worldly affairs, is a surprisingly large sum. But as the bank has assets many times that size, it is unlikely to collapse. To counter their efforts, however, I have rushed out to open an account with the bank and, thank God, I already have an overdraft.

Jewish Chronicle, 15 February 1985

Unwanted Guests

WORD HAS GONE round the criminal fraternity that Orthodox Jews do not use their phones on the Sabbath, and Friday nights have therefore become an open season for burglaries in north-west London.

As a result, some rabbis have advised their flock that if they suspect the actual presence of an intruder in their homes, they may phone the police even on the Sabbath.

But that is as far as they will go. They have not suggested that one may use the phone on the Sabbath to report a burglary, and wherever three or four burglars forgather they drink (in purloined kiddush cups) to the health of the rabbinate and to the laws of Moses and Israel.

The prohibition on the use of the phone on Shabbat derives from the prohibition on the use of electricity, which, in turn, derives from a verse in Exodus: "Ye shall kindle no fires throughout your habitations on the Sabbath day."

Sadducees and Karaites took the verse literally, which is perhaps why they are both extinct. The rabbis, bless 'em, were more reasonable about it (which they were about many things in those far-off days) and ruled that, while a Jew may not actually kindle a fire on the Sabbath, there is nothing to stop him using a fire kindled before the Sabbath, or which is kindled even during the Sabbath by a gentile.

(The ruling, of course, gave ready employment to successive generations of Shabbos goyim, but as most homes now have central heating, they are unemployed and may have taken to burglary instead—though the thieves in the north-west London forays seem so familiar with Jewish ways that I suspect they may be Jews themselves.)

Now what, you may ask, has all this to do with electricity or telephones, and the short answer is: nothing at all. A fire involves combustion, electricity does not, though it may do so in the sense that at the end of the line it is provided by a power station, which does burn fuel.

It could be argued that, by turning a switch, one is adding to the amount of fuel consumed, but one can set pumps in motion by flushing one's toilet, and, as far as I know, no rabbi has (as yet—though no doubt it will come) ruled that one may not flush the toilet on the Sabbath.

A switch, I am told, may cause sparks, but they are not inherent in the action of switching, and if that is the reason for the prohibition, one should not be allowed to wear nylon clothes on the Sabbath or have nylon carpets in one's house, for they too can (and do) cause sparks. As for phones, they do not cause sparks, nor add to the powerload.

I once raised the question with a rabbi who, in an earlier incarnation, had been a physicist and he said that, in essence, the prohibition has little to do with combustion and everything to do with the character of the Sabbath, for if we were allowed to use electricity without inhibition, the Sabbath as we know it would be finished. The same, I would say, applies to the telephone.

I have read many learned papers on why one may not use the telephone on the Sabbath and they have convinced me that even learned men can make fools of themselves when they try to defend an untenable position. But the fact is that if people felt completely free to use their telephone, there would be nothing left of their Sabbath—especially where they have teenage daughters.

I prefer not to answer phone calls on Shabbat (to be honest, I'm reluctant to answer them even on weekdays) because, if I did, they would multiply and the sublime tranquillity of the day would be lost.

If the phone rings persistently, however, I do answer it, because I begin to get uneasy and worried, and worries do not do much for one's Sabbath peace either. In other words, one sometimes has to break the Sabbath in order to keep it.

I would urge people to adopt the same attitude when it comes to burglaries, for such burglaries have become so frequent and commonplace that many Orthodox Jews now approach their Sabbath with apprehension rather than pleasure, and they have become commonplace and frequent precisely because of the inhibitions about the use of the phone.

I suspect that if some of our rabbis had been burgled themselves they would have given a more liberal ruling on the matter. But burglars know their job and very few rabbis have anything worth stealing.

Jewish Chronicle, 15 May 1987

"... a Wholly Natural Practice"

LIBERAL AND REFORM Jews, while denying the validity of the Oral Law, claim to be loyal to the Written Law as enshrined in the Good Book. But it is a qualified loyalty.

Some parts of the Good Book, they argue, are better than others; or, as Rabbi Julia Neuberger has put it, it is the work of humans "who felt themselves to be, and no doubt sometimes were, divinely inspired".

In other words, we are free to pick and choose, to invoke those parts of Scripture we like and to reject those we dislike. And Rabbi Neuberger doesn't care for the scriptural injunctions against homosexuality.

But first of all, let us be clear what we are talking about. There is no explicit biblical injunction against lesbianism, and homosexuality in this context therefore means sodomy, a word which, of course, derives from the practices of Sodom.

The story of Sodom itself may be allegorical, but the Torah conveys dramatically the repugnance with which sodomy was viewed:

"Thou shalt not lie with mankind as with womankind; it is an abomination . . . If a man also lie with mankind, as he lieth with a woman, both of them have committed an abomination; they surely shall be put to death; their blood shall be upon them."

Rabbi Neuberger doesn't try to get round that. Nor does she resort to the Orthodox practice of giving words meaning which they do not and cannot possess.

What she does do, however, is to argue that the negative attitude to sodomy of our forefathers was derived from their day, but that we are wiser and better and "now know that it is a wholly natural practice for a small section of the community . . ."

41

No doubt, but there have been societies which regarded cannibalism as "a wholly natural practice". It is certainly a wholly economic one and, as Swift argued, it could solve the problems of both hunger and over-population.

There are Indians who regard the burning of widows on the funeral pyres of their husbands as wholly natural, though I would regard it as wasteful.

There are also elderly men who think it "wholly natural" to molest small children. Some of them have even grouped themselves into a paedophilia society and, given the charity and toleration which those like Rabbi Neuberger bring to their work, some may be wondering if they shouldn't set aside rooms for prayer meetings for such men, with banners overhead declaring: "Suffer little children to come unto me."

The normality or abnormality of almost any social attitude is open to debate, but there are certain propositions so self-evidently true that in sane times and among sane people there would be no need to defend them. And one of them is that sodomy is a bad thing.

Any society which thinks otherwise is doomed to extinction, and the loathing with which most natural people approach it derives from the determination of nature to preserve herself.

People who regard sodomy as wholly natural to the point of recoiling from normal sexual relations are emotionally deformed and deserve our compassion, understanding and help. But sodomy itself remains what it always was—a hideous abomination.

Anyone who thinks otherwise has lost one of the few qualities which raise us above beasts—a healthy sense of disgust. I argued as much in this column years ago, long before Aids came on the scene. We now know it is also lethal.

Rabbi Neuberger brings many qualities to her work—colour, vivacity, optimism, great good will, a restless compassion unbridled by reason—so that she will rush hither and thither with incense and candles to sanctify anything that moves (or doesn't, as the case may be), and there is no one so irredeemable that she will not plead for his redemption.

She errs on the side of charity, but my God (and even hers), she does err, and she is a living proof that Liberal Judaism can be every bit as dogmatic as the Orthodox variety.

But I have two more serious complaints against her, the first of which is her presumption. I wouldn't mind if she espoused the causes she does, no matter how bizarre, if she didn't do so in the name of Judaism.

The second is more serious. I happen to believe in women rabbis, because I believe that they are better equipped for the vocation than most men, but every time she opens her mouth, she sets back their cause by a decade.

Jewish Chronicle, 27 March 1987

A Gay World

IN VICTORIAN TIMES, men were held responsible for everything that befell them, and although it was accepted that some had more than their fair share of misfortune, and others of luck, it was generally agreed that their fate lay in their own hands.

We have now moved to the other extreme and are asked to believe that man is responsible for nothing and society for everything. There has of late been something of a counter-reaction and the word is beginning to spread that it is possible for people to help themselves, that hard work can carry its own rewards and idleness its own penalties.

Yet no political leader has dared to utter the thought that there is also something to be said for moral conduct and that many of our ills are due less to deprivation than to depravity. The Chief Constable of Manchester has done so and the skies have fallen in upon him, but then the police are expected to deal with the consequences of moral decay and not their causes. He was speaking of Aids and said, in plain and forcible terms, that if ever a calamity was self-inflicted, this was it. Can anyone seriously deny it?

There can, of course, be innocent victims, the most obvious being haemophiliacs and others who may have picked up the infection in the course of a blood transfusion; but the overwhelming majority of cases are due not to any chance factor, but to drug abuse, promiscuity and, above all, sodomy, and the sympathy one feels for the victims and their families should not blind us to this fact.

There are laws against drug abuse which, however ineffective, at least suggest public disapproval. There are no laws against promiscuity or sodomy—nor should there be—but there isn't even an attempt to suggest that either one or the other could be wrong. Stick

44

to one partner if you can, says the Health Ministry, lamely; use a condom if you can't.

One does not expect the Government to buy air time to broadcast the Eighth Commandment, or to quote Leviticus to the effect that "Though shalt not lie with mankind as with womankind", but there is not even a concerted effort to counter inducements to depravity.

A few months ago I switched on the television and, a little incredulously, I found myself watching what was virtually a party political broadcast on behalf of gay liberation. Every university now has its gay society, which attracts no more comment or disapproval than he tiddlywinks society—one university union recently held a "Lesbian, Gay and Bisexual Week" and in some of our schools religion is being phased out and homosexuality as an alternative life-style phased in.

Aids is by far the deadliest venereal disease, but syphilis was deadly enough in its time. In its tertiary stages it was worse than death, and if promiscuity had been as rife in earlier centuries as it is now, it could have decimated the population of Europe.

I will no doubt be reminded that people in earlier centuries were not always saintly, and that the Victorians in particular, who are so often held up as exemplars of public morality, could also indulge in private vice, that we in our time are at least open, honest and frank about our habits, and that whatever we are, by God, we're not hypocrites as if men who have no standards at all are somehow superior to those who have, but fail to live up to them.

One also reads frequent references to the "guilt-ridden lives" of the Victorians, which almost suggests that one is better off without a sense of guilt at all. Guilt is to the soul what pain is to the body. It is a signal that one is doing something harmful, the only difference being that what is harmful to the body hurts instantly, while what is harmful to the soul can initially be rather pleasant. The guilt comes later, sometimes much later, not infrequently in old age. A sense of guilt or, if you prefer, a sense of shame, may not always stop people doing things they shouldn't, but there is every chance that they will do them less often.

Morals, or at least sexual morals, have in recent years been consigned to philosophers, theologians and biblical exegists. They have now become a matter of life and death and may suggest the truth of Goethe's saying: *Alle schuld racht sich auf erden*—all guilt is punished on earth.

Jewish Chronicle, 26 December 1986

45

Black Sheep and White Hopes

TWO THINGS MAY be said of the Israeli election. It was a good deal more exciting than the American election, and the results were a good deal less predictable. Nevertheless, I partly predicted them.

In the course of an extensive tour of the country, I could see that many Sephardi voters were unhappy with Likud, but not so unhappy as to vote Labour, and I forecast that Shas, which had won four seats in the last election in 1984, could win six in this one. And as I spake, so it came to pass.

I forecast, however, that Rabbi Yehuda Amital's Meimad Party might win one or even two seats, which was, I'm afraid, a classic case of wishful thinking.

Meimad is everything a religious party should be—tolerant, high-minded, far-seeing and benign—but it was utterly routed, and the religious vote went to a cluster of parties which are narrow, intolerant, bloody-minded and so removed from this world as to be almost in the next, so that the result was greeted with dismay even by many religious voters.

A friend who settled in Israel for religious reasons over twenty years ago said that were it not for the fact that his children were in the Army, he would seriously think of packing up.

One's memory of the election is filled with details so bizarre that it is difficult to believe they happened. There were, for example, the double-page advertisements put out by the Aguda Party which carried the exhortations of two famous rabbis, one of them not living in Israel, the other not living at all.

The first was Rabbi Menachem Mendel Schneerson, the Admor of Brooklyn, otherwise known as the Lubavitcher Rebbe; the second was the late Rabbi Hatzeira, of blessed memory, the sage of Netivot,

46

otherwise known as Baba Sali.

The latter should not be confused with Ali Baba and the forty thieves, or even with Israel's former Minister of Religion, Abu Hatzeira, a lone thief who, having been indicted for embezzlement and fraud, became known as Baba Black Sheep (though black sheep or not, he was a Likud candidate in the election and may, for all I know, be back in the Knesset).

Baba Sali, as I have said, is dead, but he exercises more power from his grave than he ever did in his lifetime. All sorts of miracles have been attributed to him and he has become to Netivot what St Bernadette (*lehavdil*) is to Lourdes—except that Bernadette died without issue, while Baba Sali had a son.

This son is the less than venerable Baba Baruch who, as custodian of his father's tomb, is thought to be a miracle worker in his own right and runs something akin to a franchise operation in spells, charms, incantations, invocations, amulets, panaceas, philtres and holy relics. He also, I am told, sells falafel.

Baba Baruch is regarded lightly by the mass of Israelis, but he is taken seriously by many devout Sephardim. When, with one hand on his father's tomb, he warned the faithful to vote for Aguda in terms which amounted almost to a curse on those who did not, former Chief Rabbi Ovadiah Yossef came on the screen with a whole cabal of puisne rabbis to exorcise his threat and to assure people that they could vote for the Shas Party without imperilling their life in this world or their soul in the next.

Yet Meimad, which represents all that is best in Judaism, received not a single seat, while the others, which represent all the idolatry and superstition that have attached themselves to the Jewish faith like corrosive barnacles to a ship of state, received eighteen.

With all its handicaps, Israel is recognised even by its enemies as one of the most cultured, progressive and advanced countries in the world; yet those who built it, and those who, like Rabbi Amital, could have enhanced it, have been brushed aside.

Its fate may now be decided by a handful of rabbis, most of whom do not even recognise the Jewish State and who, given half the chance, would drag it back, not to the Middle Ages—Maimonides, after all, lived in the Middle Ages—but to a Dark Age uniquely their own.

No doubt the "Who is a Jew" issue will be brought before the Knesset almost as soon as it convenes. I hope that while the debate is in progress someone will raise the issue of "What is Judaism?" and whether the variety peddled by the Lubavitcher Rebbe and the Baba Sali, *père et fils*, with all its superstition, bears any relation to the sort received by Moses on Sinai.

Jewish Chronicle, 11 November 1988

". . . sayeth Not the Preacher"

"IS THE SERMON a dying art?" asks Rabbi Norman Lamm in *L'Eylah*, the excellent journal on contemporary Judaism published by Jews' College.

I sometimes think it's a dead one, even though there are still some excellent practitioners around, including Lamm himself, but good preachers are so rare that hardly is their name made when it is unmade by promotion.

Lamm's own career may almost be taken as a cautionary tale, for after serving with distinction as a rabbi, he was snatched out of his pulpit and is now president of Yeshiva University, a good man fallen among fundraisers.

His friend and colleague, Rabbi Emmanuel Rackman, likewise a gifted speaker, has suffered an even worse fate: he is president of Bar-Ilan University. Both may still have ample occasion for public speaking, but even a good speech is only a speech, whereas a good sermon, if not quite the word of God, reverberates with divine echoes.

In *der heim*, sermons were generally given between mincha and ma'ariv on long summer afternoons (which made them seem that much longer), usually by wandering preachers known as Magidim.

Everything I remember about them suggests that they were principally actors, and the experience was theatrical rather than ecclesiastic, but then the theatre everywhere has its origins in the church.

Local incumbents could, if they were moved to it, give the occasional sermon, but they were never encouraged to do so.

The sermon as we know it now, in its comparatively compact form, is, in Jewish terms, a recent innovation and one, moreover, which is derived from the church. Jews' College in the first fifty years of this

49

century produced rabbis who not only dressed like their Anglican colleagues, but sounded like them, assuming a lofty ecclesiastical tone unrelated to their normal manner of speech.

The preparation was meticulous and sentence succeeded sentence in grammatical array with rarely a word out of place; but the effect was curiously disembodied, for the house style deprived the speaker of one of his most important qualities—his own, individual voice.

Well, we have rather more individualism today, even eccentricity, but the compilation is sometimes less than meticulous.

I am in the word trade myself and I sometimes feel that every prospective preacher should be made to serve a lengthy apprenticeship as a journalist, for the basic rule of journalism is to say as much as possible in as few words as possible, while in preaching the rule is frequently reversed.

We may have many natural speakers, but we have few natural listeners, and it takes more than ordinary talent to engage the attention of a varied, critical and sometimes reluctant audience for more than ten minutes at a time—especially if it has to be done every week.

Rabbi Lamm feels that "the burden of being fresh and original every week is beyond the powers of most mortals"—especially, I would add, if they have to base themselves on the same text year after year. But I cannot see why rabbis must always resort to Scripture when making a point.

Why can't they base themselves on something they saw on television, heard in conversation or even read on the back of a cornflakes packet? ("My friends. How often, as we reach for our breakfast cereals, do we almost subconsciously grope for some free gift, some glittering prize to brighten our day. But it's never there on top, is it? We have to search for it in the hidden depths. It's the same with Judaism . . .")

The threat to the sermon, as far as Rabbi Lamm can see, lies, however, not in the inability of the congregants to take it, but in the unwillingness of rabbis to give it. He speaks of a new generation of young, yeshiva-trained, backward-looking rabbis (or Yutbis, as I would call them) who dismiss the sermon as a soft option and attach greater weight to the halachic discourse.

I cannot see why the latter should preclude the former, though I can see why the Yutbis should prefer it. A good halachic discourse, while calling for great erudition, involves merely the transmission of received ideas, while a good sermon, even if based on received ideas, requires a capacity for original thought, which is almost unknown among Yutbis.

Those who enjoy it, employ it. Those who lack it, attack it.

Jewish Chronicle, 2 October 1987

Forbidden Fruit

A BODY CALLING itself the "Council for the Holiness of the People of Israel", which I gather is a euphemism for a collection of ultra-Orthodox London rabbis, recently produced a booklet in Hebrew and English warning of the dangers of immoral behaviour and suggesting that Aids is a divine punishment for depravity.

Immorality does, indeed, carry its dangers in this world, to say nothing of what might be in store in the next. One could also argue, as, indeed, I have argued, that most Aids victims have brought their misfortunes upon themselves, but if one brings the heavens into it, there are some awkward questions to answer.

What of people, like haemophiliacs, who have acquired the disease in all innocence? What of infants who have acquired the disease in the womb and are condemned to death even before they are born?

And if, as some rabbis often argue, the innocent pay for the sins of the guilty, how does one reconcile such divine vindictiveness with the refrain repeated thrice daily before the open Ark during our festivals: "The Lord, the Lord is a merciful and gracious God, slow to anger and abounding in loving kindness and truth; reserving loving kindness for thousands, forgiving iniquity and transgression and sin."?

I sometimes feel that we pray to one God while some rabbis have their eyes raised to quite another.

Moreover, Aids is not the only fatal disease around. Thousands of men, women and children die daily after prolonged torments from malignancies which they have done nothing to bring upon themselves. How could the "Council for the Holiness of the People of Israel" explain them? How would it explain the Holocaust?

Anyone who tries to explain human misfortunes, no matter how incurred, in terms of Divine wrath is reducing a profoundly complex theological issue to banalities and comes dangerously close to desecrating the Divine name. I can only imagine that the Council for the Holiness of the People of Israel have not worked out the full implications of their own argument.

But that is not the only piece of folly in its publication. It goes on to warn men of the danger of being alone with a gentile woman, like secretaries, or clients. But why only gentile women? Given the history of Aids it could be even more dangerous to be alone with men, even Jewish men. But the most offensive thing about the whole booklet is the inference that gentiles are always the seducers and Jews always the seduced, and that Jews left on their own are inherently virtuous. What would happen if a body calling itself the "Council for the Holiness of Christendom" issued a booklet warning Christian women of the dangers of being alone with Jewish men?

I can tell you what would happen. The Board of Deputies would immediately call on the Attorney General and demand that the Race Relations Act be invoked against the offenders; the Council of Christians and Jews would meet in special session and invite the established churches to distance themselves from them; Greville Janner would raise the matter in Parliament, and a body of rabbis belonging to the Incorporated Society of Instant Protestors, might even fly in from America for a street demonstration.

Such a publication may be inconceivable in Britain, but there was something like it in Germany between 1923 and 1945. It was called *Der Stuermer*. It was published by one Julius Streicher and it frequently warned "pure and superior" Nordic women against "defilement by Jews".

Der Stuermer was, of course, the work of a psychopath. It was designed to generate hatred and manifestly did. The booklet produced by the "Council for the Holiness of the People of Israel" is the well-intentioned work of five unworldly men but its message is almost equally repellent.

I would have ignored it as another of the bizarre little tracts which circulate in the community, but for the fact that it carries the endorsement of five leading, ultra-Orthodox London rabbis who have otherwise been known to show symptoms of sanity. In other words, they are prepared to say it purports to represent the true teachings of Judaism.

Well it is not the sort of Judaism which I've been taught, nor the sort which most of us would wish to learn.

Jewish Chronicle, 16 March 1990

If the Turban Fits . . .

NO ONE COMES well out of the "turban case", neither the plaintiff, nor the Court of Appeal, nor the race relations establishment.

One has the greatest admiration for the tenacity with which the Sikhs adhere to their traditions, and for their readiness to defend them, but there seems to be a general belief among the religious of all denominations that secular traditions, no matter how old-established or strongly held, have no validity and may safely be ignored.

The middle-class habit of clothing its school-children in uniform is, as far as I know, peculiar to England. It may seem irrational and eccentric (though no more so than many a religious tradition), and it is certainly—as I know to my cost—expensive. But it is not unattractive and it answers to a conservative trait in the English character which many find appealing. I cannot see why the Englishman who tries to defend his customs is condemned as a racist, while the Sikh who tries to assert his is spoken of as a folk hero.

Now if the uniform habit was so rigorously enforced that anyone who could not conform to it was excluded from the educational system, it would be another matter. But no one has been, nor is anyone likely to be, excluded from state schools for wearing a turban or a skull-cap or even Rastafarian dreadlocks, and most education authorities have gone to extravagant lengths to satisfy the differing needs of the different ethnic groups within their catchment areas. What seems to have been overlooked is the fact that Park Grove, the school at the centre of the storm, happens to be a private establishment, and if the headmaster had chosen to admit only red-headed boys with cleft-palates, buck-teeth, and straw in their ears he would have been at liberty to do so. In fact he has been perfectly rational in his policies, and his school is open to boys of all colours and all

54

creeds, provided only that they conform to the school rules—which include the wearing of uniforms. What the plaintiff was demanding, therefore, was not equality, but discrimination. I may add that better schools than Park Grove have been prepared to bend their rules to accommodate the turban, but if Park Grove was inflexible it should have been left at that.

And no doubt it would have been, but for the Race Relations Act, which, though conceived as a means of improving race relations, has on the whole tended to exacerbate them, for it touches upon concepts—such as ethnicity and race—which are largely undefinable. The result is that it is largely unenforceable and where attempts have been made to enforce it, as in this instance, it has generated ill-feeling against the law, the enforcement agencies, and the very minorities it seeks to protect.

In a law-abiding society, laws are part of the educational process but they should not go too far ahead of public opinion. If they do, they will be merely ignored, and if attempts are made to enforce them, they will be resisted, and the society will cease to be law-abiding.

The whole corpus of race legislation, plus the agencies which it spawned, was largely, I believe, a cosmetic exercise. The Government wanted to impress immigrant groups with its determination to do something, and something it did, but it created a climate of expectations which must inevitably be disappointed. The provisions of the Act dealing with racial hatred, for example, do not, in essence, go far beyond the 1936 Public Order Act and insofar as they do, they have been largely nullified by the action, or inaction, of successive Attorneys General. (Which is perhaps just as well. What would the Board of Deputies have achieved in the present climate of opinion if it had been allowed to haul Ken Livingstone and the *Labour Herald* before the courts for depicting Begin as a Nazi?)

One does not have to be Black to be aware that discrimination in employment is rampant, but while the Act can help one obtain redress for losing a job, it can do nothing to provide one.

To say all this is merely to suggest that the Act is futile, but I believe that it is positively harmful, and the harm lies in this. It is usual for newcomers to an established society to adapt themselves to the ways of their hosts, as the Jews did when they began to arrive in this country in large numbers a century go. The Race Relations Act, however, sought to impose the onus of adaptation on the hosts. No reasonable person would now insist that Muslims, or Hindus or

Sikhs should become English gentlemen overnight, in a generation or ever. Cultural plurality is now generally accepted and newcomers are actively encouraged to perpetuate their distinct ways of life. The only group who would seem to be actively discouraged from doing so are the English themselves. We are all aware of minority rights, but majorities too have their rights.

It was once said of the Russians that they would never become civilised because Peter the Great tried to civilise them by force. I believe that the attempt to enforce racial amity by fiat could delay the natural process of integration.

Jewish Chronicle, 13 August 1982

Flaming Rage

THERE ARE MANY lessons to be learned from the Islamic campaign against Salman Rushdie's *The Satanic Verses*, the first of which is that if you set out to ban a book, make sure you succeed, otherwise you will only promote it.

Britain's attempts to prevent the publication of *Spycatcher* made the book an international best-seller, and the Islamic campaign is doing the same for Rushdie. I half wish someone would burn one of my books in public. (A Hendon rabbi once threatened to do so, but never got round to it. I should have sent him a box of matches.)

A government has the right to expect confidentiality from its servants and I therefore had every sympathy with the campaign against *Spycatcher*.

I have none, however, for the campaign against Rushdie, not merely because he happens to be a particularly gifted author, but because every man has the right to look God in the teeth and to question the fundamentals of his faith; and if the fulminations of the book-burners are anything to go by, Mr Rushdie's questions are well founded.

I recently found myself in conversation on the issue with a cultured Muslim, who said that I should not judge his faith by the actions of the mullahs, and that Islam was basically broad-minded and tolerant.

I appreciated the point he was trying to make, because I have frequently argued that one should not judge Judaism by the actions or utterances of the rabbis; but in the last resort, Islam is as Islam does (the same, of course, is true of Judaism).

Whatever admiration one may have for Islamic culture, or for the work of this or that Muslim poet or thinker, the fact remains that there is hardly a single democratic country in the Muslim world. One must inevitably judge Islam not by the urbanities of its apologists, but by the Khomeinis and the Gaddafis, the Assads and the Saddams, and by the book-burners of Bradford.

(I will no doubt be reminded that Pakistan recently elected Benazir Bhutto as Prime Minister in a free and democratic vote, but let us see how long she remains in power and, while in power, how long she remains democratic.)

Dr Hesham El Essawy, director of the Islamic Society for the Promotion of Religious Tolerance in the UK [sic], is unhappy about the book-burning episode if only because "it has awakened the sleeping demons of racialism in so many". This may be true, but it has also evoked painful memories of what book-burning led to in Nazi Germany.

The actual book-burning may have been the work of a few hotheads, but no responsible Muslim leader has denounced it, or the threats against Rushdie and his publishers, and the whole Muslim world seems to have combined in the effort to have the book banned.

This may be an indelicate point to make by someone who is himself an immigrant, but it has to be made: the Muslims are abusing the very freedoms which have led them to seek, and obtain, a home in Britain. They are not only making things difficult for themselves; they are making things impossible for prospective immigrants, especially from the Muslim world.

Britain may not be a particularly bookish society, but it is a particularly fair-minded one, and it is intolerant of attempts to spread intolerance and interfere with free speech; and if the anti-Rushdie campaign has led to a backlash of anti-Muslim feelings—which it has—then Muslims have only themselves to blame.

But wait, who am I to talk? What of the Jewish campaign against Jim Allen's "Perdition"? Jews, to be sure, did not burn Allen's play in public, or even in private, but they did join in an effort to have it banned—and, what's more, they succeeded. The two cases, however, are not the same.

Allen's work was not a novel, but purported to be a reconstruction of recent events which touched on the personal experience of countless people still living, and which was a blatant piece of anti-Zionist propaganda.

It was, moreover, to have been staged in the Royal Court Theatre, which, unlike Penguin (Rushdie's publishers), is heavily dependent on public funds. And the play itself was trash.

Nevertheless, it is not a crime to write bad plays, or even to stage them, and, as I said at the time, it was not worthy of the wrath it provoked.

Jewish Chronicle, 3 February 1989

Mullahs of the World Unite!

FULL-PAGE STATEMENTS IN support of Salman Rushdie, signed by more than 1,000 writers, have appeared in newspapers around the world.

Not all the signatories have read his book, and not all who read it liked it, but the merits of the work are irrelevant. There is an elementary principle involved.

That principle, in the words of the statement, is "the right of all people to express their ideas and beliefs and to discuss them with their critics on the basis of mutual tolerance, free from censorship, intimidation and violence".

No one has suffered more from the denial of that right than the Jews. We are all familiar with the Nazi book-burners, but they operated within a tradition established by the Popes and the Inquisition in the Middle Ages.

In 1242, thousands of volumes of the Talmud were publicly burned in the streets of Paris; and the scene was subsequently repeated in Toulouse, Perpignan, Rome, Venice, Bologna, Ravenna, Ferrara, Mantua, Urbino, Florence and, as recently as 1757, Kamenets-Podolsk.

Not that our own record on this matter is entirely untainted. In some ways, we were the pioneers.

In 1624, the Dutch Jewish philosopher Uriel Da Costa was excommunicated and his work publicly burned by the Jewish community. In 1656, Spinoza, one of the greatest Jewish thinkers of all time, was anathemised, cursed and excommunicated in a gruesome ritual, and there was even an attempt on his life.

But the most damning incident of all came over 400 years earlier, in 1233, when the Jewish authorities in Montpellier denounced Maimonides' *Guide to the Perplexed* to the Dominicans, who promptly consigned it to the flames.

I was therefore saddened, though not surprised, by the Chief Rabbi's contribution to the Rushdie debate: here was the authentic Jewish voice of authentic Jewish intolerance.

"Both Mr Rushdie and the Ayatollah", Lord Jakobovits wrote to *The Times*, "have abused freedom of speech"—as if an expression of belief, or disbelief, was the same thing as incitement to murder.

I would not suggest that the printed word is sacred and that any thought which enters a writer's mind, no matter how vicious, has an undeniable right to publication. One should not be free to disseminate lies or to incite hatred, but the matters raised by Rushdie are precisely those which demand free expression, for the reservations he has voiced about Islam have been abundantly confirmed by the reactions they provoked.

The Chief Rabbi does not wish to tamper with the laws of blasphemy, but he suggests something worse, a ban on "the publication of anything likely to inflame, through obscene defamation, the feelings or beliefs of any section of society, or liable to provoke public disorder or violence".

If such a law were to come into effect, we could say goodbye to all our freedoms, for one can hardly utter a thought which does not offend one section of society or another, and especially those who make it their business to take offence and incite others to do so.

The Chief Rabbi's letter arose largely out of a meeting last October with the chairman of the Islamic Society for the Promotion of Religious Tolerance, which might be more aptly named the Society for the Promotion of Religious Intolerance. The purpose of the meeting was to obtain Lord Jakobovits' support against the publication of Rushdie's book.

No doubt the Chief Rabbi, as spiritual head of the Jewish community, was anxious to retain the good will of the Muslim community, but a few home truths are not out of place at such encounters.

He might have put it to his visitor that if Muslims are seriously interested in promoting religious tolerance, they must recognise that they are living in a free society, and part of that freedom is the right to say things which might cause offence. Instead, he readily agreed that the book should be banned.

There is an affinity among writers which transcends their natural rivalry, and when one is threatened, they all feel threatened.

Chaim Bermant

There is a similar affinity among the clergy—or at least orthodox clergy—which transcends their theological differences, for they all feel threatened by the free exchange of ideas.

Mullahs of the world, unite! You have nothing to lose but your manes, and you have the next world to win.

Jewish Chronicle, 10 March 1989

Cultural Insensibilities

IT IS NOW a year since the Ayatollah Khomeini passed a death sentence on Salman Rushdie for blaspheming the founder and faith of Islam in *The Satanic Verses*. I am told that the sentence is still extant, even if the Ayatollah isn't.

I am not familiar with the byways, or even the highways, of Islamic theology and if Muslim divines insist that the book is blasphemous, I, for one, am prepared to take their word for it. But no offence which Rushdie may have committed against Islam is equal to the injuries inflicted by such Muslim leaders as Dr Kalim Siddiqi, who told a Manchester gathering last October that "the Muslim community has overwhelmingly endorsed the death sentence passed on Rushdie".

I doubt if it has done anything of the sort, and any number of Muslims have privately challenged Siddiqi's assertion. If none has done so publicly, it is because they are afraid for their lives and one cannot condemn people for not acting like heroes.

But what of non-Muslims? What, in particular, of Mr Michael Day, chairman of the Commission for Racial Equality? Mr Day sounds like a benign individual and I should imagine he is opposed to capital punishment. We may take it he is also opposed to murder, but he has come perilously close to condoning the incitement to murder.

"I do think the boundary between private belief and civic behaviour needs to be re-examined," he said in an interview with the *Observer*, from which one half expected him to turn upon Dr Siddiqi. But instead he went on: "Muslims feel that the Rushdie affair is another example of the way in which few concessions are made to their cultural sensibilities . . . It only needs one fanatic bombing a bookshop or shooting a publisher to create a completely different climate. That nothing like that has happened is a testament to the discipline and restraint of Muslims in this country . . ."

Mr Day is not fully in touch with events, for there *have* been bombings of bookshops, but he has given us a new definition of the moderate—someone who does not commit murder. I would, however, ascribe the absence of actual fatalities to the security precautions taken by Mr Rushdie and his publishers rather than to Muslim restraint, and, as I have suggested, Muslim fanatics have launched a reign of terror in which it is impossible for moderates to open their mouths.

But let me return to Mr Day's reference to "cultural sensibilities". It is perfectly reasonable for minorities to demand respect for their beliefs and traditions, and, indeed, there is much in the Muslim way of life which calls for not only respect, but emulation. It also, however, includes attitudes—and Islam is not alone in this respect—which should be thoroughly condemned and which can be seen at their worst in the Rushdie affair.

Majorities, too, have their sensibilities, some of which are fairly admirable—like their dedication to free speech—and they will react with hostility if they find them threatened.

I would not suggest that the thugs who attack Muslim children on the way from school, who terrorise Muslim shopkeepers and vandalise their shops do so in defence of the freedom of speech, but the animosities generated by the Rushdie affair have created an atmosphere which has helped them to flourish; and those animosities are largely the work of Muslim fanatics.

The CRE is a statutory body established under the 1977 Race Relations Act "to work towards the elimination of discrimination and to promote equality of opportunity and good relations between different racial groups". But people like Mr Day, by attempting to defend the indefensible, have gone far towards frustrating the very aims they are meant to promote.

The Board of Deputies and other Jewish institutions have always been happy to give immigrant organisations the benefit of their experience, and the Chief Rabbi—especially in the Rushdie affair—has shown a sensitivity to Muslim feelings to the point almost of being insensitive to Jewish ones.

I would suggest, however, that until the Siddiqis and others stop baying for Rushdie's blood, Jewish organisations keep their distance not only from their Muslim counterparts, but from the CRE.

Jewish Chronicle, 2 February 1990

Of People

Menachem Begin

MENACHEM BEGIN IS the small Jew writ large, so that even in his last, sad, declining days in office, the mere threat of his resignation was enough to cause panic among his colleagues, dismay in the streets and something like a collapse on the bourse.

The plain fact of the matter is that he had virtually resigned with the death of his wife last year. Thereafter, he went about his work like an automaton, a mere shadow of his old self, but the shadow of Begin meant more to the public than the substance of anyone else.

Jews have always made impossible demands upon their leaders and have looked not only for competence and integrity but a hint of divine approval. Ben-Gurion was one such figure and, although he did not believe in God himself, he somehow gave the impression that God believed in him.

Begin, though looking like a small-town lawyer (which he was), is also in the biblical mould, but while his predecessors, and especially Ben-Gurion, had outstanding achievements to their credit, his own career as Prime Minister is largely compounded of failure.

He inherited a prosperous country with an expanding economy and a powerful Army. He leaves a nation uncertain and divided, with few friends and many enemies, the economy stagnant and on the point of collapse, and the Army bogged down in a hostile land after a long, costly and indecisive war.

Even his greatest achievement, the Camp David agreement, has cost Israel Sinai, but has yielded little or nothing in material, or even psychological terms. There has been no normalisation to speak of, no trade across frontiers. There isn't even the mutual trust which might have enabled Israel to reduce the size of its Army and ease the crippling burden of defence expenditure.

Yet, with all his failures, there is no one either in his own party, or the opposition, to approach him in public esteem. In that sense he is to Israel what Nasser was to Egypt. He has become a sort of cult figure whose popularity is unrelated to his performance. One reason for this is that, like Nasser, he has cultivated the art of defiance and elevated chutzpah to the level of statecraft. While Ben-Gurion stood up against Israel's enemies, Begin also stood up against its friends, and could be seen to be doing so on television.

His followers have frequently denounced the media for their tendentiousness and bias, but in fact they became his handmaidens. He may have been a bad Prime Minister, but he was good copy and, even when he refrained from action, he could always be counted on to perpetrate some verbal outrage to brighten the columns of the Press or enliven the dreary void of the television newscast. These, beamed back to Israel, made the country feel that it was not only the hub of the universe, but a Great Power in its own right.

He also benefited from the errors of his predecessors. The Labour alignment, which had ruled Israel for its first thirty years, had an almost Victorian faith in betterment and believed that the immigrants from Muslim lands who had poured into the country in the 'fifties could, given sufficient education and guidance, be converted into good, free-thinking, progressive Europeans. Begin was disposed to accept them as he found them, to fall in with their folk ways and to give them positions of influence they never had before.

Moreover, his determination to hold on to the West Bank and Gaza perpetuated a sub-proletariat of Arab labourers which made the immigrants feel that they had come up in the world.

Finally, he was the first Prime Minister of the Jewish State to set foot in a synagogue out of conviction rather than duty. He is not, perhaps, quite as religious as he appears to be, and his head-gear is less in evidence now than it was when he first assumed office, but he is a devout man, which is perhaps the source of his difficulty. A lesser man could not have achieved the treaty with Egypt, but a greater one would have used it as the opportunity of a lifetime to strive for a comprehensive peace settlement with the Arabs.

He was, however, hemmed in by his understanding of Scripture:

"In that day the Lord made a covenant with Abram, saying:
'Unto thy seed have I given this land, from the river of Egypt unto the great river, the Euphrates . . .'"

He has not spoken of the Nile and the Euphrates as the natural and historic frontiers of Israel, but when he speaks of "Judea and Samaria" as part of "the eternal inheritance of the Jewish people", he means just that. He is a person of perfect integrity in small things, but a lawyer in large ones, and he gave an interpretation to the Camp David agreement which stretched the meaning of familiar expressions like "autonomy" to impossible lengths.

The invasion of Lebanon followed almost as an inevitable consequence, for it was meant not only to destroy the PLO but to stifle the aspirations of the 1.3 million Palestinians living in the West Bank and Gaza and to reconcile them to permanent Israeli rule.

It failed in almost every detail, and 517 young Israelis and countless Lebanese died as a result of that tragic misadventure, and it was the cumulative effect of that misadventure, together with ill-health and the loss of his beloved wife, which finally compelled him to resign.

Menachem Begin has presided over an Israel which has turned its back upon almost every ideal of its founders. It is no longer the peaceful, egalitarian society it strove to be, with each man enjoying the fruits of his own labour, for the Arabs have become the hewers of wood and the drawers of water. The Army—the pride of the nation—is no longer a defence force but an occupying force. Agriculture, which spearheaded the national revival, is in decline, while the arms industry—which is now the country's largest employer—is growing, and Israel is beating its ploughshares into swords. Begin may believe he is striving in the spirit of the Jewish faith, and he may condemn the goyim with his last breath, but he has secured his place in history by apeing their ways.

He has no heir apparent—indeed he took some pains to have none—but he has shown that we live in a world in which audacity, persistently applied, can have its rewards, at least in esteem, and he has established a pattern of conduct which his successor will follow.

What one can see ahead are pseudo-Begins, with all the truculence of the man himself, but without his eloquence or charm. Yitzhak Shamir, a former member of the Stern Gang, which in its day out-Irguned the Irgun, has a build which made Begin seem fragile and attitudes which made him seem moderate. The thought of him as the new Prime Minister of Israel must cause many Jews to approach their New Year with more than usual disquiet.

Observer, 4 September 1983

Isaiah at Eighty

MANY TRIBUTES HAVE been paid to Sir Isaiah Berlin, the thinking man's thinking man, on his eightieth birthday.

I don't feel equipped to argue whether he is one of the most original minds of our age, though he is certainly one of the most accessible. There is no philosophy so obscure that he cannot illuminate in a line, and one reads him as much for the clarity of his exposition as for the beauty of his prose.

Yet his legendary reputation is based on a slender body of work. His entire output consists of seven or eight published volumes, most of them collections of essays.

When David Astor owned the *Observer*, he asked me to write an article on Israel's silver jubilee and I suggested that Isaiah Berlin would be the ideal man for the job.

"He would indeed," said Astor, "but to get a word out of Isaiah is like getting blood out of a stone." Which isn't quite the case, for there are two Isaiahs—the Oral one and the Written one—and the former is as lavish with words as the latter is frugal.

When I say lavish, I don't mean wasteful, for he makes every word count. But they come in a rush, like a mountain torrent, abundant in anecdote, rich in imagery and perception, glittering with wit and occasionally laced with malice.

He is, to employ a talmudic expression he likes to use, both *charif* and *baki*, sharp and profound, and with the exception of Dr Johnson, I know of no man, living or dead, whose merest asides are so worthy of collection. Indeed, I regard him as the Dr Johnson of our day.

A few years ago, I put it to my publisher, Lord Weidenfeld, that the Oral Isaiah should be committed to print—that, in other words, he

70

could do with a Boswell. I added that I had two qualifications for the job: like Isaiah, I was a Latvian and, like Boswell, I was a Scot (of sorts).

The idea was obviously not new, and Weidenfeld said: "You get Isaiah to collaborate on a biography, I'll sign the cheque and you can put the figures on it."

When I put the idea to Sir Isaiah, he did not dismiss it out of hand and asked why I wanted to do it.

I don't like flattering people to their face and I said I wanted to get rich, which he thought was a forgivable ambition. But he believed that not everything he said was worth saving for posterity and that the idea smacked a little of vanity.

He may also have felt that the presence of a rather large and gruff recording angel at his side every time he opened his mouth would have cramped his style.

His paucity of output is, I should imagine, due to perfectionism, but his work also puts one in mind of Dr Johnson's saying that a man will sometimes turn over half a library to produce one book.

Berlin is a polymath at home in every major European culture and to study his essays is to familiarise oneself with the philosophies that have dominated the thinking of our age.

His stance is that of the old-fashioned liberal and he rejects what one might call the inevitability of the inevitable—the idea that everything is predetermined.

He suggests that there is no grand system, no accounting for the anarchy of the human spirit. It is a reassuring belief, and one which has been vindicated by recent events.

The art historian Bernard Berenson noted in his diary in 1956: "If parallel lives were still being written, it would be worthwhile to write about Isaiah Berlin and myself. We come from the same kind of ghetto, came under similar Anglo-Saxon conditioning, and have both been readers, writers, thinkers.

"Yet the differences are striking. He, in moments of crisis like the last war, played a very considerable part, while I played none . . . He lectures on philosophy not only at Oxford, but at Harvard and Chicago.

"He is a Fellow of All Souls, and I have never belonged anywhere. He is idolised in official society, and I have no place in it.

"Whence the difference? Temperament, endowment, happier and better endowed than I, better technical preparation, less censorious—more genial, in short, perhaps also more brilliant, more entertaining, more good natured, although with no less malice in his talk. Why, then, a Berenson myth and almost no Berlin one?"

The poor chap was deluding himself. Thirty-three years on, who now remembers Berenson—and who will ever forget Berlin?

Jewish Chronicle, 9 June 1989

Abba Eban

I STILL TEND to think of Abba Eban as Aubrey Even, partly because I am averse to all changes of name, whether from Hebrew into English or vice versa, partly because I have nostalgic memories of his speeches as Jewish Agency delegate to the United Nations (when he was still known as Aubrey Even), and partly because the name Aubrey goes with his personality.

Though born in South Africa, he was brought up in England and quickly shed all vestiges of his crude colonial past. He is very English in his appearance, manner, dress, utterances, attitudes, style, in everything, in fact, except his cleverness.

It is not that the English are a nation of half-wits, but those who have more than their share of intelligence feel under some obligation to hide the fact, as if it were a dark family secret, whereas Aubrey (or Abba) not only refuses to hide it, but positively glories in it, like some intellectual peacock.

He has most of the talents requisite for the highest office, but he has never come—and never will come—within sight of it, and it now seems that if the Alignment should assume office (may it come speedily and in our days, O Lord), he may even be denied the Foreign Ministry.

Some politicians are overwhelmed by office, others are broken by it, others still grow into it, but Abba (or Aubrey) is nature's own Foreign Minister, the Tallyrand of our times. He has the natural eloquence, the diplomatic skill, the intellectual attainments that the office demands, plus, of course, the experience.

He was an outstanding Ambassador to the United Nations (at a time when people still took the UN seriously), and a brilliant Ambassador to Washington. He also began well as Foreign Minister, but he was viewed with disfavour by Good Queen Golda (his style wasn't hers). When she became Prime Minister, she virtually took charge of foreign affairs and he was too much of a gentleman to challenge her presumption—especially as she was, after all, a lady.

Therein lies his principal weakness. Israel, and especially her political arena, is no place for gentlemen. It is a country open to the talents, but it is open more to some talents than to others, and whatever one's gifts, they count for little if they are unaccompanied by a talent for hustling.

Aubrey (or Abba) is disinclined to use his elbows, or even to raise his voice, and he has never built up a personal following who might do it for him—partly, one suspects, because he feels he is above that sort of thing and partly because he thought he would be pushed to the fore by his natural attainments.

To many a politician the prospect of office represents not only power, but a livelihood (with a chauffeur-driven car thrown in), whereas Abba (or Aubrey) has never been short of money. He is a prolific writer and his books, deservedly, sell by the hundred thousand.

He is also in constant demand as a speaker, and in America, at least, he gets about $5,000 a lecture (in Britain he usually gets a vote of thanks) and he looked prosperous and well fed and wore a jacket and tie even in the lean and hungry 'fifties.

The Labour movement (if it may still be thought of as such) has long ago discarded its egalitarian principles, but envy remains, and it cannot quite forgive anyone who is obviously better off than anyone else.

Abba (or Aubrey) is also not quite as eloquent in Hebrew as he is in English, for the language does not readily lend itself to his style. It is too brittle. One has hardly uttered two or three words before one has completed a sentence, whereas in English he can add word to word, and clause to clause, until he has produced something of the majesty and flow of a great river.

But, with all that, who would have thought that he could be passed over as Foreign Minister-elect? Is there anyone else in the Alignment who could, by the very act of assuming the office of Foreign Minister, raise Israel's standing among nations?

Mr Yitzhak Navon, number two on the Alignment list, apparently thinks there is (or at least he has said he would like the job), and as he enjoys a large personal following, especially among Sephardim, he is likely to get it.

Like many observers of the Israeli scene, I have become an admirer of Mr Navon. Chaim Weizmann, Israel's first President, regarded the office, with all its constraints, as a squalid device to deny him real power, but Navon, with his quiet sagacity, not only enlarged the role of the presidency and enhanced its status, but gained a warm place in the affections of the nation.

But he has no experience of Government office, no knowledge of foreign affairs and only slight experience of the outside world, and the very fact that he thinks he is fit to replace someone who has become a legend suggests that his popularity has gone to his head.

Jewish Chronicle, 6 June 1984

Lord Jakobovits

DR IMMANUEL JAKOBOVITS was the first Chief Rabbi to be knighted while in office, and is now the first to be raised to the peerage.

When he was knighted in 1981, a former Chief Rabbi of South Africa suggested that it was a reward for his pro-Palestinian attitudes, and no doubt there will be voices murmuring now that he has received his peerage for political and public services to the Tory party.

Jakobovits is not pro-Palestinian, but he is a humane and far-seeing individual who is worried about the effects of the continued occupation of the West Bank and Gaza on both Jew and Arab, and has said so. He was the only orthodox rabbi of any eminence to make a public stand on the matter, and the skies opened when he did. Chief Rabbi Shlomo Goren of Israel called upon rabbis throughout the world and British Jews in particular "to spew this dangerous man from our midst". The commotion only died down in the aftermath of the Lebanese war when many of his apprehensions were confirmed by events.

He was involved in further controversy a few years later when the Archbishop of Canterbury invited his comments on "Faith in the Cities", the Anglican blueprint for revitalising the inner cities. He offered a view which, if at odds with that of the Church, was entirely in keeping with that of the Tory party and he received a letter of support signed by more than 80 Tory MPs. Yet as he laid particular stress on individual responsibility he was careful to point out the duty of society to the helpless.

Nevertheless, he is the one prelate whose preaching did not, in the view of Mrs Thatcher, give God a bad name.

They met frequently and in a sense he has become her father-confessor. She also has an almost mystical faith in Jewish abilities which, in the case of Jakobovits, is not wholly misplaced.

He was born in Kronigsberg, East Prussia, in 1921 and though he came here as a boy and is a London University graduate he still retains a slight German accent. At 28 he was Chief Rabbi of Ireland and in 1958 he became rabbi of the Fifth Avenue synagogue, New York.

He is a profound scholar and the author among other things of the standard work on Jewish medical ethics. He is also impressive both as a man and a speaker and has the distinguished bearing of a well-kempt prophet.

When Dr Israel Brodie retired as Chief Rabbi in 1965, he seemed the obvious successor, but there were fears that he would be too orthodox for the tastes of British Jewry, and he was offered the post only after two other rabbis had turned it down.

The fears proved unfounded if only because most British Jews have moved to the Right both religiously and politically. He for his part has not moved at all. As he said when he was installed, he had not become Chief Rabbi to preside over the liquidation of Jewish usage.

The Victorian values which the Prime Minister has been trying to promote have always been Jewish values, and with his large family (he has six children and 29 grandchildren) deep piety, Germanic accent and stern sense of duty, Jakobovits would have been a natural courtier of Prince Albert.

He is a fully paid-up member of the Union of Archibishops, Cardinals and Chief Rabbis and when Dr Runcie was recently under attack he felt obliged out of loyalty and friendship to come to his aid. But he believes that the Church of England, by its very readiness to adapt to change, has brought its troubles upon itself.

Though widely admired among gentiles, he has many critics among Jews. When he quoted scripture to denounce homosexuality as an abomination and Aids as a self-inflicted calamity, liberal rabbis like Julia Neuberger retorted that he was offering but one interpretation of holy writ and an outdated one at that. Many of his own followers are unhappy with the limited role he accords to women in Jewish life.

He deplores the growing polarisation in the Jewish community with the orthodox becoming ultra-orthodox and the non-observant

77

lapsing out of the faith altogether, but to an extent he has been the cause of it.

He is a sensitive man and does not take kindly to criticism but he is, for all his sophistication and scholarship, a man of simple faith and he will not be moved from the conviction that the values which have sustained Jews throughout the centuries should not only be eternally preserved, but should have universal application. That, as he would argue, is the Jewish mission.

Jakobovits is no Tory and regards himself as a man of liberal sympathies, which in some respects he is. His sponsors in the House of Lords will probably be drawn from the Opposition, but when he rises to speak their lordships are likely to discover the true meaning of conservatism.

Observer, 1 March 1988

Stanley Kalms

ONE MIGHT THINK that a man who heads a company with 1,500 retail outlets, a work-force of almost 20,000 and a turnover of over a billion would have better things to do with his time than get caught up in communal affairs; but if one becomes hyperactive, a sort of Parkinson's Law in reverse comes into play.

The more one does, the more one's time expands in which to do it. And that, I believe, is one of the secrets of Stanley Kalms' success.

He inherited a small family firm which, within a few years, he built up into a major international conglomerate; and yet, while involved in one major take-over battle after another, he has found time to direct the work of the Jewish Educational Development Trust and Jews' College.

As a communal leader, Kalms fits into the tradition of the first Lord Rothschild, who had a fairly substantial bank to look after, and Sir Robert Waley Cohen, who was managing director of the Shell Transport and Trading Company. But while the former two gave their time to communal affairs out of a sense of obligation, Kalms got caught up in them out of a sense of personal involvement.

He is passionately interested in Jewish education and has applied both his frantic energies and a good part of his personal fortune to it.

His generosity is considered rather than impulsive. I am a great admirer of the Pelech School in Jerusalem and of its headmistress, Professor Alice Shalvi, and when she was in London last year, I introduced her to Kalms.

He cross-examined her closely on her aims, methods and needs, as well as her expenditure, taking notes all the time. A few weeks later, he flew out to Jerusalem to examine the school at first hand and donated $240,000 to its building fund.

79

He was the prime mover behind the much-lauded Traditional Alternatives symposium last May, brought over the galaxy of talents who made the occasion so memorable, and paid for their stay; the whole undertaking must have cost him some £300,000.

He has raised Jews' College from the dead and has devoted so much time to the creation of Immanuel College—which promises to be the Eton of Anglo-Jewry, and which is to open its doors next September—that one had the impression he was running Dixons, Currys and the rest on the side.

Kalms is oddly misnamed, for he is neither calm in himself nor induces calmness in others, though it is entirely appropriate that he should be the biggest distributor of electrical goods in the country, for the atmosphere becomes charged the moment he enters a room, and not even his warmest admirers would insist that he is an easy person to work with.

He is brisk, brusque and impatient, and he can be moody and abrasive. He asks short, pointed questions and expects short, pointed answers, and anyone, no matter how eminent, who embarks on a speech will be cut off in mid-flow.

He is a close friend of the Chief Rabbi and has entertained him and Lady Jakobovits both in his home and on his yacht; but he cannot take the Chief Rabbi's hesitancy, and the warm feelings they have for one another have not prevented differences from emerging between them.

Kalms has a yearning for a middle-of-the-road Judaism which he feels is not shared by the Chief Rabbi, and he tends to blame him for the Rightward lurch in the community.

He has not sought office in any of the mainstream communal institutions like the United Synagogue, the Board of Deputies or B'nai B'rith, for they have constitutions and by-laws and committees and sub-committees. He prefers to work in small organisations among a handful of people who know his mind and whose minds he knows.

Why, then, his sudden resignation from Jews' College and the Jewish Educational Development Trust?

Well, high-street stores are going through difficult times and he may need to look after the shop; but I suspect it may be more simple than that. He has applied himself to Jewish education over the past decade with great intensity and he may be in need of a rest. Alternatively, he may be saving his energies for another fray.

He has strong feelings about who should be the next Chief Rabbi.

The symposium on Traditional Alternatives was, apart from anything else, a sort of talent parade of candidates, and when the selection machinery moves into gear in the coming year, I suspect we shall find him in the forefront of communal affairs.

Jewish Chronicle, 15 September 1989

Primo Levi

I WAS SORRY to read of the tragic death of Primo Levi. I had been among his devotees for many years, but I only got to know him personally last summer and had hoped to see very much more of him in the future.

Writers can be a disappointment when encountered in the flesh, for no matter how lofty the characters they create, they can sometimes be petty, peevish, self-centred and tedious in themselves, but Levi could have stepped out of his own pages. He was a slight, silvery-haired figure with a neat little beard, donnish, soft-spoken, diffident, kindly, smiling eyes behind large glasses, and the bearing of a natural aristocrat. I had to interview him for a radio broadcast and I came with a list of prepared questions: "You've been through hell," I began, at which he immediately raised a hand to stop me.

"I suppose you mean Auschwitz," he said, "Auschwitz was hell, but I was only there for about a year, you know. I was also a chemist so the Germans found it useful to keep me alive."

Which almost suggests that he had it easy. His books show otherwise, for he did go through hell, yet they are singularly free of self-pity or even rancour. He doesn't preach forgiveness or forgetfulness, but he does suggest a need to transcend experience and avoid bitterness so that his main characters emerge from their torments not only with their souls and their sanity intact, but even with their sense of humour. To be embittered, he seems to say, to harp on the past, is to give Hitler a posthumous victory.

Most of his books are concerned with the Holocaust and its aftermath, but he never became obsessed with it and warned his readers of the dangers of obsession, or as one of his characters put it: "These aren't thoughts for every day. They're all right every now and again, but if you live with them, you just poison yourself."

Levi was born in Turin and when the Germans occupied northern Italy after the fall of Mussolini in 1943 he joined the partisans, but he was betrayed and transported to Auschwitz. Yet the betrayal never rankled in his memory. There were, he said, a few Italian Nazis and a great many Italians who were afraid of the Nazis, but for every Italian who betrayed a Jew, there were countless others who risked their lives to save Jews (which, incidentally, is a point also made by another Italian, Professor Dan Segre, in his recently published *Memoirs of a Fortunate Jew*) and he went out of the way to show that we are not, and never were, constantly surrounded by enemies, and that the world is, on the whole, a rather benign and attractive place. (To which I would add that even if it isn't I can't, offhand, think of a better one.)

His books are about the best antidote to Jewish paranoia that I've come across. They have an oddly uplifting effect: one not only feels a better man for reading them, one feels a better Jew.

His most telling work was perhaps "If Not Now, When?" which has just appeared in paperback. Everyone should read it, for apart from being a particularly gripping and heartening story, it is also, in a way, his final testament. The title, of course, comes from a famous talmudic passage: "If I'm for myself, who will be for me? But if I am only for myself, what am I? And if not now, when?"

The first point which Levi makes, the need for Jews to assert themselves, is obvious. The second is rather less so, for he suggests that Jews who are too assertive and are concerned exclusively with their own survival are being untrue to themselves. The Jew in his stories comes to stand for the universal victim, and, as one of his characters says: "Everybody is everybody else's Jew. The Poles are the Jews of the Russians and Germans," to which he himself once added, "and the Palestinians are the Jews of the Israelis."

I have heard him described as the greatest Jewish writer of our age, which I think is someting of an exaggeration, for some of his characters are too good to be true and would not be out of place in the novels of Walter Scott, but he had more than talent, or even genius, he had grace.

His untimely death is a loss to literature and a great loss to the Jewish people, but one can draw some comfort from the thought that his teachings will continue to survive through his books.

Jewish Chronicle, 24 April 1987

Julia Neuberger

RABBI LIONEL BLUE, who has for some years dominated the air waves as a broadcasting personality, has now found a rival in the person of Rabbi Julia Neuberger; but while the former—as befits a man of the spirit—remains a disembodied voice on radio, the latter has materialised in the flesh on her own weekly television programme.

Rabbi Neuberger is not as amusing as Rabbi Blue, but she has his affability, his lively mind and (though these things are a matter of taste) is much prettier, and it is unlikely that she would have got her job if she weren't. A male television presenter has only to be articulate and intelligent (and sometimes not even that), whereas a woman also has to be good-looking, if only to compensate for the fact that she's not a man.

Yet to be a woman in an area hitherto sacred to men does have its advantages. There is, first of all, the curiosity value. As Dr Johnson put it: "A woman preaching is like a dog's walking on his hind legs. It is not done well; but you are surprised to find it done at all."

In the case of Rabbi Neuberger, it is in fact done very well, and she is as easy on the ear as on the eye. She has a good voice, a rich vocabulary, chooses her words carefully, and presents them coherently and volubly.

One is therefore not surprised that, apart from being rabbi to the South London Liberal Synagogue, she lectures at the Leo Baeck College, is a force in the Social Democratic Party, is in frequent demand as a media person, and last week she received the accolade of a profile in the *Observer*, which is the nearest thing to beatification in the secular world.

And the girl is only 36! Where will she be by the time he's 37? I do not question her ability, but I doubt if she would have got this far so soon had she been a man.

But even though she's a woman rabbi and a Liberal one at that (well, she would have to be, wouldn't she?), she has much in common with her Orthodox brethren in that, like them, she rarely allows an original thought to invade her pretty head; like them, she is full of certainties; and, like them, she receives her wisdom pre-packaged. But while the latter obtain theirs from holy writ, she obtains hers from the women's pages of the *Guardian*.

She has all the right (by which I mean left) ideas and embraces all the fashionable sentiments, and to catch her in full flood on a subject like sodomy is to reconcile one almost to the wildest propositions of darkest Orthodoxy. If she had been Abraham, she would not have asked God to forgive Sodom and Gomorrah: she would have designated them as holy cities.

One would not for a moment suggest that she is a dilettante, for she is obviously tenacious, and sincere in her beliefs; but the fact that they are fashionable has also helped towards her apotheosis as a media person.

The media world at the programme planning level is a fairly narrow one, dominated by people who share one another's ideas, confirm each other's prejudices and are prone to the same inclinations; and while they may take on the occasional way-out freak to show that they are open-minded, they will generally look out for the like-minded.

Julia Neuberger meets their prescription almost to the full. She is, moreover, a woman, a Jewess and a rabbi and thus, in a sense, represents three minorities in one. If she had only been a lesbian and black—or even the head of a one-parent family and black—she would have been ideal.

My complaints about her amount, in essence, to the fact that she lacks a truly spiritual dimension—which may seem unfair, for how many rabbis, male or female, Liberal or Orthodox, living or dead, have, or have had it?

Off-hand—and I have spent much of my life in ecclesium—I can think of only three, but one of those three was likewise a Liberal woman rabbi, the first of her kind, the late Lily Montagu. I knew her only in great old age, and it is not difficult for the aged to look saintly (I'm beginning to look saintly myself), but one felt improved by being in her presence, and she had a definite glow to her.

Chaim Bermant

Rabbi Neuberger also has a glow, but it is the glow of the *jeune fille*, and the sensations she instils are of this world. Yet she displays new qualities and new abilities at every turn, and who knows what she'll be like ere she becomes an ancient monument?

Jewish Chronicle, 4 July 1986

Shimon Peres

THE LAST TIME an Israeli Prime Minister visited Britain, he received a restrained welcome—and with good reason. There will be no such restraints on the welcome Mr Peres will receive when he arrives here on an official visit next Tuesday.

It is difficult enough to make a name for a nation; it is infinitely more difficult to restore a name which has been unmade, but Mr Peres has proved himself equal to the challenge. He has not only raised his own standing in Israel, he has raised the standing of Israel in the world at large.

Shimon Peres is a man in the Ben-Gurion mould, but then he was partly moulded by Ben-Gurion. The Old Man had a ready eye for talent and surrounded himself with some of the ablest young men (as they then were) in the country, including Moshe Dayan, Itzhak Navon, Teddy Kollek and, of course, Peres—and Peres was perhaps the ablest among them. He was for a number of years director-general of the Defence Ministry, and then Deputy Defence Minister under Ben-Gurion.

One of the most preposterous charges which used to be made against him was that he never served in the armed forces, but in fact he helped to build them at a time when they were undermanned and painfully under-equipped.

Nowadays, when Israel needs arms, she goes with her shopping list to the American hypermarket, picks up what she needs, and sometimes doesn't even have to pay for it. When Peres was in the Defence Ministry, Israel had to scratch around for arms wherever she could, and he built up the special relationship with France which enabled him to re-equip the Air Force and prepare the ground for the victories of the Six-Day War.

He made two great mistakes, the one out of loyalty, the other out of impatience.

When Ben-Gurion walked out of the Labour Party in 1965, Peres went with him and built up the new Rafi Party from scratch; but although the party had all the right ideas (especially on electoral reform), it fared disastrously at the polls and it fell to Peres to negotiate the way back into the good grace of Labour.

Golda, who put party loyalty above all else, never forgave him or his Rafi associates, however. It meant that he could not even be considered for the succession when Eshkol died in 1969, and he was passed over in favour of Rabin when Golda resigned in 1974.

Then there followed his second mistake. When Labour approached the 1977 election, it still had the setbacks on the Yom Kippur War to live down, and it was shaken by scandals, and Peres chose a moment to challenge Rabin's leadership when every consideration should have disposed the party to unity.

That his leadership was faulty is beyond dispute. The qualities which make a man a great general do not always make him a great politician. He was wooden, charmless, uninspiring and uninspired and had made grave errors of judgement.

Peres no doubt felt that the perilous straits in which Israel had landed called for someone of his ability, and no doubt he was right, but this was not the moment to press his claim. He failed, the party failed, and Israel was sent careering downhill upon the seven darkest years in its history.

The Likud pandered to the worst instincts of the electorate. It bribed the public with their own money and brought the economy to the brink of collapse (or actual collapse, but for the infusion of American billions). It heightened national chauvinism and deepened national divisions.

I attended a meeting addressed by Peres in the 1981 election. The Likud had sent in bully-boys to barrack and shout and the gathering assumed the character of a lynch mob. Government speakers depicted Peres almost as a traitor, and where his abilities and record should have made him an electoral asset, he became something of a liability.

It says something for the effect of the calumnies heaped against him when he all but failed to win the 1984 election. Since then, however, he has wasted no time.

Some people are seen at their worst in secondary or supine roles, and it must be admitted that, as leader of the opposition. Peres had a slightly hang-dog look. He was born for high office and, having finally been given the chance—and only half a chance, at that—to prove himself, public attitudes to him have been transformed and he is emerging as a statesman of the first rank. It will be a privilege to have him among us.

Jewish Chronicle, 17 January 1986

Jonathan Sacks

THE APPOINTMENT OF Jonathan Sacks as the next Chief Rabbi of British Jewry will come as a surprise to no one, least of all to Dr Sacks himself.

He was born in London nearly 42 years ago, took a double first in philosophy at Cambridge, and a PhD on Jewish ethics at King's College, London. Double firsts are rare in Cambridge, and very rare in philosophy, and it was obvious from the moment he entered the rabbinate that he was destined for the highest office.

The Anglo-Jewish community, however, is not large. Its ablest talents tend to go abroad and Dr Sacks himself was offered a senior post in New York a few years ago. But once he decided to remain in London it was clear that he had his eye on the chief rabbinate, and although there were other eminently suitable candidates, there was little doubt that the job would be his.

He is Principal of Jews College, London, which trains orthodox clergy and rabbis. He is a gifted teacher and superb preacher, but unlike most orthodox rabbis he appeals to the mind rather than the emotions.

He is also a brilliant broadcaster and is to deliver the BBC's Reith Lecture later this year. However, he faces one immense handicap: he will have an almost impossible act to follow.

When Chief Rabbi Brodie retired in 1965, selectors turned to Immanuel Jakobovits with something like desperation only after four other possible candidates had turned down the job. But he grew with his responsibilities, and although many feel that he is too right wing and puritanical, he has attacked his duties with frantic dedication.

Where his predecessors presided over periods of unbroken religious decline, he has presided over a religious revival, and although he would not claim it is of his own making, he has contributed richly to it.

He has also made Jewish teaching seem relevant not only to the life of the Jewish community, but to that of the nation. He has been the most energetic, and possibly the greatest, Chief Rabbi Britain has had.

The Chief Rabbi of the United Hebrew Congregations of the British Empire, to give the office its original title, was instituted with the United Synagogue by a private act of Parliament. It was designed to bring continuity and order to Anglo-Jewish religious life.

The United Synagogue, with its sister congregations in the provinces, represents the broad stream of Anglo-Jewish orthodoxy and includes about 70 per cent of the community.

The ultra-orthodox to the right and the reformed and liberal synagogues to the left do not accept the Chief Rabbi's religious jurisdiction, but they have always recognised him as head of the Jewish community.

Lord Jakobovits has been unable to check the growing polarisation of the community, with those on the left drifting out of Jewish life and those on the right dissociating themselves from secular life. There are deep differences within the 330,000-strong British community over issues such as conversion, marriage and divorce.

Dr Sacks sees his role as that of a healer and believes that there is more uniting Jews than dividing them.

His admirers are hoping that he will prove more successful in this respect and everything in his training suggests that he might bring a greater openness of mind to the task.

Dr Sacks will not be another Jakobovits, for if the two differ in background, they differ even more in character. Lord Jakobovits is large, restless, gregarious, accessible and extrovert; he is not afraid of controversy and sometimes seems to revel in it. Dr Sacks is a dapper, donnish, retiring figure who prefers the company of books and papers to the company of people, and retreats to his study at every opportunity.

Lord Jakobovits came from a rabbinical family; Dr Sacks is from a secular one. The former went only to orthodox Jewish day schools; the latter is a product of Christ's College, Finchley. Lord Jakobovits's main mentors were two Russian-born rabbis in an East End Talmudical college; Dr Sacks's greatest mentor was Professor Bernard

Williams, who tried to purge religion from his soul and then sent him on to New College, Oxford, in the hope that Oxford might succeed where Cambridge had failed.

Lord Jakobovits has rarely been exposed to a heretical thought; Dr Sacks has rarely been exposed to any other, and many people hope that he will therefore prove to be more liberal than his predecessor. That hope is likely to be disappointed if only because the very office of Chief Rabbi leaves little scope for liberalism.

The Independent, 26 February 1990

Alice Shalvi

TEDDY KOLLEK ONCE described himself as a *schnorrer*. The same, I suppose, could be said of Alice Shalvi, Professor of English Literature at the Hebrew University, and principal of the Pelech Girls' School, who'll be in London next month, though Yiddish purists will no doubt insist that I call her a *schnorreke*. But *schnorrer* or *schnorreke*, she excels at her craft for she recently managed to *schnor* a prime site in Jerusalem for a new building for Pelech from no less a person than Kollek himself. He also gave her his blessing. The one thing he didn't give her—presumably because he has none himself—is money, and she is looking for £1,000,000 to pay for the building, which is one of the reasons why she is coming to London, but there are others.

Mrs Shalvi, if she will forgive my saying so, is a woman with a mission which was summed up by Melanie Phillips in a recent interview in the *Guardian* as an attempt "to reconcile Orthodox Judaism with feminism". Miss Phillips wondered if it was not perhaps "a pointless exercise". I suspect it's a thankless exercise, but I'm afraid a necessary one, for although I regard feminism itself as the ultimate resort of the termagant, the Orthodox Jewish feminist still has a powerful case if only because she can still be the victim of blatant injustice, and Professor Shalvi gave some examples in the course of the *Guardian* interview.

As is well known, only the husband can initiate a divorce in Jewish law, and if he withholds it, the wife cannot remarry, but he, given the help of sympathetic rabbis, can. "We discovered," she said, "that between 1980 and 1985 there were 94 cases of men taking second wives, with the first wife left in a limbo because the husband had not divorced her."

She also mentioned the case of a woman who had waited 25 years for a divorce. She left her husband because he beat their child, but because she left him she was decreed a rebellious wife and therefore he didn't have to support her or divorce her.

Professor Shalvi is less inclinded to blame the halacha than the halachists for such outrages, for she feels that even a benign law can be perverted by less than benign men but—and here we touch upon a paradox—she feels that, in Israel at least, Jewish women have themselves to blame to a large extent for their situation. Instead of seeking a more active role in Jewish life they are, she believes, reverting to traditional concepts of family with the man as breadwinner and the woman content with her role as homemaker.

That, in my opinion, is not an unhealthy concept, but in an increasing number of Jewish families the wife is both breadwinner and homemaker, while the husband spends his days and nights in study (or at least, in the house of study) insulated from domestic upheaval. He is concerned with the heavens, while the earth is left in the hands of women.

It is a cosy arrangement, for the man at least, and I have tried to spread it around among my own womenfolk without much success, but it is neither just nor wholesome, and Professor Shalvi—who, one should perhaps add, is herself the mother of six children—is trying to make her pupils more aware of their own spirituality and to inculcate a greater readiness to give it public expression, not to the extent of invading the male domain, but to the extent of duplicating it. In a way she is trying to make the role of the Jewish woman more burdensome, but, of course, more rewarding. She further insists that all her pupils study the Talmud, in the belief that only the emergence of a sufficient body of women scholars can eliminate some of the handicaps from which Jewish women, particularly Jewish wives, still suffer.

She is not trying to create female rabbis, which is perhaps a pity, for the Pelech girls I have seen would make extremely attractive ones, but she is no doubt right in her conviction that a properly informed female laity will be less inclined to take no for an answer.

She is, in other words, seeking a social revolution within the parameters of Jewish law. I don't know if it can be done, but if it can, she is the person to do it. And come to think of it, she is probably the person to do it even if it can't be done.

Anyone who can *schnor* a prime site in Jerusalem from Teddy Kollek is indeed capable of absolutely anything.

Jewish Chronicle, 6 May 1988

Elie Wiesel

THERE ARE TWO surprising things about the award of the Nobel Prize to Elie Wiesel. First, that he received it now rather than 10 or even 15 years ago, and second that is was the Peace Prize rather than the Literature Prize.

The Holocaust has given rise to a vast body of literature, and Wiesel is generally regarded as the laureate of the genre. He was born in Transylvania and was 15 when he and his entire family were deported to Auschwitz in 1944. He alone survived, and since then he has become the remembrancer of what was to him one of the central events not only of Jewish history but of human experience, a period when, to use the language of the Cabbala, "God turned his back upon the world".

Other survivors have recalled their experience in terms of classical narrative, but Wiesel feels that the Holocaust was too profound an event to be approached in this way. He deals with it more obliquely, and captures the atmosphere of terror rather than the terror itself in a twilight world of seared souls and swirling mists.

He was, as a boy, deeply immersed in Hassidic lore, which is reflected in his writing. His tales abound in allegories, his figures are often symbolic rather than creatures of flesh and blood, but the effect is mesmeric, and to open one of his books is to be engulfed in a nightmare.

He found himself in France at the end of the war, and made his name initially as a French writer. François Mauriac spoke of him as a Lazarus. His work, he said, was "unique", in that "while all others have experienced life, he alone has experienced death." But it was only when he came to be published in America in the early sixties that he acquired an international reputation and began to emerge, albeit reluctantly, as a cult figure.

His mission was to impress upon mankind the enormity of what the Jews had gone through, not only for the sake of the Jews, but out of the conviction that to forget is to invite a recurrence.

In a sense, he also regards the victims of the Holocaust as a sort of sacrifice (which is, indeed, what holocaust means) for the sins of mankind, and he believes that they will have died in vain if the world is not chastened by their torments.

And finally there is the purely mystical element, the traditional Jewish belief that something of the dead survives as long as they are remembered.

It it doubtful whether he has succeeded on every count, for there are signs that the world is getting a little tired of the Holocaust, but his impact on American Jewry has been overwhelming. His books—he has lost count of their number—sell by the million, but perhaps more important than his books are his personal appearances.

He is in immense demand as a lecturer, and attracts vast audiences, and the man, spare, cadaverous, with large, haunted eyes and sunken cheeks, is almost the message. When he begins to speak in a deep, sombre voice which seems to belong to another world, his audience is caught up in the long night of Jewish travail. One comes away with the taste of ashes in one's mouth.

He has never suggested that Jews could have done more to save their brethren from the Holocaust, but he has nevertheless imbued them with guilt on that score, and if Jews react with excessive vehemence to events in the Middle East, for example, it is not so much over what is happening in the Middle East today as over what happened in Europe in the forties.

In 1968, he wrote a book on the plight of Soviet Jewry called *The Jews of Silence*. The title was something of a misnomer, for by 1968 Jews neither within Russia, nor without, were silent on the matter, but it conveyed in graphic terms what it was to be a Jew in the Soviet Union.

He did not suggest that they were threatened with another Holocaust, but they were threatened (as they still are) with spiritual extinction, and he helped to make their situation an international, rather than a purely Jewish, issue.

He has not limited himself to Jewish causes, and to an extent he uses the term Jew as a synonym for victim, so that to him the blacks are the Jews of South Africa, and the Miskito Indians are the Jews of

Nicaragua, though he has not gone as far as his fellow survivor of Auschwitz, Primo Levi, who has suggested that the Palestinians are the Jews of the West Bank.

If he regards Israel as a special case, it is not so much because of what Jews have been through, as what Israel itself has been through, and he feels that a nation born so recently out of chaos and beset with so many problems should be allowed time to find its soul.

He was for a time Professor of Jewish Philosophy at City College, New York, and is now Professor of Philosophy and Ethics at Boston University, and he is sometimes thought of as a conscience at large, so that whenever a major ethical issue crops up, television cameras zoom in upon him for a comment. It is not a role he ever sought, but he feels that someone who lives by the word cannot take refuge in silence.

His true vocation is that of rabbi, but if he has the learning, he lacks the conviction, and he is rather better at asking questions than giving answers. But rabbis in Eastern Europe were often also story tellers, itinerant preachers who wandered from town to town adding their own embellishments to tales from the Talmud and the Cabbala, to beguile, chasten and instruct. His work falls entirely within that tradition.

Observer, 19 October 1986

Fred Worms

IN THE BEGINNING there was but one Hillel House, a narrow edifice where one could move up or down, though not sideways, and which was in such a state that one could hardly move at all without demolishing some part of the fabric.

And it was a place where one could snatch a quick meal for a low price, where provincials (like me) could doss down for the night in cramped and chilly discomfort, and where Israelis could wash their smalls and drip-dry their drip-dries.

All that, however, was a long time ago, when the world was young, Churchill was Prime Minister, there were 240 pennies to the pound, and Fred Worms was hardly heard of. Today, wherever students forgather, no matter how remote their campus, there is a Hillel House or a Hillette (which sounds like a female Hillel, but is the awkward expression used to designate a mini-Hillel), or at least someone who will keep an eye on their welfare.

The Hillel Foundation is so central to the life of the community in general, and of Jewish students in particular, that one wonders how we ever managed without it; but until a generation ago there were comparatively few students and, with the exception of the handful who went to Oxford or Cambridge (where Cecil Roth and the Loewes—*père et fils*—kept a fatherly eye on them), most of them lived at home.

Today there seems to be an unwritten rule that anyone who enters a university or polytechnic will do so away from home, so that Londoners go to Manchester, Mancunians go to Brighton, and Glaswegians go to Hull, and the Hillel Foundation is a sort of *locus parentis* to them all. It is an immense undertaking and the man who has done (and is doing) more than anyone else to make it possible is the aforementioned Fred Worms.

Working with students can be a thankless and frustrating task, not because all student leaders are feckless, incompetent and stupid (though some are), but because they are necessarily ephemeral, and one has no sooner established a working relationship with one generation of leaders than one is confronted by another. Fred, however, has somehow managed to build up a tradition of confidence and trust which is among the few constants in the inconstant world of student life.

He is a self-confessed Yekke, and what is insufferable about Yekkes is that the good conceit they have of themselves is usually justified. It is abundantly so in the case of Fred, especially as he has a talent—unknown among Yekkes—for tempering earnestness with geniality.

He is the thinking man's tycoon, sparing in words, unsparing in effort, and utterly reliable, so that if he takes a task in hand it is as good as done, and all without angst.

He is now, comparatively speaking, a gentleman of leisure, but until about 15 years ago he was head of a multi-million pound light-engineering company, with factories in South Wales and Australia. Yet he still found time to involve himself actively in numerous communal projects, play an execrable game of tennis, and even go over the weekly sidra with his three daughters.

He is Orthodox in practice without being orthodox in belief, though on torrid days he has been known (may God forgive him) to forgo the pleasures of the synagogue for the pleasures of his swimming pool (though, for all I know, it could be his private mikva, in which case I apologise for the injustice).

If he has more than his fair share of ability, he has also had more than his fair share of luck. He sold out his company to a car-accessory firm shortly before the oil crisis, while the British car industry was riding high.

What is more important, he is fortunate—as anyone who has ever met Della will aver—in his wife, fortunate in his daughters, and fortunate even in his sons-in-law, and he commutes between elegant homes in Bishop's Avenue and Yemin Moshe to keep in touch with his children and grandchildren, and with his responsibilities as a governor of the Hebrew University and a director of the Union Bank of Israel. (He is also on the London Board of Bank Leumi.)

Next Thursday the Hillel Foundation and his many friends will be celebrating his 65th birthday with a dinner in the King David Suite. If I may reveal a dark secret, he was in fact 65 as long ago as last November, which suggests a degree of unpunctuality not in keeping with his nature; but as he spends half the year in Israel he may, at three score and five, have fallen in with the ways of the orient.

Jewish Chronicle, 14 March, 1986

Of Places

Lost Civilisation

ABOUT 14 YEARS ago a farmer at Tell Mardikh in northern Syria blunted his plough on a large stone object which, on exhumation, proved to be a cereal bin dating back to about the time of Abraham, the eighteenth century BC. It led to what an American archaeologist, Professor David Noel Freedman, of Michigan University, has called "the greatest archaeological discovery of the generation, perhaps of the century".

But it caused no great stir at first. Syria has felt the tread of almost every great empire in history. They all left their mark and if every remnant of antiquity was pursued with a spade, half the country would be dug up (and, indeed, one sometimes gets the impression that half the country has been dug up). The discovery did, however, excite Paulo Matthiae, a young graduate in Near Eastern studies at Rome University, not so much because of the urn itself, but because of its location. Numerous potsherds had been found in the area dating back to the middle or even the early Bronze Age (about 2500 BC) and he believed that the sands of Tell Mardikh, some 30 miles south of Aleppo, harboured greater secrets.

In ancient times when men built anew they were generally content to add to the foundations of the old and thus created artificial hills—*Tell* in Arabic—which one meets at frequent intervals throughout the Near and Middle East.

If one cuts away the side of a Tell, as has sometimes been done, one finds civilisation after civilisation, flattened and stacked, one on top of the other like the different layers of a vast multi-decker sandwich, and in each there are embedded the small objects—the handle of a jug, the base of a figurine, the bronze arrow-head—which declare their age.

103

The mound at Tell Mardikh, occupying an area of more than 140 acres, is the largest in Syria and flanks a route much used by traders, travellers and invading armies in ancient times. When Abraham "departed out of Haran" to go to Canaan he almost certainly passed through Tell Mardikh, and may well have stopped there. It also bore striking similarities to Tell Hariri, a mound by the Euphrates near the Syrian-Iraqi border which had been excavated by a French expedition in the inter-war years and which had revealed the ancient city of Mari.

Tell Mardikh, argued Matthiae, could be another Mari, perhaps even better. He was only 21 at the time and his views were treated with scepticism, but he went out to Syria to make some initial soundings and came back with sufficient evidence to convince his elders that he was following more than a whim. In 1964 he brought a small team of Italian archaeologists and technicians, recruited some Arab labourers, and began to dig into the mound in earnest.

A professional hazard is what might be called the "seek-and-ye-shall-find" syndrome, which is to say, one can start with such a clear vision of what should be in the ground that almost everything one discovers is made to reflect it. Biblical archaeologists are particularly prone to this, for Scripture tends to impose its authority on all its students, even the sceptics. Matthiae was therefore doubly on guard.

In the first few seasons he unearthed the gate and outer wall of what had obviously been a great city, and then moved inwards to uncover cisterns, granaries, homes, temples, workshops, palaces, figures in clay and stone, ornaments in bronze and gold, indicating a wealthy settlement of some 40,000 inhabitants, and all witnesses to a great antiquity, but silent witnesses, for they contained few inscriptions. Then in 1968 came a breakthrough. He unearthed the basalt form of a king which contained, among other inscriptions, the word EBLA. It was as if he had found the Holy Grail.

Ebla is mentioned in various Mesopotamian and Egyptian texts dating back to the third millennium BC as a great kingdom and commercial centre and there was considerable speculation in learned journals as to its actual location. Matthiae, though convinced from his own researches that it was somewhere within northern Syria, had not allowed himself to hope that he was touching upon the very heart of the place. Now here it was, a lost civilisation. Yet even with the basalt king he contained his excitement and sought corroboration. Six years later he was almost literally overwhelmed by it. A workman clearing what was thought to be the floor of the royal palace found himself peering into a small cavity. The hole was made bigger and the floor caved in, and there below were thousands upon thousands of clay tablets, some neatly stacked, some cracked, others crumbling into dust and comprising one of the most amazing archaeological finds of modern times. The gold, the bronze, the statues, the very stones of the city sank into insignificance. There is nothing more important to the archaeologist than the actual written word, and here was a vast library.

The tablets, of baked clay, are fairly similar in size, about 8in. by 10in., and look like overdone puff pastry, with little notches on them like one might find on the back of a digestive biscuit. These notches, which vary in size and shape, are in Cuneiform, a mode of writing widespread in the ancient Near East for more than a thousand years and which employed different shapes to represent different syllables or even logograms (the £, for example, is a logogram, so is %, so are our different road-signs).

Professor Giovanni Pettinato, a philologist attached to the expedition, at first thought the language was Sumerian, an ancient tongue which was almost the lingua franca of the Near East, and although the tablets did contain numerous Sumerian expressions, he kept stumbling upon sounds and characters which made no sense either in Sumerian or in the other great language of the area, Akkadian. At the same time he was intrigued by a formula with which most of the tablets closed—*dub-gar* meaning "tablet written"—in Sumerian. Many other tablets, however, closed with the expression *gal-balag*, which is meaningless in Sumerian, but if read as a West-Semitic language means *ikh-tub*, "it is written". Here, in other words, was a synonym for *dub-gar* and if the unknown tongue was indeed West-Semitic, then a great many other expressions, hitherto impenetrable, immediately acquired meaning.

Pettinato continued with a growing sense of euphoria, for once the expressions bearing a familiarity to other Semitic languages had been deciphered, it was but a step to extracting the meaning of those that did not, and it soon became evident that he had not merely come upon a different dialect of a known tongue, but that he had discovered a new language, which he called Eblaite, and with the discovery the whole history of Ebla lay open.

Professor "Pettinato" is a short, balding, ebullient figure, his glasses aglow with the thrill of revelation. He has none of the hesitancy or dourness of Matthiae and he has little doubt that once the entire Ebla archive has been deciphered—and it is a process which must take many years—much of the history of ancient Syria may have to be rewritten. It had always been known that Syria had flourishing urban centres like Aleppo and Damascus, but it is now clear that they must have been much larger and their influence more extensive than had hitherto been anticipated. Ebla itself, said Pettinato, was the core of a conurbation of more than 250,000 people and levied tribute from vassal settlements strung out along the valley of the Euphrates.

Ebla was clearly a business community. The written material found in most archaeological sites tends to sing of arms and of man. The Ebla tablets sing of cargoes and of corn and consist largely of accounts, inventories, price-lists which, with their regular columns, bear an uncanny resemblance to the Stock Exchange pages of the *Financial Times*. It was a major entrepôt centre, dealt extensively in timber, textiles and metals, and had trade links with Gaza, Hazor, Meggido and even, if the reference is correct, Jerusalem (which is about a thousand years before the city is mentioned in the Bible).

It was a relaxed community in which the role of women was more than merely domestic. Some appear to have been in business on their own account, and the many complimentary references to queens, wives and mothers suggest that they had an exalted place in Eblaite society.

About one in eight of the population was a civil servant—which may explain the size of the archive. As is often the case, the more the Eblaites had to fight for, the less they were inclined to fight and the army consisted of hired mercenaries, which was sufficient to keep the casual intruder at bay, but not the more determined enemy. About 2300 BC Ebla was invaded by Naram-Sin, King of Akkad, but it managed to recover its power and wealth. Seven centuries later, however, it was overwhelmed by an invasion of Hittites who razed Ebla and its suburbs, which vanished from history from that time until this.

As a kingdom, Ebla lasted for something like a thousand years and its golden age was during the reign of King Eberum in the early years of the third millennium BC when there was a constant flow of tributes from vassal kingdoms to the north and south. Professor Pettinato has little doubt that King Eberum was none other than Eber who features in Genesis as a great-grandson of Noah and the great-great-great-grandfather of Abraham and who, as such, may be considered the ancestor of the Jewish people.

The tablets also contain numerous names which, it was hitherto believed, had their origins in the Old Testament, such as Ab-Ra-Mu (Abraham), E-Sa-Um (Esau), Sau-Lu (Saul) and Dau-U-Dum (David). The name of Israel (whose literal meaning is "The Man who contended with God") was, according to Genesis, bestowed on Jacob by divine grace and acquired through him by the Jewish people. Pettinato argues that, on the contrary, it was commonplace in Ebla five centuries before Jacob, and points to the incidence of Is-Ra-El-Um in the tablets.

It is, however, when one comes to gods that Pettinato is at his most controversial. There are frequent references in the tablets to *El*, which in Hebrew is both a word for a god and a name of God, and which in Eblaite could be a purely generic expression meaning simply god. During and after the reign of Eberum, however, *El* is heard of less often and there is an increasing incidence of *Yah*, which in Hebrew is the permissible form of the unutterable *Yahweh* (which is commonly mispronounced as Jehovah). Pettinato believes that King Eberum may have introduced the worship of *Yahweh* some two or three centuries before Abraham.

He also suggests, on the basis of his own discoveries, that Abraham's Ur was not Ur of the Chaldees, but another city of the same name near Ebla and that the Israelites were derived from Syria. Here at least he may claim the backing of Scripture, for Jacob is spoken of in Deuteronomy as "a homeless Syrian", and Ezekiel describes the father of the Jewish people as "an Amorite", that is Syrian, and the mother as "an Hittite".

All of which may show that Jews may be aboriginal Syrians, but it does nothing to support the view that Judaism was a neo-Syrian cult.

Dr Michael Weitzman, a philologist at University College London, has pointed out—and he is not alone in this opinion—that Professor Pettinato has drawn sweeping conclusions from what is, so far, only limited evidence. A Cuneiform character, he said, can represent more than a dozen different syllables and the *yah* suffixes which the professor regards as evidence of a *Yahweh* cult can be read quite differently, and even if read as *yah* they need not refer to Yahweh.

The Ebla excavations are not over. Professor Matthiae and his team will be returning to Tell Mardikh next August for their fourteenth season. Given the size of the mound and their painstaking rate of progress, they will probably be returning for the next 20 years. Matthiae, who is 35, is not a young man in a hurry. He is a shortish, good-looking man with greying hair, blue eyes and a glazed expression. He moves around silent and preoccupied among his chattering helpers, breakfasts peripatetically on a cup of coffee, which he leaves unfinished, and is devoid of all Italian *brio*. He clearly lives for his work and in it, as if everything above ground—certainly everything of recent creation—was a passing irrelevance. He becomes animated only when he talks about his excavations which, even at his early age, have pushed him to the forefront of his profession.

The work on site begins at six, when the mists of early morning still swirl round the mound, and continues till noon and one comes away with *terra sancta* in one's hair, a dust which may have contained the footprints of Abraham.

All the portable finds, like the various bits of pottery, are collected in baskets and brought to the compound, where they are washed and scrubbed, and then the intricate business of sorting and dating begins. Related sherds are put together, in a slow and laborious operation, and a visitor to Tell Mardikh can get the impression that half the encampment is playing at jig-saw puzzles, which in a sense they are. They are piecing together history.

Have the discoveries affected our understanding of the Bible? In a sense it has enriched it, for even if the *Yahs* of Ebla bear no relation to Jehovah of Scripture, and Eberum is no kin to Eber, they have lent a touch of the real to the ethereal.

Observer, 16 January 1977

At Large in America

THE FAULT, AND I hesitate not to name names, was André
Ungar's—a Hungarian (but, for all that, a friend) and rabbi of
Temple Emanuel, Westwood, New Jersey. Some years ago he invited
me to tour America. Gladly, I said, but how will I pay for it? Talk, he
said.

Talk? In Britain one may be paid a pittance for writing, but one
gets nothing at all for talking. Indeed when I was secretary of a
learned society in Glasgow it was our custom to invite moneyed men
to address us from time to time in the hope—usually forlorn—that
they might make a small contribution to our funds.

There we have the great difference between our two cultures. In
Britain one expects to be paid to listen; in America one is paid to talk.
I understand that even rabbis, God's own talkers, are so paid, at least
when speaking ex cathedra. And I am told that there are laymen so
well trained in the matter that they reach for their cheque books every
time their rabbi says good-morning. "Talk," said Rabbi Ungar,
"and the money will come down like manna from heaven." He
introduced me to a friend, who introduced me to another, who
introduced me to the matchless Lily Edelman, cultural director of
B'nai B'rith, who waved her hand and presto!, I was presented with
an itinerary of a coast-to-coast tour.

I was brought up in a house of words. I am descended from a long
line of rabbis on my father's side, and from a long line of women on
my mother's, and I became familiar with the various gradations of
speech at an early age. At the very bottom of the scale there was
malicious rumour and then, in ascending order, low gossip, high
gossip, a chat, a schmooze, a talk, a speech, an address, a sermon, a
discourse—and finally, at the very apex of the spoken word, the

lecture. A lecturer enjoys a certain social standing, at least in Britain. I'd been asked for a series of lectures. Therefore I buried myself in books and papers and prepared a course which would have produced a master's degree *summa cum laude* in sociology or Semitics, or even both, for anyone who had cared to accompany me on my tour. I gave each venue a choice of subjects and in Washington my hosts invited me to speak on "European Jewry—Today and Tomorrow".

The synagogue auditorium contained about two thousand seats, most of them filled. The largest audience I had faced up to then was in a hall of some two hundred economics students, where I began at the sound of one bell, was cut short by the sound of another fifty minutes later and that was that. Here there were no bells, only this vast audience. For the first time in my life I experienced the drug of numbers and, having exhausted my prepared lecture on today and tomorrow, I went on to speak of yesterday. As I had something like a thousand years to cover I could have continued infinitely, and almost did. It was only when my voice began to give out that I had a closer look at the audience and noticed that it too was giving out. My host for the day said to me later, "You've got it all up there," by which I think he meant that I should have kept it all up there.

From Washington I flew in a large plane to New York, from New York in a smaller plane to some place in Pennsylvania and from there in a smaller plane still (I had the feeling it flapped its wings) to some place at the back, or maybe the front of the Alleghenies. The runway seemed to be a dirt track and the terminal was a wooden hut. Chickens fled from our path as we pulled up and I half expected to see Li'l Abner and his Maw come bounding by my window. As I came down the stairs I was greeted by two men with gnarled faces, a portly woman in a fur coat and a huddled elderly figure in a wheelchair who was introduced to me as the founding father of the local Jewish community. He greeted me unenthusiastically with a mittened hand. He had been bedridden for some months and his family had persuaded him to dress and come out in my honour, but he had not carried the honours to the point of putting in his teeth.

The town, which I shall call Hicksville, consisted largely of one long street that began in the hills and ended abruptly at a grimy lake with old tyres and dead fish floating on the surface of the water. Jews had been among the first settlers in the neighbourhood in the early part of the 19th century, and the elderly gentleman could, by the look of him, have been among their number. There were about two hundred Jews in the town, nearly all of whom looked alike, which was only to be expected, for they were nearly all related. There was a surprisingly well-appointed synagogue and communal hall and, even more surprising, a full-time rabbi—a short, sad man from Germany, who had a good library and ample time to peruse it. "Nothing happens here," he said, "no one is born, no one even dies." It seemed that I myself was something of a happening, for I was taken on arrival to the local broadcasting studio where I was greeted by a young man with a smooth voice and rough hands and led to a seat beside him.

"We are proud and privileged," he began in a voice like a fanfare of trumpets, "to have with us in the studio today, straight from London, England, best-selling novelist Chaim . . ."

At which point I interrupted to say that I was not a best-selling novelist, and all but added that I would hardly have shlepped out to this neck of the woods if I were. The announcer looked at me open-mouthed, lost, for a moment, for words. I suppose he had never met anyone before attempting to devalue his own currency. I was not, however, acting out of modesty, but I lived on words and did not like to see them used in such a way as to deprive them of their true meaning. But I learned later, my hosts in the listening audience felt badly let down.

This "best-selling novelist" business kept happening to me until a kindly chairman drew me aside to explain that the buildup was not for my benefit but was necessary to warm up the audience. "If they think you're a best seller you've got them eating out of your hand before you start, but if the word gets around that you're nobody you've got to make every word count."

That night I had to make every word count. The entire Jewish community was there, of course, as were clergy from the various churches (including a gentleman with a very large cross whom I took to be a bishop), the police chief, the fire chief, the mayor and—for all I know—the governor of the state. So was the elderly gentleman in the wheelchair, wearing his teeth now and making clicking noises like castanets. The place was packed.

About an hour before the meeting I was told by the president of the synagogue, who a little improbably was from Brooklyn (he had married into the local family), that my lecture was part of the local Civil War centenary celebrations.

"But I arranged to talk on the Anglo-Jewish ruling class," I protested.

111

"Yeh, yeh, so make it de Anglo-Jewish ruling class an de Civil War."

"But I don't know anything about the Civil War."

"You ain't hoid of Abe Lincoln?"

I had heard of Abe Lincoln and somehow I was able to drag him into my talk, but it didn't really help. It transpired that, although the geography of the place indicated otherwise, Hicksville had in fact fought on the Confederate side and everyone was waiting for a reference to Robert E. Lee.

From there I travelled via planes of growing size and increasing airworthiness to the suburbs now of Boston, now of Dallas, now of Cleveland, now of Chicago. I was never quite sure which was which. I flew in identical Boeings tended by identical stewardesses, serving identical food, landed in identical termini and plodded along the same endless corridors, to be greeted on emerging by identical delegations from the local temple or chapter of the B'nai B'rith. In fact the delegations, which usually consisted of women, were at first glance like stewardesses in mufti and one half expected to be greeted with "Fasten your seat belts, please". Very short hair was then the fashion and I kept seeing Mia Farrows everywhere. Some of the women were grandmothers and were remarkably well preserved. It was the American men, I discovered, who put on the years.

I suffered occasional mishaps. In New England I found myself in the pulpit of a vast temple bristling with electronic gadgets. One button, and the ark opened; another, and it closed; a third, and the choir screen unfolded. I have a habit of flailing with my hands as I speak and inadvertently pressed a fourth, whereupon the pulpit, with me still in full voice, vanished from view and I found myself in the basement. Was it, I wondered, designed to allow the rabbi a quick getaway, or to illustrate the story of Korah?

Another time I found myself in a town much favoured as a health resort, especially by people suffering from rheumatic and respiratory disorders. When I walked onto the stage of the Jewish community centre, below me were row upon row of middle-aged and elderly people in wheelchairs, with crutches and walking sticks. I didn't know whether to address them or bless them. I had been invited to speak on a light topic, in this case, "A Litvak Fallen Among Scotsmen", and as if that wasn't light enough, to do it in *mammeh-loshen*, which I said I would, and which may have explained the age of the audience. As soon as I began there came a loud crackling as the entire audience, almost in a body, adjusted their hearing aids. I speak what I call the Queen's Yiddish, which is to say the Lithuanian variety, while the audience was composed of Galitzianer, and they didn't understand a word.

Such incidents, happily, were uncommon and in most cases I faced a fairly straightforward routine. I was generally met at the plane and taken out to lunch at a smart local restaurant where the local rabbi and I were about the only male guests among a dozen or so smartly groomed, bright-eyed, lacquer-nailed females. The rabbis generally bloomed; I wilted. The most difficult company invariably consisted of those who had actually read my books.

My novels are, or at least are meant to be, vaguely amusing, and presumably some of the ladies had enjoyed them sufficiently to want to hear me in person. In America there are no degrees of attainment. If one sells at all, one is a best seller, if one is funny at all then one is Groucho Marx, Mark Twain and Oscar Wilde rolled into one. I must have been so heralded around some of the suburbs for I was frequently surrounded by eager-eyed groups waiting breathlessly to laugh at the first aphorism to fall from my lips. While I occasionally shine, I am in fact a large and gloomy man and at most times of the day and all times of the night I can put a dampener on even the most cheerful gathering. I'm a poor traveller and after a long and turbulent plane journey I generally need a period of time to let my pancreas and kidneys recover their moorings—but such is the level of expectations that I only had to ask for the toilet to occasion a tinkle of laughter all around me, and appreciative remarks on my earthy English wit.

I was offered a lot of hospitality and at first stayed exclusively in private homes. These tended to be very long and very low, though on closer inspection I discovered that they largely consisted of garages and that most of the rooms in the actual houses were bathrooms. Very dirty the Americans, I thought, or very clean.

I was generally allowed perhaps an hour or two for a rest and change and was then taken to a cocktail party where I was expected to shine and where, after a sufficient intake of dry martinis (America's greatest contribution to civilisation), I usually convinced myself that I *was* shining. From there we retired to yet another meal, and thence, fattened and fed like a Nebraska ox, I was hoisted to the stage of the local community centre and asked to do my piece.

The meetings were flatteringly large and the audiences flatteringly attentive. The questions were intelligent and searching and suggested not only a wide area of reading but a sense of concern for what was happening in the Jewish world which one did not always find in England, and I was sufficiently stimulated by the meetings to emerge gradually from the stupor induced by the dining and wining. Still when each meeting had ended I was ready for bed, but my host for the evening was not, and he generally invited a few friends back for late night drinks. He may have invited only a few, but generally several dozen came (nothing is quite as open as an American open house). If there is an art of disengaging yourself from a gathering brought together in your honour I have not mastered it, and I found myself going to bed at one, two or three in the morning and, where I had an early plane to catch, not going to bed at all. Now that sort of thing is not too harmful, even after a long plane journey, if it happens once or twice a week, but if it happens four or five nights in a row one begins to show the effects. I finally showed mine in one city, when I rose to get off a plane and my legs sagged under me in the gangway, and I was taken off in state (and in a state) on a stretcher. It was a matter of simple exhaustion and I would have been discharged from the hospital after a few hours, but my recovery was delayed by a succession of visitors each of whom came bearing gifts and one of whom bore a cheque for the lecture I hadn't delivered and wouldn't be delivering. When I refused it (how ill I must have been!), he said to me in a low whisper: "You'd better take it—you'll need it when you get the bill." But I found when I rose that somebody else had paid the bill.

I was six weeks in America, travelled from Maine to Alabama and from New York to Los Angeles, gave thirty different lectures in thirty different towns, and by the end of the tour had worked out my own rules for survival, the first of which is: BEWARE OF AMERICAN HOSPITALITY.

The hospitality is always well intentioned. One finds oneself among people who take pleasure in giving pleasure. Their sociability is infectious but, after a time, murderous, and after my initial collapse I made it a rule never to stay in a private house but always to book into a hotel.

What I could not work out was how to come to terms with American politeness. Americans regard themselves as gruff and uncouth, and I used to think of them as such myself. When I noticed Texas and Arizona on my itinerary I was half afraid that if I bored my audiences they might reach for their guns. I even contemplated appending a notice to my lectern: "Don't shoot the speaker. He is doing his best." But if anything I found them extravagantly affable. In England if someone tells you that your talk "was *rather* good", you know from the tone of the *rather* that it was fairly dreadful. American politeness is prodigal and Americans who express an opinion do so in superlatives ("Great!" . . . "Fabulous!" . . . "Sensational!") so that anyone new to the game, as I was, comes to think that he really is great.

It was Rabbi Ungar who put me wise. The superlatives, he explained, are not an expression of opinion but of guilt. When someone hasn't followed a word of what you said the least he feels he can do is to praise you for the way you said it. "There is," he concluded, "only one certain way of knowing you were good—if they ask you back."

I wasn't asked back.

Present Tense, Vol. 2 No. 4, Summer 1978

All Roads Lead To . . .

THE MOST SURPRISING thing about Roman Jewry is that it should still exist, for it shows, and has for long shown, all the symptoms of a community in the process of dissolution. It is small, assimilated, with a slight level of Jewish knowledge and an even slighter level of observance, and it has always kept itself a little distant from the major centres of Jewish life.

As a community it is the oldest in Europe; its records go back to Hasmonean times, about a century and a half before Christ. It thrived under pagan rule, but beginning with the rise of Christendom it has suffered frequent periods of harassment and oppression. Yet, until the Nazi era, Roman Jews never suffered the expulsions or massacres that took place in other parts of Europe. Papal rule, while despotic, could be benign. The 12th-century Jewish traveller Benjamin of Tudela found a small but cultivated community of some 200 souls enjoying a high social status and—this was unusual for the period—paying no special levies. In Renaissance times, Roman Jews, though still formally restricted to their ghetto (the very term is of Roman origin), enjoyed a standard of living and a degree of cultivation unknown among Jews elsewhere in Europe. They were among the last in Europe to be formally emancipated, yet among the first to find their way into the mainstream of European life.

The community's unique experience has given it unique characteristics. Its traditions and rituals are neither Ashkenazi nor Sephardi, but Roman. It has its own liturgy and its own chants—which, given the rich musical traditions of Italy, are surprisingly tedious and bring to mind the buzz of hornets on a hot afternoon. Many northern towns, such as Milan and Trieste, which still have sizeable Jewish communities, were under Austrian rule until modern times, and thus

116

were open to northern influences and the influx of Ashkenazi Jews, but Rome itself has always remained comparatively insulated.

There have never been more than 50,000 Jews in Italy; there are only about 35,000 now, of whom about half are concentrated in Rome. It is usual in such small communities (and indeed in larger ones) for Jewish life to be sustained by the next group of immigrants off the boat. Italian society is somewhat less absorptive than others—notably the French, which quickly draws in most new-comers—but there is something Italianate about the Jews (or maybe something Jewish about the Italians) which has hastened the process. When the Nazis began rounding up Jews for destruction in 1943, they were sometimes hindered by the fact that they could not always tell Jew from Italian. It was thus easier for Italian families to offer refuge to Jewish neighbours—to which one must add that they were also more disposed to do so—than elsewhere in Europe.

When the great trek of Jews from Eastern Europe began at the end of the last century, few Jews found their way to Italy, and fewer still to Rome. Roman Jewry has therefore been living substantially on its own resources and its own resourcefulness. In recent years, however, there has been an influx of about 4,000 Jews from Libya, Italy's former North African colony, but, unlike most immigrants, they were prosperous, cultivated and already half assimilated to their country of adoption. Libya's Jewish poor had moved to Israel in the 1950s. Those who arrived in Italy in the 1960s had been to Italian schools and universities, and were not so much aliens as Italian Jews who happened to have had their homes on the southern shore of the Mediterranean.

These former Libyan residents now number about a quarter of the Roman community. They tend to be somewhat devout, more rigorous in their observance, more Zionistic, but they are not so different from the rest as to affect the underlying character of the community. In the main, they do as the Romans do—or, rather, don't. Which is to say that Roman Jews have the same sort of relaxed attitude toward their Judaism that other Italians have toward their Christianity. They cherish their Judaism, but it is marginal to their existence. They like colour, they love ceremony, they venerate antiquity and tradition, but do not allow anything to interfere with their habits or pleasures. They are so much a part of Italian life that they have never needed reforms to ease the process of assimilation, or to adapt their creed to their times.

117

Reformations presume a concern with theology, an intensity of belief, a religious fervour, a fanaticism even, which are un-Italian, and certainly un-Roman. The faithful may change, but the faith remains changeless. Thus it is with the Romans, and thus it is with the Jews. The Roman Jewish community is Orthodox; Roman Jews are not. They do not quarrel with the orthodoxy, but merely do not practise it, and do not practise it with aplomb.

In Britain, any member of an Orthodox congregation who drives to synagogue on the Sabbath will do so furtively and with circumspection, and will park his car at a discreet distance. In Rome he will pull up in full throttle before the very gates of his synagogue. In Britain some women bring their handbags to synagogue; in Rome many arrive with carrier bags, either on their way to their morning shopping or on their way from it. In Britain even Reform Jews hesitate to smoke on Shabbat; in Rome they light up on the very steps of the synagogue. A friend who bumped into an Italian acquaintance in the synagogue was asked if he would like a drink after the service and, thinking he was being invited home for *kiddush*, said yes; instead he was taken round to a nearby bar. There are deeply devout Jews in Rome who are meticulous in their every observance, but they form an insignificant minority and are rarely of Roman origin.

There are four synagogues in Rome and, to judge by the size of the congregations even on a Friday night, communal worship is taken fairly seriously. But the impression is misleading, for, if many come, few pray. As a result, a visit to the Great Synagogue in the Lungotevere Cenci can be a particularly dispiriting experience.

This synagogue, which stands on the banks of the Tiber near the Ponte di Garibaldi, was built early in this century on the site of a cluster of five smaller synagogues (the *Cinque Scoule*) which had served the nearby ghetto for several hundred years. The building, perhaps the most magnificent synagogue in Europe, is a baroque extravaganza, massive, lofty, domed, with the sort of basilica one might expect in one of the grander Renaissance churches. Only the array of candelabra in the apse behind the Ark suggests that this may, after all, be a synagogue.

As a rule, congregations in the larger synagogues behave with a decorum one rarely finds in the small ones because, apart from anything else, the very proportions of the building impose a certain restraint. The great synagogue in Rome is an exception. The service is long, the chatter is incessant, the children are unruly, there is a constant traffic of people going hither and thither, and the cantor can hardly be heard above the hubbub. The *kriath hatorah* (reading of the Torah), the most important part of the service, which seems to go on for hours, and to which numberless individuals are called up, cannot—unless one is sitting near the front—be heard at all.

Apart from the Chief Rabbi, Dr. Elio Toaff, five or six officiating clergy sit on the platform by the Ark, all in black canonicals. One is not sure what their function is and neither, it would seem, are they. They chatter ceaselessly, like fishwives at a herring stall, their black birettas bobbing excitedly, during *sheacharith* (the morning service), during the *kriath hatorah*, during *musaf* (the additional service), and even when lined up as a guard of honour by the Ark for the ceremonial opening. Meanwhile the Chief Rabbi remains on his throne, a book before him, serenely oblivious to the clamour about him which, amid the echoing spaces of the synagogue, assumes the volume of heavy waves crashing upon a rocky shore. I was finally moved by curiosity to ask if he was deaf. "No," I was told, "he no like to interfere." That, indeed, may sum up his career.

One of the strengths of Italian Jewry is that, though it is small, its scholastic traditions are such that it has always been able to recruit its clergy from its own ranks. Anglo-Jewry, which is ten times as large, has had only one English-born Chief Rabbi in the past hundred years. Dr. Toaff's father was a distinguished rabbinical scholar and head of the Collegio Rabbinico Italiano (which in the last century was the most celebrated rabbinical seminary in Europe) and he himself served for a time as rabbi in Ancona and Venice before being invited to Rome in 1951.

A Chief Rabbi has many functions, of which one—some would say the supreme one—is to represent his community to the outside world. No community could hope for a better ambassador than Dr. Toaff. He is a handsome, dignified, well-groomed, well-spoken figure, with a bearing which suggests that Judaism is a superior if somewhat this-worldly faith. He radiates well-being rather than spirituality. One cannot imagine him upbraiding his congregants for their religious deficiencies or attempting to rouse them to a higher level of piety; he would perhaps be less popular if he did. He is a complacent man, inclined to accept the world as he finds it and his congregants as he finds them. In any case, Roman Jews have been doing things their way for too long to be radically changed.

The Italian Jewish community is a formally constituted body, established by law. Any Jew who wants to have his son circumcised, to celebrate a *bar mitzvah* or wedding in a synagogue, or to be buried in a Jewish cemetery has to be a registered member of the community and pay its taxes. (The state pays a subvention to the church, but not to the synagogue, so the Jewish taxpayer is in fact doubly taxed.) There is, however, a considerable number of Jewish left-wingers who have no contact with Jewish life and are not even interested in Jewish burial (perhaps the ultimate act of dissociation), and others, of no particular affiliation, who recall that the Germans used the community lists for their round-up operations in 1943, and therefore refuse to be registered. Still others resent paying the communal taxes. Therefore it is possible that the real number of Jews in Italy is closer to 50,000 or 60,000 than the 35,000 on the official register.

I asked an Italian how many Jews he thought there are in Rome. He paused for a minute, then said: "A hundred thousand, certainly not less—they are very good" (by which he meant "very successful"). "They own half the Corso (Rome's Fifth Avenue). They have shops in the Via Veneto. They are everywhere."

They are fairly, perhaps even very, successful in business and the professions, and some of the capital's most prominent doctors, dentists, lawyers, architects and engineers are Jews. But the average Roman Jew owns a fairly small shop, which often has to support a fairly sizeable family. One is sometimes taken aside to be told of the fortunes amassed by this or that individual—but though individuals may be wealthy, the community itself is not. For example, the nearest thing it has to a youth centre is a suite of shabby rooms on top of one of the older synagogues, and even this was brought into use only through the efforts of Carmi Schweitzer, a stocky, robust, whirring dynamo of a man, who was sent by the Jewish Agency to infuse some life into the community.

Schweitzer admires the relaxed spirit of the people about him. "I wish I could be so relaxed," he said. But this attitude can also fill him with despair, as when he tried to organise a symposium on anti-Semitism, for which he brought in nationally known speakers and sent out more than 3,000 invitations—and attracted an audience of about twenty-five. At such times he finds Roman Jewry not so much relaxed as comatose.

The community has a network of schools attended by some 2,000 children, but they are substantially secular schools whose pupils and teachers happen to be Jewish. The amount of time devoted to Jewish studies is about an hour to an hour and a half a day. It is doubtful whether there are teachers available to offer more, and in any case the parents do not want more. "I don't want my sons to be rabbis," said one father, echoing a sentiment which seems to be fairly universal among Jewish parents.

There are still about a thousand Jews living in the old ghetto at the back of the Great Synagogue. The streets are narrow, too narrow one would think, to take vehicular traffic, but through which vehicles still race (give an Italian an inch, and he'll use it as a freeway). The courtyards are dark and damp, the staircases crumbling and rickety, and everything about the place speaks of narrowness and constriction. Yet the inhabitants haven't the pinched, pale appearance one looks for in such surroundings, but seem to be well dressed, well fed and in good health.

One cannot always tell ghetto dwellers from outsiders, because in Rome Jew likes to meet Jew on every conceivable occasion, and many drive to the ghetto on Sunday to promenade, to sit in one of the outdoor cafés or stand around on the polished cobbles, to talk over old times and to sigh over old scenes. They also crowd the synagogues frequently and in large numbers, because these are occasions to meet their fellows. Perhaps that is also the reason why they display so little decorum inside the synagogue itself.

The man who goes to synagogue once or perhaps twice a year approaches it with a sense of occasion, perhaps even a feeling of religious awe—but to someone who is there two or three times a week the synagogue is almost an extension of his home. It becomes more a house of the poeple than a house of God.

In this very tendency to get together and stay together one finds the secret of Roman Jewish continuity. Gregariousness, fellowship, the sense of sharing a common past are at the source of the community's religion; actual observance or belief hardly enter into it. One might call these Jews without Judaism—who have discovered the secret of surviving without invisible means of support. Any threats they may face arise not from disintegration from within, but from forces without.

Rome is bespattered with aerosol graffiti, like the New York subway, and the Magen David has been sprayed on most of the shops in the Via Portico d'Ottavia, which runs through the heart of the ghetto. Here and there one hears anxious whispers about a possible resurgence of fascism. A far more imminent danger, many believe—

121

some speak of it as an unavoidable certainty—is the prospect of Communist rule. The Communists are already the largest single party in Italy; the Christian Democrats are kept in office with the help of Communist votes. What would happen if the Communists and their allies should win an overall majority? Or grab power by other means?

An elderly Jewish dentist with a large and fashionable practice near the Via Veneto (Rome's Park Avenue) said that he, for one, looked forward to a Communist takeover because it would bring to Italy the thing the country most needs—order. Others comfort themselves with the thought that the Communists would, after all, be Italians and would bring to their Marxism the same easy tolerance that they brought to their Christianity.

But most Jews one encounters in what is, after all, a bourgeois business community view the prospect of Communist rule with frank alarm. This does not mean that they are on the eve of a mass exodus. Some have moved to Israel, others are planning to move, but most are inclined to batten down until the storm passes. They are too Italian, too well established to contemplate any drastic change of environment. When people have been in a place for 2,000 years they are inclined to regard Communism—as they once regarded fascism—as a passing aberration.

Present Tense, Vol. 5 No. 2, Winter 1978

Cold Comfort

IN RECENT WEEKS Israel has been like England. Wherever people have met they've rarely indulged in low gossip, or high gossip—they didn't even talk about the Stock Exchange. Only one topic has dominated conversation—the weather. The subject has also crept into news bulletins and the press. It has made me feel at home.

Now I believe that God in His infinite mercy has given the weather as a gift to the English, for they are otherwise tongue-tied and if they hadn't the weather to talk about, they would say nothing at all, and their very speech organs would atrophy.

The same cannot be said of Israelis for, whatever their deficiencies, they are neither short of words nor topics and if they should find themselves talking about the weather it is not for want of something better to talk about. In Jerusalem recently, in the course of one day—in fact, in the course of a few hours—we had: rain, hail, sleet and snow, all swept by high winds, sometimes singly, sometimes together: all that was lacking was fire and brimstone, though by way of compensation one had cold mists which darkened the city and penetrated the soul. One can have good days and bad, but if the bad days persist for an almost unbroken period of three months one begins to feel that it's not so much the weather, as a conspiracy. We have prayers to invoke rain; have we none to stop it? I sometimes think the Ministry of Agriculture may have something to do with it, because farmers have been smiling, and when farmers smile, it's a glum time for everyone else.

And it is not only a matter of staying wet or dry. In England the difference between good days and bad is the difference between going out with a mackintosh and umbrella, or just going out with a mackintosh; in Israel it is the difference between bankruptcy and

123

solvency. Where we live, each flat has its own central heating unit. I have just received my heating bill for January and February, and it has come to—prepare yourself—34,138 shekels and 27 agorot, which may lead you to believe that we have a flat as vast as Hechal Shlomo, that we have the furnace blazing day and night, and that we keep our room temperatures at blood-heat. We in fact have one living-room, three small bedrooms and a tiny study. I work at home so that we have had the heating on all day, and sometimes into (but not through) the night, and always at a low point, and if that is the sort of bill one has to face to keep accommodations habitable in Jerusalem, then it would be quite literally cheaper to burn shekels.

Our London home had twice the cubic capacity of our present one, and last winter was one of the most severe in human memory, but our fuel bill for the three months of January, February and March came to less than a third of our present one, or 13,851 shekels, which I thought was high enough; I therefore appealed against it. The system here, apparently, is to pay first and appeal later; otherwise one pays interest on the bill, and interest on the interest, pending the outcome of the appeal. I haven't paid the bill yet, and I don't know if I shall pay it—indeed I don't know if I *can* pay, for apart from the difficulty of raising the money, it has given me such a shock that my hand is not steady enough to sign the cheque.

I was not the only one affected. Wherever one saw two or three persons talking in hushed voices, as if some great calamity had befallen them, they were probably discussing their gas bills.

One of the reasons why gas is so expensive in Israel is that it is still carted around in bulky cylinders, as if the country was a scattered community of weekend campers. It may be difficult to pipe gas from a central conversion plant to remote areas like the Negev and the Galilee, and it may be impractical to tear up the streets of the main centres of population like Tel Aviv and Jerusalem to lay gas pipe-lines, but I cannot understand why new towns and housing estates have no central depot. The present distribution system allows few economies of scale, because greater consumption means more trucks and more cylinders, which presumably stand idle when consumption declines.

However, the main villain of the piece, here, as elsewhere, is the building contractor. There is an assumption in Israel that if a building excludes rain, the builder's work is done. No thought is given to retaining heat, for Israel seems to be thought of, or at least thinks of itself, not merely as a Mediterranean country, but as a subtropical one in which winters, when they occur at all, are mild and short and, indeed, pleasant. It has taken Jerusalem 3,000 years to reconcile itself to the fact that snow is an annual occurrence, and to equip itself accordingly. (I must add that in England, the railway boards think of snow as something which doesn't, or at least shouldn't, happen, and whenever there is a blizzard, as there is almost every year, the whole railway system is paralysed.) If flats in Tel Aviv are built like holiday homes in Miami, it is one thing, but if Jerusalem builders are guided by the same principles, it is another; this is the fourth winter I have spent in the capital, and although some have been colder and longer than others, none have been mild, and one can reckon that there are at least three months of the year in which one has to have heating every day, and sometimes all day. And the nights are, of course, even worse. I am not complaining, for, on balance, Jerusalem enjoys the most attractive climate in the country, but it would seem more attractive still if builders could be induced to take fuller account of winter temperatures.

It is already difficult enough for a person with modest means to acquire even a modest home in Jerusalem: given the present costs of heating, it may become impossible for him to live in it.

Friends tell me that my heating system may be inefficient and that I should get myself a new boiler, or go over to oil. I have a less extravagant idea. I shall buy myself an axe. I live right opposite the Jerusalem forest and next year, please God, I shall go over to solid fuel.

The Israel Economist, April 1983

Next to Godliness

ISRAEL HAS MANY claims to fame, but the fact that Mrs Thatcher should have singled it out for its cleanliness, of all things, is a measure of her infatuation with the place. The towns she actually saw were Jerusalem, Ashkelon, Ramat Gan, and the Weizmann Institute in Rehovot. (Her forays into the Beersheba region were too brief to count.)

It is true that the area round the King David Hotel (where she was staying) has always been tolerably clean and Teddy Kolleck has done his best to keep the rest of Jerusalem reasonably tidy, and—against all the odds—has largely succeeded. Ashkelon and Ramat Gan were also nicely tarted up for her visit and the Weizmann Institute, with its elegant buildings and beautifully kept grounds, would have impressed anyone.

As for the rest of Israel, Mrs Thatcher saw it as through a bullet-proof glass darkly, and flittingly, behind an army of police outriders. I was caught up in her convoy at one point, and all sideroads were closed off so that we could proceed unhindered at 90 mph. It's the only way to travel, and made me see that being Prime Minister has its compensations, but it's not the best way of seeing a country.

There are islands of tidiness in Israel, as, for example, in the kibbutzim, which have the immaculate appearance of an American country club estate. Moshavim are rather less immaculate, but it's in town that the trouble begins, for while people may take great pains to keep their own homes spotless, they tend to regard anything beyond their doors as a waste-disposal area.

I am not sure if Israelis are more untidy than anyone else, but they have more occasion for untidiness if only because they eat more, and as they spend much of their life in the open and, so to speak, fress

126

alfresco, they leave much of their mess in the open. "Unto everything a season," sayeth the Preacher, and unto every season its own seasonal litter, orange-peel during the citrus season, melon-peel during the melon season, banana-skins during the banana season, and in season and out, discarded sweet-wrappers, ice-cream wrappers, yoghurt-cups, bottles, cans, over-ripe fruit, under-baked pizzas, half-eaten pretzels, sesame seeds, mangled pizzas and mouldy bread.

There are also the so-called non-perishables which accumulate in perishing heaps, usually topped by a perished cat. Some areas are worse than others and the worst of all is Tel Aviv bus station, which is part terminus, part market, and part midden, and I have never been able to understand how a city as proud and as splendid as Tel Aviv can tolerate a place which assaults every sense and outrages every sensibility.

Economists usually measure the wealth of a nation by what it earns, but there is, I think, a truer measure to be had from what it discards and by that index, at least, Israel, even in its present straits, is doing well. Yet if Israel is not uniquely clean, one could hardly single it out as uniquely messy. Off-hand, the only country which has impressed me in recent years as particularly clean is the Soviet Union, but then, being a comparatively poor country, it has little to discard, and the authorities have ways of enforcing cleanliness which are not available in a free society. I also found Spain—given the fact that it's a Mediterranean country—rather clean, but Franco was still in charge when I was last there, and he too had his ways of keeping it clean. I daren't think what it's like now that it has become a sort of torrid Blackpool. Italy has never been renowned for its tidiness, and Athens (the only part of Greece I know) is like Tel Aviv bus station.

I think one acquires a higher tolerance for untidiness under sunny skies, and I suspect what coloured Mrs Thatcher's attitude was not so much the transition from a clean country to a messy one, as the transition from a sunny climate to a bleak one. When the very heavens are dark and oppressive, one tries to draw some comfort from one's immediate surroundings on earth, and there was none to be found between Heathrow and Downing Street. In Israel, it was roses, roses all the way: in London, it was litter, litter. No wonder she was impressed with the one and depressed by the other. Britain has acquired a Mediterranean tolerance to squalor without the compensation, or excuse, of Mediterranean skies.

Jewish Chronicle, 13 June 1986

Last Stop

I HEAR THEY'VE closed one of the most beloved of all Israeli institutions (beloved, that is, by me)—the Jerusalem-Tel Aviv railway line.

It was said to be losing money. There are few railways anywhere which aren't and, off-hand, I can't think of any public institution in Israel which is actually making money.

It is also said that it is quicker to travel by bus. Well, there, I must confess, critics may have a point, for I suspect it may also be quicker to travel by bicycle, and there are times when it could be quicker to go on foot.

Middle Eastern railways are not renowned for their speed, and it is possible that the Children of Israel took forty years to cross Sinai because they took the slow train from Kantara, stopping at Ramses, Succoth, Etham, Baal-Zephon, Migdol, Pene Hahiroth-on-Sea, Marah, Elim Spa, the Wilderness of Sin, Dophkah, Alush, Rephidim (the same is Bir Gaf Gafa), Kibroth Hattavah, Hazeroth, Rithma, Rimmon Perez, Libnah, Rissah, Kehela, Haradah, Makeloth, Tahath, Terrah, Mithka, Hashmonah, Mesoroth, Bene Jakaan, Hor Hagidgad, Jotbah, Abronah, Etzion Geber, Kadesh Barnea and Mount Hor (which, for Aaron, at least, was the terminus) and all stations to Jericho.

The Jerusalem-Tel Aviv train made scheduled stops only at Beth Shemesh and Ramleh. It sometimes made an unscheduled stop to let a camel cross the line or to allow a goat to browse on the greenery between the lines, and took about two and a half hours to cover the forty miles.

As buses take about 45 minutes, the railways are not a favoured means of travel for men in a hurry, but just in case they should be, the

128

railway company located the terminus on the southern edge of Tel Aviv, miles from anywhere, so that even those who might be tempted to travel by train still had to take a bus to get to their destination.

It was a journey to yesterday, an excursion out of time, and although I must have made the trip (as far as Ramleh, at least) more often than I've had hot dinners, I made it yet again every time I was in Israel.

There is (or was), first of all, the railway station itself, an imposing edifice built by the Turks nearly a hundred years ago and still in fairly good shape. Bus stations in Israel are like a grinding vortex, but the railway station, even in the rush hour, is almost like a retreat; one half expects to hear the sound of bells summoning one to matins.

The train, though by no means magnificently appointed, was never crowded and set off slowly, clattering through the streets of Baqa like a tramcar.

Once out of town it gathered pace and, a few miles on, it moved gracefully through the charming Arab village of Beit Safafa. Before 1967, Beit Safafa was in Jordan while the railway line was in Israel, so that one had only to lean out of the window to be in enemy territory.

From there the train entered upon a biblical landscape as it wound its way, slowly and majestically, round the Judean hills, with the river Sorek gurgling below.

We were in what one might call the Samson country, for Samson "loved a woman in the valley of Sorek whose name was Delilah", and there was something along every inch of the line to beguile the eye and the imagination.

When the Orient Express to Venice was resuscitated a few years ago, I put it to some moneyed friends that they would do something for Israel, and themselves, if they bought a number of Pullman cars which could be attached to the train for the scenic run between Jerusalem and Ramleh.

Ramleh, for all its undoubted appeal, is not quite Venice, but if they served good food and wine en route, with pretty waitresses togged up as Delilahs (to give it local colour), it would be an immense tourist attraction.

Unfortunately, my moneyed friends are not very adventurous (which is perhaps why they are still moneyed) and the idea was left in abeyance, and since fuller use was not made of the line, the economic case for closure was indeed overwhelming.

Chaim Bermant

Closing the line is an act of wilful desecration—and worse. Tradition hath it that the Messiah will come to Jerusalem on a donkey. I personally believe that, if he will come at all, he will come by train (on a Pullman, probably). No train, no Messiah.

Jewish Chronicle, 23 May 1986

130

Bus Fuss

TEL AVIV BUS station has one thing in common with the Temple: we pray for its rebuilding, but we don't believe it'll happen in our day.

They had a crack at rebuilding it about twenty years ago, but they cracked before they did so. The remains are still there, a monument to the futility of human endeavour and bad taste, for if there is anything in Tel Aviv uglier than the old bus station, it is the remains of the new one.

It is, however, the nearest thing the city has to an ancient ruin and, given another few years, it might become a tourist attraction as a sort of secular Wailing Wall (an apt name, come to think of it, given the number of people who lost their shirts on it). But in Israel they cannot leave well—or even ill—alone and a Jerusalem contractor called Jonah has plans to complete it.

One should not, of course, read too much into a name, but it seems to me that this Jonah is a man with a mission who hopes to do for Tel Aviv what his namesake did for Nineveh.

Nineveh, it will be remembered, "was an exceeding great city of three days' journey". Tel Aviv is the same and it takes three days to cross it, because its roads are so congested. If the old Jonah saved Nineveh from sin, the new one hopes to save Tel Aviv from paralysis.

There is no rush hour in Tel Aviv. They rush all the time and the more frantic their efforts to get around, the longer they stay in place. In fact, I doubt if there is a city in the world where people spend so much time and energy in getting nowhere.

One of the main causes of the immobility is the central bus station, which was never built to cope with the volume of traffic it attracts and which, being congested, spreads congestion throughout the city.

A new station with good approach roads would thus be like a cure

131

for thrombosis, but there are too many people—including half of Tel Aviv's criminal fraternity—interested in preserving the old, and too many obstacles to surmount. I doubt if Mr Jonah will get very far. I must also confess that I shall be sorry if he does.

One would not, as I have suggested, call Tel Aviv's bus station stylish or ornate, but it does have a certain tatty glamour, like the film set for an oriental extravaganza. It may not have dancing houris in diaphanous silks—and any that are around tend to be in khaki—but it has teeming crowds and colour and commotion and noise.

There are street vendors crying their wares, soothsayers saying their sooths, deformed beggars displaying their deformities, bearded Chabadniks snarling up travellers with tefilin, harassed mothers screaming at straying infants, and harassed fathers roaring at scream-ing mothers. Music wafts forth from a thousand tape-recorders amplified a thousandfold, competing with hooting horns, steaming buses and steamy bawds. Black-clad skeletal figures dart hither and thither with hunched shoulders and eyes averted from the profanities around them, and bewildered bands of Christian pilgrims gaze about them as if they have stumbled on Gehenna—which in a sense they have—while wide-eyed men with matted hair proclaim the end of days.

In Russia, they used to say that the flames of hell burn for seven parasangs round Odessa. They also burn in the Tel Aviv bus station, only they are used to fry falafels and roast kebabs, and the resulting aroma hovers over the place like a profane *shechina*.

And yet, with all the rush and commotion, there is geniality and warmth. I like the verbal exchanges, the small dramas—and large—played out on every corner, the sheer variety of faces and attire, the small bouquets clutched in grubby fists on the eve of festivals, and the cries of "Chag sameach". It is a place for instant friendships (and, if one is not careful, instant enmities). It is street theatre at its most enthralling.

Israel reveres the ancient and the modern, but anything in between is at risk. This is particularly true of Tel Aviv, which as a city is the sworn enemy of the familiar. Its biggest crime was to demolish the Herzlia gymnasium—the one building with character in the city—and replace it with the most hideous slab in the Middle East.

The central bus station has its drawbacks, but I cherish it as about the only part of Tel Aviv which has remained virtually unchanged for the past forty years.

Jewish Chronicle, 14 October 1988

Jaffa Jews

TEL AVIV HAD but one public building of distinction, the Herzlia gymnasia at the top of Herzl Street, which they pulled down about twenty years ago to make way for the tallest, and almost certainly the ugliest, building in the Middle East—the Shalom tower. Well, the Society for the Uglification of Israel (SFUI), which seems to be able to sweep everything before it, plans to do the same for Jaffa harbour.

The northern coast of Israel has many attractive features, especially round Acre, but south of Caesarea there is nothing to gladden the eye, and a great deal to sadden it, until one gets to the towers and minarets of Jaffa, or Joppa as it was called in the olden days, a small port of great antiquity and infinite charm, built round a lofty promontory and buffeted by the blue waters of the Mediterranean Sea.

It was the point of entry for the great cedars of Lebanon used in the building of both the First and Second Temple: "And we will cut wood, of Lebanon, as much as thou shalt need, and we will bring it to thee in floats by sea to Joppa; and thou shalt carry it up to Jerusalem", and when Jonah sought "to flee from the presence of the Lord", he "went down to Joppa and he found a ship going to Tarshish". (And a fat lot of good it did him.)

It is also the home of Andromeda's Rock, which should not, however, be compared to Brighton rock. Andromeda, an Ethiopian princess, was, according to legend, chained to a rock near the harbour mouth to assuage the wrath of a sea monster until she was freed by Perseus.

I am not sure if Andromeda ever existed and, if she did, whether she was chained to that particular rock, and if she was, whether Perseus swooped out of the skies to rescue her, but it's a good story, and in any case how many people would put their hand on their heart and swear that, say, King David's tomb on Mt Zion actually contains the remains of King David? Antiquity should never be scrutinised too closely.

It is some years since Jaffa had any significance as a port but it still offers a livelihood to about two hundred Arab fishermen, and it has all the bustle and colour which goes with the trade, the small craft bobbing in the harbour, the nets drying on the sands, the tarred warehouses, the cobbled quays, the shrill cries of seagulls, the pungent smell of fish, and the tanned, leathery features of the fishermen themselves.

For me, as for many others, the pleasures of a visit to Tel Aviv lie mostly in Jaffa, and they are all under threat, for there is a $20 million conspiracy afoot to banish the fishermen and the fishing-boats, to bury Andromeda's Rock itself under concrete and to convert the ancient port into a vast marina for eight hundred yachts.

Eight hundred! As is well known, most yachts in Israel are owned by dentists. Could there be that many dentists in the country? And if so, are they all that prosperous?

People are now making strenuous efforts to save what there is left of "old" Tel Aviv, by which they mean buildings which date back to the nineteen thirties, but they seem to lack the determination to save Jaffa, which has real claims to antiquity, from the developers.

Large parts of the sea front are no longer accessible to visitors, and one area is defaced by a hideous high-rise building (with a penthouse at the top which was one of the several homes of the late Moshe Dayan). Old buildings have been demolished and replaced by expensive edifices in a mock-antique style housing expensive art galleries and boutiques, and plushy apartments, and the non-rich are being prised out and priced out of Jaffa. The plans for the port, however, have gone a little too far, and they have aroused local resentments to the point where Jew and Arab have made common cause to withstand any further depredations. They deserve the support of everyone who prefers the old and the mellow to the brash and the new.

Mr Shlomo Lahat, the Mayor of Tel Aviv-Jaffa, though with impeccable Right-wing credentials, has found that what is good for the developers is not always good for Tel Aviv. I think he will find that the same is even more true of Jaffa.

Jaffa as Jaffa is unique. Jaffa, as yet another marina, would be commonplace. *Jewish Chronicle*, 14 August 1987

Hi Hi Haifa

I AM TOLD that Rishon le Zion is about to overtake Haifa as the third city of Israel.

I remember Rishon when it was still a charming little town with tiny red-roofed villas, a place with character which still bore traces of its settler origins.

After the Six-Day War, however, it began to spread in all directions, like a muddy river which has burst its banks, and it has now inundated a large area from Holon in the north to Rehovot in the south.

Many peope live there, and may even work there, but that doesn't make it a city, for the term suggests a thriving centre of civilisation and culture.

Rishon has neither. At best, it could be described as the Slough of Israel (and a fairly despondent Slough at that), but I'm surprised it should be contending with Haifa even in the matter of size, which suggests not merely that Rishon has grown, but that Haifa is in decline.

Nowadays, of course, one travels to Israel by air, but until the mid-1960s one generally went by boat, so that Haifa represented one's first sight of Israel.

And a glorious sight it was—an array of lights glittering in the darkness, and then, as one approached in the early dawn, the pink and white buildings on the flanks of the Carmel emerging slowly from the mists; and finally, as the sun came through, a dazzling panorama of green and gold and blue.

In a way, it was overwhelming, for Israel could never live up to everything Haifa promised. All seaports are exciting, much as all airports are dull, but Haifa in those days was in a class by itself.

Haifa is an ancient city, but it owes much of its present character to the work of one man, Abba Khoushi, who, until his death in 1969, was mayor and father of the city.

Other mayors have to work with coalitions. Khoushi suffered no such impediments. He was head of the Labour Council, which controlled the city, and he was boss. He was on good terms with the local Arabs and Druze and integrated both into the life of the city.

He also made the Haifa area the principal industrial zone of the country, though in this respect he may have been a little too success-ful, for there are times when half the city is lost in smoke.

It was said that, while Tel Aviv danced and Jerusalem slept, Haifa worked, which in the 'fifties and 'sixties was not a reputation to be ashamed of. At the same time, Khoushi was anxious to enhance the cultural status of the city and he was responsible for the creation of both the Haifa municipal theatre and Haifa University.

The latter, in particular, gave rise to charges of megalomania, for Haifa, of course, was already the home of the Technion and there was no obvious need for another major academic institution.

The huge skyscraper erected by Oscar Niemeyer (architect of Brasilia) to house the university also had its critics, but whatever one may think of the building, the university itself rapidly proved its worth.

I recently revisited Haifa after an interval of twenty years and, though it remains the beautiful city it always was, it has lost some-thing of its buoyancy and self-assurance.

Every major city is the service area for a large hinterland. Haifa's hinterland is Galilee, and Haifa has suffered from the neglect of Galilee since the Six-Day War, while the opening of the port of Ashdod has robbed it of much of its traffic.

Moreover, for several decades, especially while Khoushi was around, it was always known as "red" Haifa, and although its redness was of a fairly pink variety, the city thought of itself as forward-looking and in the vanguard of progress.

Redness, or even pinkness, is no longer in favour; Labour is no longer the force it was; and Haifa has lost the ethos without acquiring another.

The heavy industries which brought in prosperity—and smog—are in decline (though that may be a blessing in disguise) and it still has its magnificent setting—the Carmel range on one side, the sea on the other, and the hills of Galilee but minutes away. It has, or could easily acquire, everything necessary to make it the tourist capital of Israel.

I only wish someone would reintroduce regular sailings to Haifa. The greatest deterrent to visiting Israel is the thought of the long wait at the airport, and the cramped journey in the plane, trapped in one position like an oversized foetus in an undersized womb.

Jewish Chronicle, 8 September 1989

Point of Arrival

THE EAST END, being near the docks, was for many years the point of arrival for successive waves of immigrants, the French Huguenots in the 17th century, the Irish in the middle years of the 19th century, and the Jews, who descended in a great torrent between 1881 and 1914.

The Huguenots had fled from religious persecution, the Irish from hunger, the Jews from persecution and hunger, and they were by far the most conspicuous, and therefore least welcome, group of newcomers.

If the Huguenots spoke a different language, they were of the same faith; if the Irish were of a different faith they spoke (approximately) the·same language, but the Jews were different in language, in religion, in culture, in appearance, in manner. Over 100,000 of them poured into the East End in the course of a generation and Whitechapel, in particular, assumed the look of a small East European town, or *shtetl*, as it was called in Yiddish.

Yiddish shops and Yiddish shop-signs replaced English ones; Russian rye bread and bagels replaced the English cottage loaves and pan loaves; the pungent smells of salted, smoked, soused, pickled and marinated herrings hovered like a mist over the shopping parades, there were Yiddish posters on the hoardings and the sound of Yiddish filled the streets. Derelict churches were converted into synagogues and derelict music halls into Yiddish theatres, and many a local school had to close on Jewish holidays because some four-fifths of their pupils consisted of newcomers.

Local inhabitants were, understandably, not particularly happy with the changes; a local paper, while insisting that "actual race hatred is very far from our thoughts", went on to declare that the

138

manners and customs of the newcomers "are a distinct menace to the public health not only of East London, but of the metropolis as a whole and the nation in general. Whitechapel, St George's East and parts of Mile End and Bethnal Green baffle description. Here huddle poor creatures who live in a state of semi-starvation; they eat the garbage in the streets and live in rookeries and cellars."

Give a Jew an inch, it was said, and he put a bed in it, give him two and he took in lodgers and one famous magazine compared the manners of the Jews "to that of a not very particular pig".

Yet Dr Shirley Murphey, Medical Officer of Health for the London County Council, was amazed to discover that the death rate among the Jewish newcomers was a good deal lower than among their gentile neighbours, and ascribed the difference to their more wholesome way of life, while the Rector of Spitalfields, the Reverend R.C. Billing, whose parish was overwhelmed by the newcomers, felt moved to declare: "Go to the Jew, thou Christian, consider his ways and be wise."

Many immigrants were in fact desperately poor, but the more prosperous Jewish families had set up a host of charities to help them, like the Jewish Board of Guardians, and the Jewish Soup Kitchen, and the Boot and Shoe Guild, and the Coal and Fuel Society, and the Grocery for the Poor Society, so that it was rare for any of them to be supported by the parish.

They were also sustained by their faith. For six days the Jew laboured, often in a sweatshop owned by his co-religionists, his slight frame bent by his exertions, his clothes bedraggled, his face begrimed, stopping now and then to snatch a hunk of black bread or a piece of stale herring. On the seventh he was king; his person purged at the local steam bath, his suit pressed, his boots polished, his house cleansed, his wife and children in their Sabbath finery, his table laden, and all caught in the warm glow of candlelight. The Sabbath was quite literally his recreation.

The Jewish character of Whitechapel was sustained by successive waves of immigrants, but once immigration stopped it gradually became Anglicised. No local authority in those days felt obliged to preserve the customs and culture of newcomers, while the newcomers for their part were impatient to assimilate, and the older Jewish families established a host of institutions to convert the crude progeny of the ghettos into English gentlemen.

Even the Jews' Free School in Bell Lane, which was largely paid for by the Rothschilds, and which, with about 4,000 pupils, was probably the biggest in Europe, was less concerned with Jewish education than instilling the essence of Englishness, and it succeeded beyond its expectations.

Young Jews began to claim places in English grammar schools and English universities. They prospered in business and the professions and they began to move out of Whitechapel and into Hackney and Stamford Hill and beyond, to Cricklewood, Ilford and Golders Green.

The Second World War and the blitz merely accelerated what was already an irreversible trend. Abraham Stenol, the Yiddish poet, continued to haunt the area until his death in 1983, and to celebrate it in his poems, for he regarded Whitechapel as the last *shtetl* in Europe; and Bloom's, the kosher restaurant, is still flourishing, for Jews are sentimental and they come there to savour not only the food but the memories; and here and there one can find Hebrew lettering on what was once a synagogue or philanthropic institution. But Jewish Whitechapel is no more.

London Daily News, 25 May 1987

Odd City Out

NOW THAT SUMMER is over the question may perhaps be safely asked: How did Glasgow escape the riots which overwhelmed parts of London, Liverpool, Manchester, Birmingham, Leeds, in fact almost every major urban centre in Britain? Certainly if the reasons suggested for the troubles elsewhere are at all valid, Glasgow should have been among the first to go up in flames.

Unemployment? One in six of the working population is jobless: among the young, the ratio is about one in three.

Deprivation? About 40 per cent of the population are poorly housed, poorly fed and without access to amenities which most of us take for granted.

Racial tensions? Glasgow has a large and growing immigrant community.

Police harassment? There has never been any love lost between the local police and the working-class population, and Glasgow is now overwhelmingly a working-class city.

Political agitation? "Red Clydeside" is as red now as it's ever been, and in some respects, redder.

Added to which is Glasgow's own problem of alcoholism. Between 1960–80 hospital admissions for alcoholism increased sixfold for men, tenfold for women.

Yet while there were rampaging mobs in the south, Glasgow remained strangely quiet. Last week I went up to Glasgow to ask why, and was given a number of answers, some of them light-hearted, but even these contained more than a grain of truth:

"Glasgow's Scotland, you know, and Scotland's no England."

"Our blacks are 'nae as black as yours."

"We don't have tae wait till the summer for a punch-up wi' the

141

polis—we have it every week-end."

"You cannae loot Glasgow shops, they're a' grilled up like banks."

"Who in Scotland wud start lobbin' petrol-bombs wi' petrol at nearly two quid a gallon?"

There was almost a defensive tone to some of the replies, as if I was impugning Glasgow's hard-earned reputation as the home of mayhem.

One sometimes wonders how Glasgow came by its reputation, because every visitor to the place remarks upon the openness, friend-liness and geniality of the people. Even football rowdies in Glasgow are now less violent than they are elsewhere, and there are no racial aspects to their violence. Religious undertones remain, and Rangers v Celtic matches can give rise to pitched battles, but these are hardly more than a form of violent banter, the stylised restaging of ancient feuds.

Even these confrontations are not what they used to be, partly because the Scottish football league has been reorganised and Rangers and Celtic now meet five or six times a year so the matches have lost their sense of occasion. "You can now take your auntie to Ibrox," I was told.

Glasgow is not what it was. All Britain's urban centres have undergone great changes since the war, but Glasgow has suffered a metamorphosis. Apart from anything else, while its area has grown, its population has shrunk by a *third*. Motorways swirl through what used to be the town centre and the heavy industries on which the city grew have all but vanished. Blast furnaces no longer light up the night sky. The air is less gritty, cleaner, softer. Distant prospects are clearer. One can now raise one's eyes unto the hills and see the hills.

An improved environment is, of course, no consolation for declin-ing job prospects, but a recent poll commissioned by the *Glasgow Herald* showed that while many youngsters were jobless, few (5 per cent) complained of any feeling of rejection; very few (3 per cent) thought it was embarrassing to be unemployed and most were confident that with a bit of effort they would be able to find work in a matter of months. Unemployment is, unfortunately, not a novel experience to Glasgow, but there is, with all the folk memories of hardship, a sense of optimism and, above all, a feeling of self-reliance. The rise in the unemployment figures has not been paralleled by any sharp rise in crime and the young have not felt tempted to vent their frustrations upon the police. Indeed—a little surprisingly—the opinion poll referred to above suggested that young people had a high regard for the police, and placed them well above churchmen and teachers in their esteem.

Glasgow is no Dock Green and the "polis", as they are called locally (with the accent on the first syllable), are no Dixons. The Glasgow comedian Billy Connolly recalls in an autobiographical sketch: "The police came round to St Gerard's just before we left, to tell us how cosy it was being a policeman. The guy wasn't exactly laughed off—just laughed off in complete silence. They were regarded as the common enemy. Them and Us, very much so." The police in his own particular locality, however, "were terrific": "They were magic big guys. Talk about 'finger on the pulse'—they knew exactly what was going on."

The police still try to keep their "finger on the pulse" and in 1975 they formed a Community Involvement Branch to foster good relations with the public. Men have been taken out of their cars and put on the beat, and they stay longer in the same place to familiarise themselves with their locality and its problems. But as Professor S.G. Checkland, a distinguished economic historian observed in a revised edition of *The Upas Tree* (to be published by the Scottish University Press in November), "in spite of some striking successes, and in spite of some real efforts to be accepted as friends of the community, the police have attracted hostility in some parts of society".

The hostility, however, is not the sort which would induce people to take to the streets. Even their enemies do not feel the police are there to be loved. A young man who had been in police hands more than once (and claimed that he had marks to prove it) told me: "They're tough, the polis, but Christ they have to be. They wudnae last a day if they wasn't." He even seemed to take a pride in their toughness.

Glasgow has an immigrant population of about 20,000, consisting mainly of Pakistanis, with a few Indians and Chinese. Most of them are self-employed. Many are shopkeepers and show a flagrant disregard for the shopping hours acts, but they otherwise pose almost no problems to the police. "You'll get Paki shops broken into and Pakis robbed," a young officer told me, "and they'll think they've been set upon because they're immigrants; but you don't have to be an immigrant to be robbed in Glasgow."

Mr Bashir Mann, 54, a prosperous businessman who is a leader of

143

the immigrant community and a city councillor, served for a time as chairman of the Glasgow Police Committee. "David McNee (the Metropolitan Police Commissioner) was Chief Constable at the time," he said, "and when people press him about his attitude to immigrants now, he tells them that when he was in Glasgow, his boss was an immigrant, and that he never had any difficulties. And it's true, we've always had good relations with the police."

The same may be said of their relations with the general public. The Scots, possibly because of their own migratory streak, have always been hospitable to newcomers. The Jews, who made their home in Glasgow at the turn of the century, settled without difficulty and prospered without friction, and the Pakistanis are reliving their experience. They moved into the south side of the city as the Jews moved out and, where they are beginning to prosper, they are spreading into the suburbs. Being self-employed they do not compete for jobs, and as they live in owner-occupied properties, they do not compete for homes. If one speaks to individuals, rather than community leaders or police, one hears stories of tension, or vandalism and muggings, but overall I doubt if there is a city in the British Isles where the immigrant feels as secure as in Glasgow.

A Pakistani who lived in England and now lives in Glasgow, told me: "Both the English and Scots are lazy bastards, but the English resent it if you work hard, the Scots don't."

Finally, to a delicate question. Would the experience of Glasgow have been different had it had a sizeable West Indian community? Bashir Mann thought not. He suggested that the conduct of newcomers is determined largely by the attitude of its hosts, and he believed that West Indians would have felt less alienated in Glasgow. Others were less sanguine, and made the point that the attitude of the host society is largely determined by the conduct of the newcomers.

Sir William Gray, a former Lord Provost of Glasgow, did not think race was a major factor in the recent troubles, but it was a factor, and if there was no trouble in Glasgow it was partly because it had no immigrant ghettos, and partly because the city had always been fortunate in the character of its immigrants. "The Pakistanis," he said, "are hard working and ambitious, with a strong family structure which ensures a sense of responsibility, and while I have no specific knowledge of other immigrant groups, I doubt if the same is true of the black communities in England where trouble has occurred."

Observer, 6 September 1981

Sodom and Glockamorrah

YOU'VE NO DOUBT heard or read of the discovery that the Promised Land is not Palestine, but quite another place entirely. I can imagine Shamir or Peres, or a compound of the two (Sheretz?), reading the report and saying to his colleagues: "OK chaps, we've made a mistake—pack!"

The fact is—as anyone who has been to Sinai will aver—the roads in the area are notoriously badly signposted, and it is the easiest thing in the world to take the wrong turning, especially where one isn't too sure where one is heading for in the first place.

I am reminded of the (apocryphal) story of Moses (forgive me if you've heard it). The old man lay dying and Joshua was at his side.

"We have been wandering in the wilderness for forty years now," said Joshua. "Will you tell me, O Master, where we are trying to get to?"

At which Moses slowly sat up and drawing the last breath in his body, he began:

"Ca, ca, ca . . ."

"Yes, yes, yes, O Master."

"Ca—ca—ca . . ."

"Yes, yes, yes."

"Ca—," but before he could finish, he died.

"He must have meant Canaan," said Joshua, but he was mistaken, for he meant California.

Well, according to Dr Kamal Salibi, Professor of History at the American University of Beirut, he didn't mean California either, but a place in south-west Arabia called Asir. He bases his belief on a gazetteer published by the Saudi Government showing that Asir abounds in biblical place names, such as Hebron, Jericho, Gaza,

Bethlehem, Sodom, Gomorrah, Beersheba and Qa'wat Sian (which he translates as Zion Hill). I, however, happen to have a copy of a gazetteer published by Her Majesty's Stationery Office which proves quite conclusively that the true Promised Land was, and is, the British Isles, for it too abounds in biblical place names.

If my theory is true an awful lot of people have been barking up the wrong tree. Think of all those people who have gone on what they thought was aliya when it was, in fact, yerida. If, however, you should set foot in Oxford Street or Brent Cross you will find a great many Israelis have discovered the mistake and have returned to Zion.

The very name of Britain is compounded of two common Hebrew words, *Brith ain*, meaning, "a covenant, there isn't", as there wasn't before the various parts of the British Isles became the United Kingdom. But apart from that, there's a Hebron in Northumberland, a Joppa (or Jaffa) in Edinburgh, a Hadzor (or Hatzor) in the Midlands, a Mt Ephraim in Tunbridge Wells, while Bethnal Green is obviously a corruption of Bethlehem.

There are also two Bethels and two Nebos in Wales, a Sion Mill (for which read Zion Hill) in Ulster, a Garth in the tax-haven of the Isle of Man (hence the saying, "tell it not in Garth"), and Sodoms in one guise or another all over the place. There is no Gomorrah, but there is a near cousin (in Ireland, of course) called Glockamorrah, which inspired the famous question, "How are things in Glockamorrah?" and the even more famous retort, "Don't ask!"

There is a River Eden up north, and even an Eden Valley, but no River Jordan anywhere in Britain, which need not worry us, for as Professor Sillybilly has rightly pointed out, the Jordan is never specifically referred to as a river in the whole of Scripture. It could well be a place and there is a Jordan, or in fact Jordans, in Buckinghamshire. Against this, however, one must put the story of Naaman the leper who was advised to bathe in the Jordan as a cure for his leprosy:

"Then went he down and dipped himself seven times in the Jordan, according to the saying of the man of God: and his flesh came again like unto the flesh of a little child, and he was clean."

All of which suggests that Jordan, if not a river, was at least wet, but Naaman could well have had a sand-bath, or a mud-bath, or even a blood-bath.

We finally come to Jerusalem where Professor Sillybilly is, on the face of it, on stony ground, for he can point to an actual City of

David, whereas I can only point to a Davidstown, which is in Co Wexford, in southern Ireland, and a Holytown (but not Holy City) in central Scotland. On the other hand Jerusalem has been called many things in its time, and in some respects it is better known by its ambience than its name. Thus when one reads verses like: "It is builded as a city which is compact together", or "Or it is a city in which the spirit of the Lord doth dwell eternally", or "Peace reigns within thy walls and prosperity within thy palaces", one place immediately comes to mind—Hampstead Garden Suburb.

Jewish Chronicle, 17 August 1986

Of Zion
and Zionism

All Israel's a Stage

TO ENJOY ISRAEL these days one should avoid politics and politicians and confine oneself to artists and the arts.

Perhaps the arts only flourish amid disaffection, but the place, for all its troubles—or possibly because of them—dazzles with talent. Here is a country with only four million people which has three major theatre companies and half a dozen minor ones, two major ballet companies, three symphony orchestras, several chamber ensembles and, it would seem, budding virtuosi in every household.

Impresario Victor Hochhauser who travels to Israel three or four times a year to trawl for talent is almost embarrassed by the richness of his catch, and he rolls off the names of a long list of instrumentalists, all of them in their teens, who, he is convinced, will become virtuosi of world rank.

They include Shira Ravin (violin), who has already appeared with major orchestras in America and Europe, Maya Weltman (piano), who has played with the London Philharmonic, Sharon Batzaly (flute), Shalev Adel (harpsichord), Zvi Plesser (cello) and many others.

But, as one might expect in a Jewish state, it is the written word which has brought forth the greatest talents and provoked the greatest controversy, for there is a tradition of commitment in Hebrew letters, and writers are expected not only to tell a story, but to assume the mantle of the Prophets—and they have done so enthusiastically. To which one must add that they are widely regarded as false prophets.

Israel is divided between the narrow and the universalistic, between those who are obsessed with the past and those who look towards the future, between those who believe in a greater Israel and

151

those who would abandon territory for the sake of peace, and most Israeli writers are on the liberal side of the divide.

In fact the only notable exceptions are Moshe Shamir (no relation to the Prime Minister), who began life on the extreme Left of the political spectrum and is now on the extreme Right—a sort of poor man's D'Annunzio; and Aharon Applefeld, who confines himself largely to writing about the Holocaust and its aftermath and never utters a public word on contemporary issues.

All the rest, A. B. Yehoshua, Amos Oz, Yehuda Amichai, Aharon Megged, Yoram Kaniuk and others less eminent, though they are staunchly patriotic, have consistently pointed to the dangers which have lately overtaken Israel and warn of the even greater dangers ahead.

The same is true of Israel's dramatists, who excite even greater controversy if only because where a book offends it offends in isolation, but where a play offends it offends in public and the offence is shared. Moreover, nearly all Israeli theatres are publicly subsidised, and as someone put it to me: "I don't really object to blasphemy or even sedition, but I do object to blasphemy and sedition being paid for out of public funds."

Israel's most prolific playwright is Yehoshua Sobol and one can rarely go to the theatre in Haifa, Tel Aviv or Jerusalem without seeing one or other of his plays. One of his most recent works, "Jerusalem Syndrome", was denounced by the Chief Rabbi of Haifa as an act of desecration. The Rabbi had not seen the play (orthodox Rabbis never set foot in the theatre) but he had heard about it—as well he might, since one heard of little else when it was first staged about six months ago. It was concerned with the Jewish revolt against the Romans in AD 70, and there are obvious parallels between the religious and political fanaticism of ancient Judea and modern Israel. To bring the point home, actors were dressed not as Romans, but in Israeli army uniform.

Right wingers bought a large bloc of seats and disrupted the opening performance. If they tried to disrupt every play to which they took exception it would become a full-time occupation: for whether one goes to the plays of Sobol, or of Hanoch Levin, Shmuel Hasfari or Motti Lerner, there is hardly a drama to be seen in Israel which does not, in one way of another, deal with fanaticism or bigotry in fairly merciless terms.

This is true even of revivals, like the current production of

"Mother Courage" at the Habimah (Israel's equivalent of the National Theatre): Brecht's picture of the devastation caused by the religious wars of the 17th century has more than passing relevance to contemporary Israel.

Fanatics and bigots do not normally go to the theatre, but there are quite a few people who think of themselves as moderates who feel that the theatre of protest—and in Israel there is hardly any other sort—doth protest too much.

Israelis approach the written word (except as written in the daily press) with something like veneration, and if writers or dramatists receive few material rewards (one writer, with an almost legendary reputation, told me that his last royalty return would just about pay for a packet of cigarettes), they do enjoy an exalted place in Israeli society. But they are regarded by the public with a mixture of pride and bewilderment—pride at their talent, bewilderment at the fact that they should use their talent in such negative ways.

There are, it is true, nihilistic strains in some of the plays; for if they are obviously *against* militarism, fanaticism, superstition and hypocrisy, it is less easy to see what exactly they are *for*. But in broad terms Israeli plays, like Israeli novels, are infinitely nearer in spirit to prophetic teaching than any speech one is likely to hear in the Knesset or any sermon one is likely to hear in the synagogue. If Israel should eventually find her way out of her present difficulties, it could be due more to the efforts of her men of letters than her men of war.

The Daily Telegraph, 22 April 1988

Patriot or Traitor

ISRAELIS HAVE A good conceit of themselves, which is forgivable. What is perhaps less forgivable is their conviction that every one else is stupid—though I'm coming round to the view that, when it comes to America, they may be right. Here is an ally which has sustained Israel from the earliest days, hailed her triumphs, overlooked her excesses, supported her when the rest of the world condemned her, gave her special privileges as a trading partner, armed her with the latest equipment, and poured billions into her coffers, only to find an Israeli spy purloining her secrets.

Israel has tried to explain away the whole Pollard affair as "a rogue operation". But in case anyone, even in America, should take her explanation seriously, she has promoted both the principal rogues involved and has from beginning to end acted on W. C. Fields's dictum that one should never give a sucker an even break.

There is, no doubt, regret in Jerusalem about the damage to Israeli-American relations. There will be none about the harm to the American Jewish community, for, as I wrote when the story first broke in December, 1985: "There are people on the extreme right of Israeli politics—and Likud, in this context, is extreme enough—who resent the continuing stability and prosperity of the American Jewish community because it affronts their belief that the diaspora is a passing phenomenon, who would not be unhappy to see it destabilised, and who must regard the embarrassment brought upon American Jewry by the scandal as a bonus."

Mr Benjamin Netanyahu, Israel's UN Ambassador, has claimed, by way of mitigation, that Pollard was motivated by Zionism, as if that were an excuse for betrayal. Pollard, in fact, received monthly hand-outs from his minders, and further sums were paid into his

Swiss bank account.

Right-wing Zionists would, in fact, like to see the entire diaspora destabilised. Last month, for example, Jean-Marie Le Pen, head of the French National Front, who is regarded by French Jewry much as Mosley was regarded by British Jewry, was entertained to lunch by Mr Jacques Torczyner, a leading Right-wing American Zionist.

There is an obvious affinity of interest between them, for while Le Pen would like to see the Jews out of France, Torczyner would like to see them settle in Israel—though Torczyner himself, one must add, is content to stay in New York. (I should say that there is, of course, a precedent for all this, for Jabotinsky flirted both with Simon Petlura, the Ukrainian nationalist leader and foremost pogromchik of his day, and with the Italian fascist dictator, Benito Mussolini.)

Right-wing Zionists have never recognised diaspora communities —not even the six million Jews of America—as legitimate entities in their own right, but as satellites at the service of Israel, so that they might give money where they have it, exert influence where they command it, and, above all, act as reservoirs for potential immigrants.

During the 20 years in which the campaign for Soviet Jews has been in operation, no major Jewish leader—with the honourable exception of the late Nahum Goldmann—has suggested that we should not only demand that Soviet Jews should be free to leave Russia, but that they should be free to live as Jews within Russia; yet the idea was never seriously considered because Israel is not interested in human rights for Russian Jews, only in Russian Jews as aliya fodder.

Any doubts one might have had on the matter have been dispelled by the formal request made by Mr Shamir to President Reagan that America should withhold refugee status from Soviet Jews. Could there be a more abject confession of moral bankruptcy? If Le Pen should ever attain office, I can see Shamir's successor asking the Americans to withhold refugee status from French Jews. The whole effort is not only shameful, but futile. No American President is likely to accede to such a request, and even if he did, there are always—as many South African Jews are discovering—the attractions of Australia.

Mr Shamir and his colleagues should know their fellow Jews better. The greater the efforts to corral them towards Israel, the greater their determination to go elsewhere.

Jewish Chronicle, 20 March 1987

Pathways to Heaven

THERE HAVE BEEN almost constant demonstrations in Jerusalem against the building of a Mormon University campus adjacent to the Hebrew University on Mt Scopus, and one of the most telling placards carried by the demonstrators asked: "Isn't Utah Big Enough?"

Utah, the American home of the Mormons, is indeed a very large state, but the question misses the point at issue. Jerusalem has a grip on the imagination, not only of Jews, but of anyone familiar with the Bible. It is more than a place, it is a concept, and it is as natural for an academic institution concerned with the fundamentals of existence to seek a foothold in Jerusalem, as it is for American and British institutions concerned with art or archaeology to have schools in Rome and Athens.

Jews may have a unique relationship with Jerusalem, but they cannot overlook its universal appeal, nor should they wish to, and I regard the desire of the Mormons to build a university on Mt Scopus as a tribute to the universality of prophetic teaching. I only hope that the obstacles they have had to face, and the calumnies and harassment to which they have been subjected, will not discourage others from following their example. It would be nice to see the hills which ring Jerusalem crowned with seats of learning of whatever persuasion. Mayor Teddy Kollek has been criticised for allowing the Mormons such a prime site, but one cannot run up a university in any odd corner, and in any case, even if it had been hidden away among the slums of Katamon, the protests against it would have continued unabated because of the widespread belief that it will engage in missionary activity.

Now it must be said that the Mormons are active proselytisers, and

156

they would not have achieved their present size and importance without a readiness to knock on doors and spread their teachings, but they know why Jews regard missionaries with particular abhorrence and they have solemnly promised that there would be no missionary activity. But that isn't all. They have, I am told, also undertaken not to admit Jewish students to their courses at all. No such undertaking should have been sought, and none should have been given. One cannot claim to build a university on grounds of academic freedom, and then go on to exclude students on non-academic grounds. Israelis have an insatiable intellectual curiosity, and although they are not short of universities themselves, if another is to open on their door-step they will wish to make use of it and I would like to see anyone try and stop them.

The people leading the campaign against the Mormon University would also close down the Hebrew University if they had their way, or, indeed, any other seat of learning which did not conform to their narrow teachings. They are substantially the same people who have led demonstrations against the excavations near the Temple Mount and who have succeeded in making archaeology a semi-clandestine activity in Israel. In this particular campaign they can draw on wider support because the cry of missionaries engages Jewish emotions more readily than the cry of bones, but it is based either on ignorance, or wilful distortion, or both, for there are people who know the facts, but are ready to exploit the emotions of those who don't. I have heard that same cry against churchmen who have devoted their lives to service to Israel and the Jewish people, and much as there are antisemites who claim they are only anti-Zionists, there are bigots who claim they are only working against missionaries when they are in fact hostile to the very presence of churchmen and church institutions in the Jewish state.

A man secure in his convictions can face alternative ideas with equanimity and broaden his knowledge without impairing his beliefs, but the self-proclaimed defenders of our faith know what they know and are afraid of what they don't, and seem to feel that Judaism is so frail a creed, and Jews so fickle a race, that they must be shielded against external influence. This is a fight not only for religious tolerance, but academic freedom, for if they should succeed in preventing the Mormon University from rising on Mt Scopus, I am not sure for how long the Hebrew University will remain safe in its place.

Jewish Chronicle, 3 January 1986

Think Big

IF YOU WANT to be a criminal, think big. That is the most obvious of the many lessons to emerge from the Israeli bank scandal.

If you're going to be a petty operator and steal a thousand here or divert a thousand there, the chances are that you will not only be caught and punished, but you will be shunned by your friends, ostracised by the public and stigmatised for life as a malefactor. If, however, you should think in terms of millions and operate under the guise of a banker, you're safe.

When the Likud came to power in 1977 it cast off numerous controls and set the people free—to rob one another. Vast development schemes were undertaken in the occupied territories which poured millions into the pockets of contractors and sub-contractors, and an artificial aura of economic well-being was induced which helped the Government win the 1981 general election.

One drawback to it all was that, as the government increasingly resorted to the printing presses to pay its bills, money kept losing its value and the rate of inflation, which had been at about 30 per cent when the Government took office, shot up to 100 per cent, 200 per cent, 300 per cent; but there was—or at least there was thought to be—a hedge even against that in the form of bank shares, which rose in value even faster than inflation. Hyper-inflation can (in the short term) in itself be good for banks. No one wants to hold on to money and there is a constant inducement to pass on what one has and to borrow what one hasn't. The banks, for their part, lent liberally, especially as a good deal of the money they were lending went into their own shares, which in turn jacked up their value; but, if that weren't enough, the banks jacked them up further by making purchases on their own behalf.

158

I am not a banker, nor even a speculator, but I think I recognise daylight robbery when I see it. Yet, when I commented on it at the time, I was advised that, even if it were not ethical for banks to hype their own shares, it was legal and that, in other words, the banks acting severally and together were more or less at liberty to perpetrate a gigantic fraud upon the general public. Very few people were in the dark as to what was happening, yet they continued to press every shekel they had—and quite a few they didn't—into bank shares in the belief that they would thereby get their portion of the loot.

In the inter-war years, many British investors lost money on dubious mining shares, but in that instance, at least, the gold could conceivably have been in the ground. In this instance, everything was up in the air.

The accounts were there to be studied and one could see at a glance that the market value of the bank shares bore no relation to the value of the capital assets or even the earning potential of the banks.

Yet, in a crude way, the whole crazy operation made sense, because in the last resort one couldn't lose. The small First International Bank of Israel (or FIBI, as it's known) kept out of the racket, but the big four—Bank Leumi, Hapoalim, Discount and Mizrachi—were in it up to their navels, and all had grown to such a size that no government could afford to let them fail, so that punters could enjoy the profit potential of speculative stock, but suffer few of the hazards. The shares were virtually gilt-edged.

It could not last, of course, if only because the very fabric of the economy was beginning to come apart, and once investors made a headlong rush out of paper and into real money—such as dollars—the game was up.

A judicial inquiry has now revealed the full scale of the chicanery, and has named the guilty men, but I think the whole episode reflects rather sadly on a large section of Israeli society and the extent to which people were caught up in the speculative frenzy.

The real losers, however, are the honest to goodness members of the general public—and difficult though it is to believe, they exist in considerable numbers—who are not interested in speculation, are not avid to get rich quick, and are happy with their portion, or would be—if it were not consistently stolen from them.

They are never among the profit takers, but are always, as in this case, among those who are called upon to settle the final account.

Jewish Chronicle, 16 May 1986

Tarnished Hand-Shake

THERE SEEMS TO be no limit to the greed of the very rich.

It is not so long since the head of Burton's decided to pay himself £1 million a year. No one is worth that much money—certainly no one needs that much—and if my own experience is anything to go by, one can jog along very nicely on half that sum.

As if a million weren't enough, however, that same gentleman has now proposed an option scheme which would given him even more. But Burton, at least, is making money—and lots of it.

What is one to say of Bank Leumi, which is not doing too badly now, but which was nearly done for three years ago and which yet proposed to pay its former chairman, Ernest Japhet, nearly $5 million, plus a pension of $360,000 a year, by way of a *golden handshake*?

A golden handshake? He should have been given the metal-capped boot. In Britain, the chairman of Guinness was dismissed without a penny for boosting his company's shares in the course of a takeover battle, but in Israel, Bank Leumi (in concert with the other major banks) had been doing the same thing, openly and blatantly, over a period of years, until the bubble finally burst and the Government had to intervene to save the entire banking system from collapse.

The fact that Japhet wasn't the only guilty party doesn't make him innocent. The only thing which could possibly be said in mitigation is that Israel's bankers have for so long been used to dealing with funny money that they have lost all sense of proportion when dealing with the real stuff.

Bank salaries in Israel are not particularly extravagant, but at the very top they are astronomical, and the sum which Japhet hoped to

160

get away with is a measure of the annual salaries which he and his senior colleagues have been paying themselves.

The most shameful part of the whole business, however, is that they tried to keep it dark—as well they might—and it only came to light through the vigilance of the Israeli press.

The Bank of Israel, the Treasury and the Knesset finance committee, which are meant to act as watchdogs over the operations of the commercial banks, have proved to be lapdogs. But the body which has shown the greatest dereliction of duty has been the Jewish Agency.

Bank Leumi, Israel's oldest and largest bank, is a successor to the Anglo-Palestine Bank, established in London in 1902 as a subsidiary of the Jewish Colonial Trust, which in turn was founded by the Zionist Congress.

The founders' shares are still vested in the Jewish Agency, which holds them in trust for the Jewish people, and the chairman of the Jewish Agency, Mr Aryeh Dultzin, is, technically at least, the *capo del capo*, the supreme head of the bank. If he didn't know of the payment to Japhet, he should have known, and if he did know, he shouldn't have allowed it to have been made.

In either case, he may be wondering what the whole fuss is about, for one gathers that the emoluments and perks he receives are not dissimilar to those enjoyed by the top people in the bank, while the spending habits of the Jewish Agency are such that the sums Japhet hoped to get away with must seem fairly commonplace.

The Jewish Agency operates in a twilight world of smart accountants and limited accountability. The Israeli taxpayer knows the earnings of Cabinet Ministers, Knesset Members and civil servants, but no subscriber to the JIA or the JNF—whose funds, of course, flow into the giant maw of the Jewish Agency—have the slightest inkling what Dultzin or any of his colleagues get.

The JIA often has fact-finding tours of Israel and subscribers are taken to witness at first hand the poverty of development towns like Dimona; but it might also be instructive if they were shown round the suite in the King David Hotel frequently occupied by Mr Dultzin.

It is possible that I, in common with other journalists, may be doing Mr Dultzin an injustice and that the rumours circulating in Israel of his extravagance are unfounded, but the only way to kill rumours is to tell the truth.

Chaim Bermant

Silence in such a situation is tantamount to confirmation. An organisation, dependent on public funds, which is not prepared to take the public into its confidence, does not deserve the confidence of the public.

Jewish Chronicle, 23 January 1987

The Godless and the Godly

CHIEF RABBI SIR Immanuel Jakobovits recently had some controversial things to say about Zionism and he was attacked not so much for what he said, but for where he said it—in *The Times*.

Whether we like it or not—and I suspect that most of us do like it—what happens in the Jewish state is of interest to more than Jews, which is why the Chief Rabbi's opinions are so often sought by the media.

It so happens that I disagreed with some of his conclusions, but his arguments were well put, and if the resulting controversy showed that Jews do not always think alike, it suggested that they at least do think, and I, for one, prefer honest divisions to spurious unanimity.

Sir Immanuel's main point is that Zionism took too little account of the fact the Jewish national aspirations were at source religious and that the attempt to create a secular state was therefore doomed to failure.

But Zionism, as he must know, evolved in the teeth of religious opposition. One could find a Moshe Mohliver here or a Rav Kook there who were prepared to go along with it, and even bless it, but the mass of religious leaders condemned Zionism with bell, book and candle, not because it was secular, but because it was presumptuous. The Jewish state, they believed, could be restored only by divine intervention.

There was a paralysis of will in the great ghettos of eastern Europe. Zionists had to be secular to get off the ground at all—and by God they did.

They drained swamps, laid roads, set up kibbutzim and moshavim, established schools and institutions of higher learning, built cities, fought and won a prolonged war against impossible odds, and

163

created a state out of chaos.

They took their fate into their own hands and succeeded with fifty years of strenuous effort where two thousand years of prayer had failed.

But that was not the limit of their achievements. A country with fewer than a million Jews, bled white by war and on the brink of bankruptcy, immediately applied itself to the ingathering of exiles and absorbed more than 600,000 immigrants, most of them penniless and few of them skilled, in three years, without economic upheaval or civil strife. I doubt if any nation in history, large or small, surmounted so many difficulties in so few years.

And yet Sir Immanuel talks of failure. If that was failure, what is success?

Mistakes were made, of course, and the country had its critics, but in the main it was a source of wonder and for a while Israel— unashamedly secular though she may have been—was "a light unto the nations", a model of what a small, democratic country could achieve.

She was crowded with delegations from other new nations who hoped to learn from her experience and emulate her ways. She had (to adapt the words of Pitt) saved herself by her exertions and hoped to save others by her example.

Israel is now, in formal terms, an infinitely more religious society than it was thirty years ago. There are more synagogues, yeshivot and religious day schools and a far greater degree of religious observance.

But would Sir Immanuel lay his hand on his heart and say that it is therefore a more just, tolerant and equitable society?

I would invite him to quote one action or utterance of a leading Israeli rabbi or leader of a religious party to suggest a concern with humanity or justice, for I could quote any number to show a perversion of everything that Judaism has traditionally stood for.

Yet Sir Immanuel is right. Zionism *has* failed, though not because it was secularist, but because it has abandoned secularism and been hijacked by messianism.

In the last resort, however, the Chief Rabbi and I are arguing about words. I believe that a man is religious if he acts religiously, and not because he festoons himself with the appurtenances of religion and spouts religious teachings. In that sense, Israel was a good deal more religious in its secular phase than it is now.

Murmurings of a Licensed Heretic

Abraham Isaac Kook, the first Ashkenazi Chief Rabbi, who always defended secular Zionists against their religious detractors, argued that godless men can sometimes do the work of God. The corollary of that is that godly men can sometimes do the work of the devil.

Jewish Chronicle, 26 June 1987

False Façade

YOU'RE FAMILIAR WITH the question, who is a Jew? Well, let me pose another: who is a Jewish leader?

I am moved to ask by the invitation from Israel's Prime Minister, Mr Yitzhak Shamir, to "Jewish leaders" to go to Jerusalem for a global conference designed to show the world that the Jewish people is at Israel's side.

And who are the Jewish leaders? One of them is Mrs Vivien Duffield, a charming young woman who happens to be the rich daughter of a rich father (the late Charles Clore) and who has been fairly generous to various Israeli causes.

Generosity is indeed a commendable quality, but it does not in itself mark one out as a leader.

Another is Robert Maxwell, a less than charming, rather elderly man who for many years insisted that he wasn't even Jewish, whose six children have been raised as Anglicans, and who isn't even particularly generous.

Which more or less answers my question. Who is a Jewish leader? Someone who is very rich and who is unlikely to question Mr Shamir's policies in public or in private.

To be fair, one must add that a considerable number of people of real eminence were invited, men of the calibre of Sir Isaiah Berlin, but, as Sir Isaiah has said, "talking to the present Prime Minister of Israel is like talking to a stone wall".

Several friends who are highly regarded in the community, who may be construed as leaders in the true sense of the word, and who were likewise invited, have told me that, although it was not easy to ignore a signed invitation from the Prime Minister of Israel, they were boycotting the conference because they could see no point in it.

166

Who, after all, is the conference meant to impress?

The Jewish world? Jews are too familiar with the sad truths of the situation to be impressed by yet another display of hand-shaking, back-slapping and yea-saying.

Israel? The country has been chortling over the conference ever since it was first mooted.

The outside world? The conference, far from being a display of Jewish unity, has highlighted the divisions which have arisen within it.

Where there is real solidarity over a particular issue, it is self-evident. Where one has to organise a conference to display it, it is a confession that it doesn't exist.

The conference bears all the marks of haste and desperation and it is entirely appropriate that it should have been held over Purim; though it seems to me that delegates should have been invited to come in fancy dress or, at least, in funny hats.

The only thing that may be said for the conference is that it must have helped Jerusalem hoteliers, who have been going through a rather bad patch.

It may be readily conceded that the entire Jewish people do have a sense of solidarity with Israel, especially during a crisis; but at such times there is no need for the Israeli Government to organise freebie solidarity conferences, because people rush to Israel of their own accord and at their own expense.

There is no great crisis now, and in so far as there is one, it is benign, for world opinion—including America—has been urging Israel to do what in all conscience it should have done of its own accord—talk to the Palestine Liberation Organisation.

The PLO are, by any standards, an unsavoury pack who are not entirely in charge of their own house and who will find it difficult to deliver any promises they may feel compelled to make.

But Mr Shamir himself vetoed the attempts of Shimon Peres to set up talks with Hussein, and any Palestinian leaders who emerged in the occupied territories have either been deported or detained, so that there is hardly anyone left to talk to except the PLO.

It has been suggested that local elections might be held so that Palestinians could choose their own delegates; but then, such elections were held in 1976 and were won outright by pro-PLO candidates, which is why they haven't been held since.

Mr Shamir's insistence that he will never talk to the PLO means in effect that he will not talk at all.

Mr Shamir assures everyone that he wants peace, which I don't doubt for a minute, but he wants peace only on his own terms.

The solidarity conference he has scratched together is merely a claque to applaud his do-nothing approach. It is in no way a representative gathering of the Jewish people.

Jewish Chronicle, 24 March 1989

Holy Disneyland

MENAHEM GOLAN, THE film producer, is the Cecil B. de Mille of Israel. Cecil B. de Mille (for the benefit of younger readers) was the man who brought the Ten Commandments to America, while Menahem Golan is planning to bring the Ten Plagues to Israel.

And not only the Ten Plagues, for I gather he also plans to re-enact the expulsion from Eden, the erection of the Tower of Babel, the Great Flood, the destruction of Sodom and Gomorrah, the binding of Isaac, Jacob wrestling with the angel, the rape of Dinah, the massacre of Shechem, the sale of Joseph, the dreams of Pharaoh, the building of Pithom and Raamses, the parting of the Red Sea, the Golden Calf, the giving of the Torah, the sun and the moon standing still over Ayalom, the collapse of the walls of Jericho, Samson and the lion, Samson and Delilah, Samson in the temple of Dagon (methinks Samson will need a section of his own), Saul and the Witch of Ein Dor, David and Goliath, the building of the Temple, the arrival of the Queen of Sheba, the division of the Kingdom, the Assyrians descending like a wolf on the fold, the siege of Jerusalem, the Babylonian captivity, Daniel in the lions' den, Shadrach, Meshach and Abednego in the fiery furnace, Jonah in the whale, the hanging of Haman, Ruth amidst the alien porn (I know it's usually corn, but with Golan it will be porn). Belshazzar's feast, the Writing on the Wall, the return under Ezra and Nehemiah, and, for good measure, Jesus walking on the Sea of Galilee (how's that for a whirlwind tour of the Old Testament *and* the New?).

I am told that Mr Golan also intends to throw in Tobias and the Angel, but that at least is apocryphal.

Golan was obviously inspired by Disneyland. One tours Disneyland by monorail; one will presumably tour Goland by a fiery chariot

169

of the sort which took Elijah up to heaven. It will be driven by Jehu. ("The fiery chariot now standing at platform three is the 2.55 for Sodom, Gomorrah and the five cities of the plain.")

In Disneyland, one is greeted by Mickey Mouse, Donald Duck, Goofy and Pluto. In Goland, I should imagine, one will be greeted by the Serpent (hotfoot from Eden), the Golden Calf, Balaam's Ass, and any number of other animals, some coming two by two, some seven by seven, many of them ringstraked, speckled and grisled.

Children and teenagers will be invited to eat spiked apples from the tree of knowledge and to inscribe their own writing on the wall.

Drinks will be available for all the family in Lot's shebean. Noah's Ark will be selling Vin du Patron 354 (a vintage year), and there will be a Gay Bar in Sodom. Boutiques will be selling couturier-designed fig-leaves, coats of many colours and a wide variety of prophets mantles (only one previous wearer).

Fast-food counters will be selling matzot, and paschal-lamb kebabs, and there will be any number of speciality restaurants, one selling manna, another quails; a third—to be managed by Wheeler's—will be selling loaves and fishes.

The Prodigal Son chop-house will be selling fatted calves, while the truly carnivorous may wish to repair to the Shadrach and Meshach barbecue and the Abednego grill.

There will also be an establishment, open only in the evenings and catering for parties of thirteen or more, which will be serving the last supper. (Table d'hôte menu only: last orders at midnight.) Pork, and kids seethed in their mothers' milk, will not be available.

A dentist will be in attendance for children whose fathers may have eaten sour grapes (and whose teeth may therefore be on edge), and there will be a moral and physical Yom Kippur health farm for those suffering from every form of over-indulgence, so that even though their sins were as scarlet, they will emerge as white as snow.

Five-star accommodation will be available in the Tents of Kedar, four-star in booths half-open to the skies (minimum stay, seven days), three-star in the Cave of Adullam, and two-star in a manger.

There will be no room at the inn (which has been fully booked for VIPs), while the impecunious will be free to lie down in green pastures, or try their luck at the Inn of the Good Samaritan; and to make sure that visitors do not go astray, they will be guided by a pillar of cloud by day and a pillar of fire by night.

Mr Golan anticipates millions of tourists who, he believes, will be agog at the sights. Agog? I think they'll be Agog and Magog.

I presume that Mr Golan must be a supporter of the Greater Israel movement, for lesser Israel is too small to accommodate his theme and his scheme. Indeed, if he plans to site the Garden of Eden and the rest in their original locations, he will have to incorporate Syria and Iraq as well.

But all that is quibbling with details in what is, after all, a grand design.

Jewish Chronicle, 19 April 1985

Jews on Horseback

"I know two things about a horse, and one of them is rather coarse."

But then being Jewish I am not expected to know much. The late Lenny Bruce (*zichrono livrocho*) once prepared a long list of things which were Jewish and things which decidedly were not:

"Instant potatoes are *goyish*, TV dinners are *goyish*. Fruit salad is Jewish. Black cherry soda's very Jewish . . . Trailer parks are so *goyish* that Jews won't even go near them. Chicks that iron your shirt for you are *goyish* . . ."

But he failed to mention the most *goyish* thing of all—horses.

No Jew, even in extremis, would offer a kingdom for a horse, though he might be induced to part with a tidy sum for a horse and cart, provided it was comfortably appointed. One meets horses in plenty in the stories of Mendele, Sholem Aleichem and Agnon, but they are all tied to a wagon, much as the horses one meets in Scripture generally come with chariots. When Elijah went up to heaven he travelled by chariot. When Mohammed did the same he travelled by horse—which is possibly why Disraeli referred to Arabs as "Jews on horseback".

The only horseman of note in the Old Testament was Esau. I am aware that there is no explicit reference to him on horseback, but he was spoken of as "a cunning hunter", and he would not have been very cunning if he had hunted on foot. He was, moreover, "a man of the field", and what does that suggest if not horses and horsemen and perhaps even hounds? I have always imagined Esau as the Jorrocks of the Canaan hunt.

Esau has never been treated with sufficient kindness and understanding by our commentators (as distinct from Jacob, who has been treated with too much understanding) and I suspect that one of the reasons why the horse has such a lowly place in Jewish esteem is that it is subconsciously associated in Jewish minds with the rider. Another are the rather unkind references to the beast in Psalms: "Be ye not as the horse, or the mule, which have no understanding . . . A horse is a vain thing for safety; neither shall he deliver any by his great strength."

Both statements are debatable, but as a result the horse has descended into Jewish lore as something of an ass. To call somebody a *ferd* in Yiddish is to call him a fool. To call someone a "horse" in English—though the expression is rarely used in this way—is to suggest that he is an honest, plodding toiler, I think our horses have deserved greater consideration from us.

I was therefore delighted to read a recent article in the *Jerusalem Post* which suggested that horses were being rehabilitated in the Jewish state, and that if Israel's economy as a whole is in decay, Israel's riding schools are experiencing a boom.

I once hired a horse from a so-called riding school in the Negev. It looked like a reject from a knacker's yard and I was nervous of mounting it, not because I was afraid I'd fall off, but because I was afraid it might collapse under me, which it nearly did. Some weeks later I read of a kashrut scandal in which non-kosher animals somehow found their way into purportedly kosher wursht, and now every time I look at a plate of wursht I see that poor beast staring up at me.

I, however, understand that there are now at least six properly regulated riding schools in Israel, and that one operated by a Miss Jill Lerner in Rishon leZion, is not only fully booked, but has a waiting list of over a hundred, which is almost enough to man a cavalry regiment. (I have always felt that there should be a cavalry brigade, and perhaps even a camel corps, in the Israeli Army, if only for ceremonial purposes.)

Miss Lerner, I understand, is from England, where she was a member of the Surrey Union Hunt, while her brother was an MOF in Yorkshire. Bless her. I believe her efforts represent the most important contribution of Britain to the rebuilding of Zion since the Balfour Declaration.

I must admit that I myself have a weakness for donkeys because, apart from anything else, they are easier to park and less expensive to maintain than horses.

The first of the many times that I lived in Israel I could not afford a car, bicycles were too hazardous, and I therefore acquired a donkey. I don't know what it would be like in Tel Aviv, but it is ideal for getting around Jerusalem, especially the stepped narrow streets of the Old City, and one doesn't even have to feed it, for it helps itself to the vegetation in the surrounding gardens.

I also have it on good authority that when the Messiah comes he will do so not in a Volvo, or even on horseback, but on a donkey, and what's good enough for the Messiah is good enough for me.

Jewish Chronicle, 9 August 1985

Shaky Justice

I HAVE ALWAYS thought that being a judge was about the most sublime occupation open to man, and it is one of the few which is divinely ordained: "Judges and officers shalt thou make thee in all thy gates, which the Lord thy God giveth thee, throughout thy tribes, and they shall judge the people with just judgements."

And, with the occasional lapse, it is generally accepted that they do. Their standing is high, their expenses are low (no overheads except wigs, and they're paid for), their perks are many, their duties are few, their burdens are light, their recompense is heavy, and they have a security of tenure second only to that of Orthodox rabbis. No wonder most of them live for ever—or as near for ever as counts.

But all that, it would seem, applies only to England, for I was startled to hear that an entire bench of Tel Aviv judges, six in number, and all good men and true, are demanding compensation for the "tension-filled atmosphere" in which they have to work and which, they say, has given them all heart ailments.

They claim that, before being raised to the bench, they were bursting with health, sound of limb and fleet of foot, that they would do forty press-ups and jog round the city's perimeter before breakfast, and the same again after lunch, without as much as pausing for breath; but that ten years on they were doddery old men, hardly able to get about, broken in body and maimed in spirit (though, if their claim is anything to go by, the judges are still fairly agile in mind).

Asked to furnish further and better particulars, one judge said he had had a bypass operation, another spoke of a flyover, a third an underpass, and a fourth (if I understood him rightly, which I probably didn't) said he had been filled with cones for an arterial counter-

175

flow system, all of which reminded me a little of our motorways, which, I will admit, are in a fairly parlous state.

The National Insurance Institute, from whom they are making their claim, has, however, regarded their case with scant sympathy. Or rather, it has given them a great deal of sympathy, but no money.

I dare say that if one judge had sought compensation for his ailments, it would have been one thing, but when an entire bench of judges all succumb to the same ailment, and flash their X-rays to prove it, it begins to look like an epidemic, if not a conspiracy, which may explain the negative attitude of the NII. The trouble with all insurance institutions is that, while they are fairly prompt in paying for the fully dead, they are disinclined to compensate the half-dead. The Tel Aviv six, however, feel that the NII should, on the grounds that they half-killed themselves in the course of their work.

In other words, they believe that their ailments arise wholly, solely and exclusively from their occupation and that they would like to put judges' hearts on a par with housemaids' knees, clergymen's sore throats and journalists' livers, and to that end they have taken the NII to court. "Judge not lest ye be judged," sayeth the Good Book. I would not like to be the judge who will have to preside over the hearing, for he will need the wisdom of Solomon and the stamina of Samson.

Can a judge hearing the claims of fellow judges be impartial in his judgement? I fear that long before the hearing is over, he will himself fall prey to a heart ailment and sue the NII for compensation.

Whatever the outcome, I shall be following the case with more than academic interest, for before I became a scribe and a pharisee and embarked on this column, my head was a cascade of golden curls and my beard a russet brown, so that men turned in the street and each said to the other, "Verily, a god walketh among us"; but now, alas, my head is bare and my beard is white and I, too, feel entitled to compensation from someone. It may be argued that no one has died of a bald head or a white beard, but the Tel Aviv judges, for all their complaints, are also alive (may they live to be 120), which, as I have suggested, is the root of their trouble.

Perhaps they should have compounded their disorders, and instead of filing six individual claims for ill health, they should have put in for three fatalities and shared out the proceeds among each other. But whatever the outcome of the hearing, they deserve full marks for trying.

Jewish Chronicle, 10 October 1986

Fruity Farce

IN THE STATE of Israel, everything that matters (including everything that doesn't) is a matter of state.

About twenty-five years ago, someone proposed inviting the Beatles (of blessed memory) to tour Israel. I can't remember now if the National Religious Party threatened to leave the coalition if the Beatles as much as set foot in the country, or if Ben-Gurion came out of retirement to deal with the issue.

What I do remember is that the Cabinet went into secret session and, after a long and acrimonious debate, in the course of which the Minister of Education and Culture called the Minister of Health and Hygiene a snivelling idiot (or words to that effect), it was decided that the Beatles shouldn't come.

Little did they know that a mere twenty years later the JNF would seek to plant a forest in memory of John Lennon. (What, incidentally, ever happened to the John Lennon forest?)

Well, a similar crisis has now erupted over "The Idler's Song", Israel's entry to the Eurovision Song Contest, and in particular its lyrics, which go:

Hoopa hoopa hoopa
Hoola hoola hoola hoopa.
In the afternoon I sent my dog with
a shopping basket made of straw to buy strawberries.
When he gets back I prepare a
meal for the two of us because the
birds have finished all the seed.

It is notoriously difficult to render Hebrew into English, but I suspect that, even in the original, the words are not quite in the

Psalms class, and I cannot see them finding a place in the canon of the Bible; but I think they compare favourably to the words of one of the most beloved of all Yiddish songs, which go:

Cherry bim, cherry bom,
Cherry bim bim bim bim bom bom.
Cherry cherry cherry bim bim bim, bom, bom,
bim bim bim . . .

And so on, *ad nauseam* and, indeed, *ad infinitum*, but then Cherry Bim (or if you prefer, Cherry Bom) was written (if written it was) long before the State of Israel was in being and, what is more to the point, it was never an entry for the Eurovision Song Contest, and the matter of the entry has aroused strong, indeed violent, passions in Israeli political circles.

Again I am not sure if the National Religious Party has threatened to leave the coalition if the song is not withdrawn, or if Mr Begin is to come out of retirement to deal with the issue; but the Minister of Science and Technology, Mr Gideon Patt, has vowed a great vow that he will move heaven and earth (and, as Minister of Science and Technology, he has the means—including the Dimona nuclear reactor—to do just that) to have the song blocked, and he hopes to persuade Mr Yitzhak Navon, the Minister of Education and Culture, to join him in the endeavour.

The song, he believes, will "besmirch the name of Israel before 200 million viewers and cause shame and anguish to the three or four million Jews living in those countries where the Eurovision Song Contest will be televised".

The most innocent words, both in Hebrew and English, can have hidden sexual meanings these days and, for all I know, "a shopping basket made of straw" is an unspeakable obscenity, while "strawberries" may be another word for you-know-what. Otherwise I can't understand what the fuss is about.

"The Idler's Song" may not be poetry, but taken at face value is it any worse than "A-Ba-Ni-Bi", which actually ran away with the first prize at the Eurovision Song Contest a few years ago?

One should not look for truth (or, at least, the whole truth) in an obituary, or for wisdom in a pop song, especially since the lyrics, no matter how beautiful or grotesque they may be, are rarely if ever intelligible.

The one area of Israeli life from which one can continue to draw unalloyed pleasure is the arts. One can rarely open an intelligent paper these days without reading a tribute to an Israeli writer or painter or instrumentalist.

Israel's composers, at least of classical music, are less celebrated (perhaps with good reason), but her pop composers are outstanding. They are about the best ambassadors the country has. I wish I could say the same of Israeli politicians.

Jewish Chronicle, 10 April 1987

Of Politics
and Politicians

Government by Jews

I AM NOT prone to paranoia, but I did feel that there was an element of antisemitism in the "Brittan must go" campaign. And now that Brittan has gone, Alan Watkins, in the *Observer*, has reached the same conclusion:

". . . There has always been a suspicion of Brittan among Conservative backbenchers," he writes. "This is the consequence partly of straight political jealousy, partly of that antisemitism which still exists in parts of Westminster.

"After 1983 the jealousy and the antisemitism reacted upon and reinforced each other through Mrs Thatcher's appointment of other Jewish Cabinet Ministers: Mr Nigel Lawson, Sir Keith Joseph, Lord Young and, most recently, Mr Malcolm Rifkind."

When General de Gaulle landed in London in 1940, he is said to have complained, on looking round his immediate supporters, that they almost comprised a synagogue. I have heard Mrs Thatcher's Cabinet spoken of in much the same terms, or even as a Sanhedrin.

Jews form less than 1 per cent of the population and it would have been unnatural if people had not remarked on the fact that, until Mr Brittan's resignation, they formed something like 25 per cent of the Cabinet.

There was a time when it was almost impossible for a Jewish Conservative candidate to get into Parliament at all, let alone the Cabinet, and until about 15 years ago there were only two Jews on the Tory benches—the late Sir Henry d'Avigdor-Goldsmid and Sir Keith Joseph, both of them rich, both titled and both of good pedigree.

The great change came with the rise of Edward Heath to the leadership of the Tory Party in 1965. Heath was a self-made man and

183

did his best to ease the grip of the old-boy network on the constituencies and make the party more open to talent.

Jews, by then, had ceased to be an immigrant community. They had risen in business and the professions. They were as likely to vote Tory as Labour and were less hesitant in seeking an outlet for their political ambitions through the Conservative Party.

In 1970 the number of Jewish Tory MPs had increased to nine, but there were still 31 Labour Members in the House. Today there are 17 Jewish Tory MPs and only 11 Labour, and, with the transformation in the character of the Labour Party, I anticipate that their number will further decline.

Most Jews are conservative both by nature and by training (conservatism, indeed, is the principal force which has kept them Jewish) and, given acceptance and stability, they will tend to veer towards the Right—as they have done, for example, in America, and as they are doing in this country.

The number of Jews holding high office in the present administration, however, cannot be ascribed solely to the increasing Jewish involvement in Tory politics, and it seems to me that Mrs Thatcher—like Harold Wilson—has an almost mystical belief in Jewish ability.

This may be seen not only in the number of Jews in her Cabinet, but in the appointment of David (now Sir David) Wolfson as her *chef du Cabinet*, and of Stuart Young as chairman of the BBC, which, given the place of the electronic media in our lives is, I believe, one of the most important offices in the land.

It is uncertain whether this is good or bad for the Jews—or, what is more important, whether it is good or bad for the country—for, as Mr Watkins has suggested, not everyone in the Parliamentary Tory Party is convinced that her faith is wholly justified.

It used to be said that the Jew had to work harder, do better and be brighter to get anywhere in politics, or even to get anywhere at all. I am not sure if this is still the case, in Britain at least, and Jews (and especially Jewish lawyers) may sometimes be credited with qualities they do not possess through the very fact that they are Jewish—which, however, means that they are less easily forgiven for failure.

Alan Watkins believes that Mr Brittan had to go because there were too many Jews in Mrs Thatcher's Cabinet and that he paid the price "of other men's preferment".

Murmurings of a Licensed Heretic

I think that among men brought up on Greek and Hebrew myths, there is an instinctive inclination to throw someone overboard whenever a political storm blows up, if only to propitiate the gods, and who better to play Jonah than a Jew?

Jewish Chronicle, 31 January 1986

Foxes and Jackals

THE SCALE OF the outrage would have been comparatively minor—what, after all, are 380 innocent lives these days?—but its viciousness was unique.

Here was a man who had courted a girl over a period of years, had impregnated her and promised her marriage, and had then planned to use her, and his own unborn child, as a detonator to blow up an El Al Boeing, its passengers and crew. It would have been one of the most despicable crimes in history, and if it failed, it was not for want of trying.

Deranged individuals are capable of any enormity, but Nezar Hindawi was, of course, not acting alone, and the fact that the Syrian Ambassador was personally implicated is proof, if proof were needed, that it had all been planned at the highest level.

It was an act of war, more treacherous, if less blatant, than a border crossing, and Israel would have been entirely within her rights had she countered by invading Syria. Unfortunately, little would be gained from doing so.

Syria is, and always has been, Israel's most aggressive and most obdurate enemy, if only because it's obsessed with its own history. It was a great power under the Seleucids in the third century BCE and again under the Ummayads in the eighth century CE.

When the Ottoman Turks became the overlords in the sixteenth century, they treated Syria and Palestine as one administrative area and, after the collapse of the Ottoman Empire in the aftermath of the First World War, the self-styled General Syrian Congress demanded sovereign rule over Syria and Palestine (including Transjordan).

Palestine and Transjordan, however, passed under British rule, while the French took over Syria, which they dismembered further by

186

making Lebanon independent, and by ceding the northern province of Alexandretta (which had a large Turkish and Armenian population) to Turkey.

Syria, which became independent only in 1946, was the last Arab country to sign an armistice with Israel (in 1949) and was never quite reconciled to it. The border was always tense and was the scene of frequent skirmishes and occasional pitched battles, until Israel finally flushed the Syrians out of the Golan Heights in the course of the Six-Day War and advanced to within thirty miles of Damascus.

A truncated country with dreams of empire can make a particularly dangerous adversary, and it would be difficult to think of a more murderous head of state than President Hafez al Assad, who is sometimes styled the "fox" of the Orient, but who could more appropriately be called the jackal.

Yet I doubt whether Israel would wish to see him replaced, for he has been in power since 1970, far longer than any of his predecessors; and, unlike his predecessors, he has, with recourse to the occasional massacre, been able to maintain his authority over his unruly subjects.

One reason why no responsible Israeli politician would countenance the emergence of a Palestinian state is that it would be a second Lebanon, and a Syria reduced to chaos would be more dangerous even than the first Lebanon.

I thought that Britain acted with commendable, if uncharacteristic, decisiveness and speed in breaking off diplomatic relations with Syria.

Most Arab states (with the predictable exception of Libya) have maintained an embarrassed silence over the affair, but Russia has waded in with shrill cries of "provocation!" and "intimidation" and the claim that the whole case was a British invention staged at the behest of the Americans. Lies so blatant and absurd are extravagant even by the standards of mendacity to which the Russians have accustomed us.

It has been argued that Russia as a great power would have to be included in any international negotiations to secure a Middle East peace settlement, but this case highlights in dramatic form the virulence of her hostility to Israel. She is no longer a mere friend of an enemy, but is emerging as an enemy in her own right.

As for Britain's so-called European allies, they did all that one expected of them, which is to say, nothing. They all make pious resolutions about the need to stamp out international terror, but when they are offered palpable proof of terror, they look to their short-term interests and retreat into ambiguities.

Germany wants to sell the Syrians machinery, France wants to sell them arms, and the Greeks want to sell their soul.

Jewish Chronicle, 31 October 1986

Chic Chiracery

THERE ARE LIARS, damned liars and Chiracs, and the name of the Prime Minister of France may yet enter the English language as a byword for duplicity and falsehood. It even has the right sound.

There is, in fact, another French name, Tartuffe, which serves almost the same purpose, but Tartuffe was a fictional creation, whereas Chirac is only too real.

In September, when terrorist bombs were exploding almost nightly in the streets of Paris, and after eleven innocent people had died and a further one hundred and fifty had been wounded, M. Chirac declared that he would stop at nothing to bring terror to an end.

By this he meant that he would stoop to anything, and the opportunity came last month when Britain broke off diplomatic relations with Syria.

For one country to break off diplomatic relations with another is a drastic step, and no country, least of all Britain, does so lightly. But she could hardly do anything else in the face of irrefutable evidence that the Syrian authorities were directly involved in the attempt to blow up a civilian airliner with four hundred passengers and crew.

The facts which emerged at the Old Bailey trial of Nezar Hindawi were damning enough, but the Foreign Office had further proof of Syrian complicity which it could not make public, but which it divulged to its so-called European allies in the hope that they might follow its example.

They didn't, but M. Chirac went further and told a Washington newspaper editor that the Hindawi affair could have been instigated by Israeli and Western intelligence to discredit President Assad; and when the report caused a furore, he denied having made the remarks in the first place.

189

It is this which distinguishes Chiracery from common or garden falsehood. The ordinary liar tells his lie and sticks to it; the Chirac tries to cover up one lie with another, and perhaps even with a third, so that by the time he is finished, he is no longer too sure himself what is truth and what is falsehood.

One thing may be said in mitigation. Apart from the slaughter on the streets of Paris (of which Monday's murder of the Renault boss is but the latest example), there are several French hostages in Arab hands, and it could be argued that a lie, or even several lies, is not too high a price to pay for a human life. Indeed, M. Chirac did obtain the release of two hostages.

The trouble with hostages is that, while one knows whom one is saving, one does not know whom one is putting at risk; and—as President Reagan has found—one is therefore under immense pressure, not least from the families of the hostages, to come up with a deal of some sort.

Everyone, including Israel, has said that there can be no dealing with terror, and everyone, including Israel, has made a deal, so that M. Chirac is not singular in this respect. Where he is singular is in the degree of his mendacity and abasement.

There has always been rivalry between Britain and France in the Near and Middle East. In 1920, the Syrians proclaimed Feisal, a British protégé (and a brother of Abdullah of Transjordan), as king in Damascus. The French promptly expelled him and imposed their own rule, which, while bringing certain material and cultural benefits to the country, rode roughshod over Arab susceptibilities; and in 1945 the Syrians made a desperate effort to obtain their own independence.

The French countered by bringing in Senegalese mercenaries and bombarding Damascus, and Britain—which, to prevent German infiltration, had occupied the country in 1941 (Moshe Dayan lost his eye in that operation)—moved in and ordered the French back to barracks, thereby virtually bringing French hegemony in the area, which dated back to the Crusades, to an abrupt and inglorious end.

The French have never forgiven the British for that humiliating episode, and now that Britain seems to be siding with Israel (an aberration which is unlikely to outlast Mrs Thatcher), I suspect that M. Chirac is using the occasion both to settle old scores and to worm his way into Arab favour by taking the side of a beleaguered Syria.

It won't work, because the Arabs, to their credit, recognise unctuousness when they see it and regard such efforts with contempt.

Nor have they all that much affection for Assad, and even the Syrians themselves have too many memories of French brutality to be thrilled by a French embrace.

Jewish Chronicle, 21 November 1986

National Frontiersman

THERE SEEMS TO be some dismay at the thought that a Jew, Sir Alfred Sherman, should have invited Mr Le Pen, head of the French National Front, to a fringe meeting of the Tory Party.

In fact, six months ago the selfsame Le Pen was guest of honour at a luncheon in New York given by Mr Jacques Torczyner. There were some protests from the leaders of the French Jewish community, who know what M. Le Pen stands for, but no one else uttered a word.

Sir Alfred is a private individual acting in a private capacity who happens to be on the extreme Right of the Tory Party, whereas Mr Torczyner is president of the World Union of General Zionists, which is an integral part of the World Zionist Organisation and which, in turn, presumes to speak for the Jewish people.

There were some two dozen guests at his table, all of them leading members of the American Jewish community, including Dr Israel Singer, executive director of the World Jewish Congress. (It was Dr Singer, of course, who launched the vendetta against Kurt Waldheim some two years ago and who has been pursuing it with undiminished vigour since, though one would have thought that what Waldheim may, or may not, have perpetrated in the distant past is less significant than what Le Pen may yet perpetrate in the near future.)

It should perhaps be added that the FNF should not be spoken of in the same breath as the British National Front. The latter is a minuscule clique led by faceless nobodies who are regarded with contempt by the general public, whereas the former is a large, growing and influential party, and Le Pen is a leading politician who could conceivably become Prime Minister.

He is not a Nazi or even a fascist, but he does evoke unpleasant memories of Charles Maurras and the pre-war Action Française movement; except that where Maurras was anti-Jewish, Le Pen is anti-Arab (there are over a million Arab immigrants in France), which does not mean that he has particular affection for Jews. Where one minority is singled out as an enemy of the people, then all are threatened.

There was a special relationship between France and Israel during the drawn-out struggle for Algerian independence, and it was one of the reasons why France joined with Britain and Israel in the 1956 Suez campaign. But the relationship ended when Algeria became independent in 1962, and five years later de Gaulle used the Six-Day War as an opportunity to distance himself formally from Israel and seek a rapprochement with the Arabs.

There are Zionist leaders—and one suspects that Mr Torczyner is among them—who think that with the help of Mr Le Pen the special relationship could be restored and that an anti-Arab government in France would necessarily be good for Israel, even if it were also antisemitic. Indeed, there are not a few Israeli politicians who would regard such antisemitism as a bonus if only because it would mean an increased influx of Jewish immigrants.

Many right-wing Zionists believe that the diaspora is doomed, that antisemitism is ineradicable, and that wherever Jews settle in any number, their gentile neighbours will sooner or later throw them out; and some would like to give what they regard as an inevitable process of history a helping hand.

I happen to think that the diaspora is here to stay and that the very existence of Israel, by heightening Jewish consciousness, is helping to ensure its survival, which does not, however, mean that there are no dark clouds on the horizon.

I can see several, and Mr Le Pen is one of them, but the prophets of doom should not draw comfort from Jewish discomfiture: bad news for the diaspora is not good news for Israel. A victory for Le Pen would no doubt have an unsettling effect on the huge Franco-Jewish community—now the biggest in Europe—and a considerable exodus might ensue, but if the experience of Iranian and South African—and, indeed, Russian—Jewry is any thing to go by, few of the migrants would make their home in Israel.

There is a sad irony in the fact that where Jews feel compelled to uproot themselves, the last place they turn to for refuge is the Jewish State.

Jewish Chronicle, 4 September 1987

Twice Blessed

IF, AS GEORGE Bernard Shaw said, "the devil quotes Scripture", I cannot see why a Prime Minister shouldn't. Yet Mrs Thatcher's invocation of the Bible in support of her policies has been treated in some quarters as a sort of blasphemy.

One can quote the Bible in support of anything, short of cannibalism and incest, and there are ample sanctions in both the Old Testament and the New for her stress on individual responsibility. But she did, I think, come dangerously near to suggesting that the opulent are twice blessed in that they enrich not only themselves, but those around them.

The New Testament's denunciations of the rich and riches ("It is easier for a camel to go through a needle's eye than for a rich man to enter into the kingdom of God") are well known, and even the Old Testament, which has been quoted in recent years as if it were a plutocrat's charter, if not a Tory manifesto, has its reservations on the matter:

"Be not envious of him who is made rich, when the glory of his house is increased, for when he dieth he shall carry nothing away, his glory shall not descend after him" (Psalms).

"There is he that maketh himself rich, yet hath nothing; there is he that maketh himself poor that hath great riches" (Proverbs).

"The sleep of the labouring man is sweet, whether he eat little or much; but the abundance of the rich will not suffer him to sleep" (Ecclesiastes).

The most telling indictment of wealth, however, comes from Job, who was in his time both rich and poor and could therefore speak with double authority:

"The rich man shall lie down, but shall not be gathered: he

194

openeth his eyes and he is not. Terrors take hold of him as waters; a tempest stealeth him away in the night."

It could be argued—as, indeed, it has been—that all this is an attack not on the rich, but on the accumulation of riches; or, as Mrs Thatcher put it, "it is not the creation of wealth that is wrong, but love of money for its own sake".

Unfortunately, one cannot even escape poverty without a passing affection for money, and among the rich it often becomes a ruling passion.

I once asked a very wealthy man how much he was worth, and he replied that anyone who knew how much he was worth could not be worth all that much—to which he added, without undue modesty: "But if I can't tell you how much I've got, I can tell you how much I've given away." And, to do him justice, he had parted with fortunes.

Such people, however, are untypical. One knows of benefactors through their benefactions. The Rothschilds, for example, became legends not so much because of their wealth, but because of their generosity.

But there have been—and there still are—many very rich men who accumulated vast fortunes without allowing a penny to pass outside their family circle. Munificence is public, avarice is private, sometimes very private.

There is a well-known saying from Proverbs, "Better a poor and upright man than a rich and corrupt one," to which one is tempted to add, better still a rich and upright man. But such people are rare.

Among Jews poverty was often taken as a mark of virtue, whereas wealth carried hints of chicanery. All that has changed and we tend to regard the poor, and even the non-rich, as lazy, feckless and useless, whereas wealth is often treated as a form of grace.

It takes great strength of character to combine wealth with probity, and greater still to combine it with compassion. All of which suggests that Mrs Thatcher has excessive faith in individual responsibility.

Individuals are best left to their own devices when it comes to getting rich, but not to sharing their riches, as one can see in most South American countries, in many Arab countries and, to an increasing extent, in Britain itself.

One can see it even in the Anglo-Jewish community, which has never been more affluent, but whose welfare and cultural institutions have never been in such dire straits as they are today.

Disraeli, who is often spoken of as the father of modern Conservatism, described England as two nations—rich and poor—and
stressed the duties of the former to the latter. One hears few such
exhortations from Tory leaders in our time, and what we are witness-
ing is not a reversion to Victorianism, but the sanctification of
materialism.

Jewish Chronicle, 11 September 1987

New Germany
and New Germans

MOMENTOUS EVENTS ARE crowding upon each other with such wild rapidity that they are difficult to absorb, and one sometimes has the uneasy feeling that the world is running out of control.

First glasnost and perestroika in Russia, then free elections in Poland and Hungary, and now the collapse of the very monument of Communist domination, the Berlin Wall.

The events in East Germany were the least expected because the German Communists, unlike their counterparts in Hungary, Poland or Russia, approached their responsibilities with the grimness and fervour of true believers.

They showed that, in so far as Communism could be made to work, it was working, and their economy, at least compared to those of other Warsaw Pact countries, was fairly productive and efficient. But even they have finally given way to popular clamour, and now that the wall is down, the next step would seem to be the reunification of Germany.

It is understandable that Jews should view the prospect of such a step with the darkest foreboding, but though I have come across some wild prognostications, the wildest of all came from an Irish commentator, the usually sagacious Conor Cruise O'Brien, who warned that a united Germany would be a Hitlerite Germany—which shows that, when faced with the totally unexpected, even the wisest of men can go off their chump.

If a united Germany could revert to Hitlerism, so could a partitioned one, but the Federal German Republic, though the most powerful and populous state in free Europe, has shown no signs of doing so, or any sign that it might do so. None of the forces that made Hitler possible—the economic collapse, the fear of Bolshevism, the

197

injustice of the Versailles treaty, the raging xenophobia—is now extant.

Hitler and Hitlerism lasted for 12 years. The Federal German Republic has now lasted for 40, and it is not only a model of almost everything a democracy should be, it is a symbol of human resilience.

No nation in history has sunk as low as Germany, and none has risen so quickly, and if it has become the dominant force in Europe, it is due entirely to the hard work, self-discipline and ingenuity of its people, and a determination to shake off the attitudes which had made it the curse of Europe.

Even so, whether united, or even divided, its very strength would be worrying were it not for the fact that, in Europe at least, we no longer live among warring nationalities, and Germany is gradually being absorbed into a united Europe, though its dominance will, of course, be felt even as part of the larger entity and it will become to the rest of Europe what Prussia was to the rest of Germany.

Jews have always been drawn to the dominant culture within their host society and, until the war, German was the *lingua franca* of the European Jewish intelligentsia.

Kafka, Wërfel and Kraus, for example, three of the greatest writers of this century, though natives of Bohemia, all wrote in German rather than Czech, and Jews as a whole, whether in Bohemia or Moravia, Galicia or Hungary, Bosnia or the Baltic states, were unwitting agents of Germanisation.

The fact that German happens to be the core of Yiddish is no accident of history, for German language and culture have always had a powerful—some might say, fatal—attraction to the Jew. I feel that the love affair is about to be resumed.

I anticipate that once the various members of the EC become the United States of Europe, and Britain is linked to the Continent by the Channel Tunnel, Jews from every part of the union, including Britain and France (and not a few from countries outside it, like Russia and Israel), will flock to Germany, much as Jews from the outlying provinces of the Hapsburg Empire used to flock to Austria.

I should imagine that the German Jewish community, which, since the war, has always thought of itself as transitory, and which now numbers only some 25,000 souls, will within a generation or two revert to its original size.

The most exciting possibilities, however, arise out of the likelihood that Russia, too, will one day shake off Communist rule and become part of a free Europe. If it does, the Jewish world, which is now, of course, dominated by Israel and America, will see the emergence of a third force almost as large as the other two, but with its own distinct cultural character.

Jewish Chronicle, 17 November 1989

What Have We Got
Against America?

THE FINAL ECHOES of the bombs which fell upon Tripoli and Benghazi last month have not yet died away and they will no doubt reverberate for some time to come.

One may legitimately question the wisdom of the American raid without being anti-American, or the prudence of Mrs Thatcher's support for the raid without being anti-Tory. Nevertheless, the moment the bombs fell there emerged an instant unholy alliance of Right and Left who find something reprehensible in almost everything America does, or fails to do, plus the usual rag, tag and bobtail of political malcontents who saw in the public disquiet which the bombings aroused an opportunity to settle old scores with Mrs Thatcher.

I would not for a moment suggest that the Rt Hon Edward Heath fell into the last-mentioned group, but I thought his contribution to the debate on the Libyan bombings did not show him in the happiest light. He reminded the House that during the Yom Kippur War he, as Prime Minister, refused, on the grounds of neutrality, to let the Americans use bases in Cyprus in the airlift they had mounted on behalf of Israel.

Britain has been about as neutral between Israel and the Arabs as the so-called non-aligned nations are neutral between East and West, and Mr Heath, in citing the Cyprus precedent, seemed to be recommending a similar type of neutrality between America—our Nato ally—and Colonel Gaddafi.

America is not without faults, but with all the mistakes it has made in the past forty years, no great nation in history has used its power with such restraint, or its wealth with such generosity.

There are elements in British society who have never quite forgiven the Americans for their revolt against his Britannic Majesty, George III. The rise of America almost coincided with the decline of Britain, and the citizens of a declining power are not disposed to regard the actions of a rising one in a particularly friendly light.

Moreover, generosity on a national scale (and perhaps even on a private scale) has never endeared the giver to the receiver. And there is, finally, the element of simple envy. The poor, and even the rich—the latter more than the former—resent the hyper-rich.

Which brings me—somewhat reluctantly—to American television. Very few people know much about American life, and the little they do know is derived largely from American films and television, and especially from staple fare like "Dallas" and "Dynasty", with their pictures of high life at its lowest, and debauchery tempered by mayhem.

No reasonable man would judge a country by its television, but there are any number of unreasonable men who have come to think of Americans as so many Ewings.

To all of which one must add the ingrained anti-Americanism of British liberals, like E. P. Thompson, of CND fame, who pretend to an impartiality between the conflicting claims of the great powers and carry it to the point of being impartial between truths and lies.

Their attitude is perhaps typified in a recent utterance of Thompson himself. "West Europe," he declared, "has got to get out from under American domination, just as East Europe must get out from under the Soviet Union."

What, I ask you, can be more fair-minded, even-handed and impartial than that?—except that, of course, in so far as West Europe is under American domination, it was freely assumed and could be as freely shrugged off, while Soviet domination of East Europe (and, indeed, a substantial chunk of central Europe) was imposed by force and is maintained by force.

Dr Thompson, one must add, is an historian by profession, and recent events may be outside his field of expertise, but men like him have made benign expressions like "liberal" and "liberalism" by-words for mendacity.

And there are, finally, men who make no pretensions to liberalism, and who are against America precisely because it has the resources, the determination and the belief in the principles which gave it birth to check the spread of tyranny and terror.

Together they made a formidable coalition, and it is useful at such a time to recall the words of Burke: "When bad men combine, the good must associate; else they will fail one by one, an unpitied sacrifice in a contemptible struggle."

Jewish Chronicle, 9 May 1986

Horses for Courses

WHO OR WHAT is Sir Anthony Meyer? Until a month or so ago, few of us had heard of him, and a month or so hence few will remember him. But for the time being he is enjoying his moment of fame as the "stalking-horse" in the challenge to Mrs Thatcher's leadership of the Tory Party.

I am not sure what a "stalking-horse" is, but—if one can forgive the use of Yiddish in such a context—Sir Anthony does strike me as a bit of a *ferd*.

If he were even as remotely Jewish as he is said to be, he would have had more sense than to stand against Mrs Thatcher, who, for all her errors of judgement, is not only the best Prime Minister we have, but the best one we are likely to get.

The derisory result, though, will do Sir Anthony little harm. He has, after all, fought against overwhelming odds, and Britain admires a loser (if only because it has of late had little else to admire).

But how Jewish is Sir Anthony? His mother was Christian, his father was a convert to Christianity, and he himself is not only a member of the Church of England, but an actual churchgoer.

He is, moreover, an old Etonian, an ex-Guardsman with a town house in London and a country seat, and, to crown it all, a baronet. In other words, he has all the equipage of an English gentleman.

Yet the moment he is exposed to public scrutiny, his Jewishness is touched on as if it were a dominant characteristic, and the *Spectator*, after commenting on his other qualities—of which more later— referred to him last week as "a representative of the enlightened *haute juiverie*".

All of which raises the question of how ex-Jewish does one have to be before one is accepted as a goy among goyim?

It is a question which, I should imagine, Mrs Edwina Currie has often asked herself. She is not, to be sure, a member of the *haute juiverie*, enlightened or otherwise, for her father was a tailor; but while she did marry in church, which is as formal an act of dissociation as one could imagine, one can rarely read an article on her which does not describe her as Jewish.

Is there anything sinister in all this?

Mrs Currie herself has complained of undercurrents of anti-semitism in the controversy that led to her resignation from the Department of Health, but one does not have to be an antisemite to regard Mrs Currie with less than affection—though I dare say it helps.

Where a person is disliked, his or her alleged Jewishness adds an extra dimension to his or her unpopularity, but it can sometimes work the other way round.

Let us take the case of Disraeli, who once described himself as "the blank page between the Old Testament and the New". He was baptised in boyhood and had he been a Jew he would not have been able to enter Parliament when he did, let alone become Prime Minister.

As Prime Minister, he was responsible for all senior church appointments, yet he was never regarded as anything other than a Jew. Gladstone, who loathed him—with good cause—was convinced that he sided with the Ottoman Turks against Russia out of hatred for Christendom.

Yet Bismarck, who was no Judaeophile, said of him admiringly: "The old Jew, he is the man." This was at the Congress of Berlin in 1878 which Disraeli dominated and which saved Europe from a major conflagration.

(When he returned, Queen Victoria wanted to make him a duke, to which a member of Gladstone's entourage suggested that he be made Duke of Jericho and dispatched to look after his duchy.)

It is a long jump—in more ways than one—from Disraeli to Sir Anthony Meyer, but it may be interesting to read what the *Spectator* said of him in full:

"Sir Anthony's claims are not negligible. He is a dignified and gallant man. He was Captain of the Oppidans at Eton; he served in the Scots Guards in the Second World War and was wounded; he was a conscientious public servant before entering Parliament; he is a representative of the enlightened *haute juiverie*; and he has a lovely house in Brompton Square.

"If you like all these things—and every Tory should like them—you should do the honour of taking him seriously."

There is, of course, an element of irony in all this, but it does carry the suggestion that Jewishness in England is not only forgivable, but commendable, if it is accompanied by sufficient other qualities.

Jewish Chronicle, 8 December 1989

Green for Stop

WHEN I HEAR the word green, I see red.

When I first came to Britain, green was a bad word. To be green, or rather "a greener", was to be outlandish, foreign, uncivilised.

Today, green is in. It is everything and everywhere, like St Patrick's Day in New York.

We are all greeners now—the Prime Minister and the Leader of the Opposition, the Archbishop of Canterbury and the Chief Rabbi— and anyone who isn't green is an enemy of the earth.

I am wary of any cause which becomes the object of mass enthusiasm, for it will almost inevitably be carried to extremes, as the green cause already has been in Britain and Western Europe.

The Green Party, with its plans to cut the population of Britain by a third, shows that it cares more for animals and plants than for people, and that if it had its way we might have a healthier environment, though not all that many people around to enjoy it. Nor, given its bossy attitudes, would it be all that enjoyable.

I am not, in fact, all that worried about the aims of the party itself, for as the small print of its manifesto becomes known, no one with any sense will care to vote for it.

But the environment lobby has already affected public attitudes to the point where no farmer can drain a ditch or plough a field without fearing that he might be accused of disturbing the habitat of the knock-kneed centipede or the hairy-shanked greenfly.

Farming itself has become a dubious activity, while any builder who actually plans to put a roof over people's heads has to do so furtively, as if engaged in a misdemeanour.

And yet, if wary of greens in general, I feel there is ample scope for a Jewish or, if you prefer, a kosher Green Party, because Jews, if not

206

insensitive in other respects, have become almost blind to their environment.

One can quote innumerable passages from the Psalms, the Song of Songs and the Prophets which suggest an acute awareness of the environment, and Succot itself is an extended celebration of nature.

Something died, however, in the Jewish soul during the long Babylonian exile and, although one finds many expressions of the love of God and the fear of God in the Talmud, one finds little awareness of the beauty of God's creation. Instead, we have this well-known passage:

"He who is walking by the way and studying and interrupts his study to say, 'How lovely is that tree, how lovely that fallow,' it is as if he has forfeited his own life." Which is to say, the admiration of nature is almost a capital sin.

I have heard innumerable interpretations of the passage, all of which stretch the meaning of words a bit far; and in any case, whatever the interpretations, the passage itself does reflect prevailing Jewish attitudes, at least in the Orthodox world.

I have been a sermon taster for nearly 50 years now, and I am almost inclined to say that anyone who walks by the way admiring this tree or that fallow, but pauses to read a sermon, it is as if he has forfeited his senses, though there is no accounting for habit.

Some sermons are well worth reading and I have, over the years, come across one rabbi—and only one—who has shown the slightest appreciation of the fact that in physical terms, at least, we happen to live in a beautiful world. Let me quote:

"Jews today are the most urbanised nation on earth, and as a result many of us have become divorced from nature and insensitive to its thrills and quiet inspiration.

"Most Jews somehow seem to prefer the loud clanging of a dance orchestra to the mystic eloquence of a mountain stream, or the sweet soothing music of a humming bird."

The words come from a sermon given in the Fifth Avenue Synagogue by Rabbi Immanuel Jakobovits in 1959 and he was thus a greener long before the Greens were heard of (much as he was a Thatcherite long before Mrs Thatcher was heard of).

The Chief Rabbi is as untypical in this respect as he is in so many others, for we are not only divorced from nature, we are divorced from beauty.

This is not, of course, true of every Jew, or even of every Orthodox

Jew, but I can think of very few Jewish institutions built in the past 50 years which are not an affront to the eye.

One of the worst examples of despoliation that I have come across is the so-called "Great" Synagogue in Jerusalem, which must shrivel the soul of anyone who sets foot in it.

Jewish Chronicle, 13 October 1989

Daughters
of Eve

Women Rabbis

THE CHURCHES HAVE been in turmoil over the question of women priests, but they have theological difficulties in that Christ's successors—the twelve disciples—were all men, which suggested that the Christian ministry should be eternally vested in men (though, by way of compensation, women have been able to take holy orders as deaconesses or nuns).

We, on the face of it, have similar problems, for, to quote the Pirkei Avot (or, as we used to call it in cheder, "The Perky Abbot"): "Moses received the Torah on Sinai, and passed it down to Joshua; Joshua to the elders; the elders to the Prophets; and the Prophets to the men of the Great Synagogue." To the *men* of the Great Synagogue, be it known, and not the women.

The declaration could hardly be more emphatic, except that we know very little about the members of the Great Synagogue, and the little we do know suggests that they were not rabbis.

The word "rabbi" does not appear in the Old Testament and, although it features in the New, it is used as a term of respect in the sense of Master, rather than as a title. Nor were the rabbis, ravs or rabbans who people the Talmud rabbis in the contemporary sense of the term. They were certainly men of great piety and learning, but their scholarship was rarely the source of their livelihood.

It was only in the Middle Ages, after the Jews were scattered throughout Europe, North Africa and the Orient, that the rabbi emerged as a stipendiary spiritual leader; and it was only in the nineteenth century that he came to function as a preacher.

In Jewish terms, therefore, the very office of rabbi is something of an innovation, and the rabbi himself is a parvenu, an upstart, without claims to Apostolic succession and without any direct connection to

211

the sages of old.

Even the old custom of the laying on of hands, which might have made it indelicate for a rabbi to ordain a woman pupil, has lapsed and, as far as I can see (which, some readers may object, is not very far) there are no theological obstacles to the creation of women rabbis.

Nor would anyone seriously suggest (though some have done so in the past) that women are inherently incapable of acquiring the wisdom, piety, learning, compassion, spiritual depth or sense of dedication which the calling demands. Women, indeed, are more likely to possess them, which does not mean, however, that one is attracted to the idea of (even attractive) women rabbis.

In an inconstant, wavering world, where everything seems to change by the day (if not by the hour), the synagogue—or at least the Orthodox synagogue—is a haven of constancy, and people resort to it not so much for spiritual solace as for the solace of the familiar.

The fabric may have altered, the interiors may be more ornate, but everything else remains the same—the due events in their due season, the ancient ceremonies, the familiar order of service, the familiar words sung to familiar tunes, and familiar exhortations couched in familiar terms.

Even the gossip one hears (or communicates) tends to be unchanging and a man anxious to revisit the scenes of his childhood need only repair to the nearest synagogue, where everything that was is, and where all that has been will continue to be.

Here is one environment which remains intact, one habitat which has been largely untouched by time; and women rabbis would transform it out of all recognition. They would bring new sights, new sounds, new sensations (not all of them holy), and even if they remained loyal to old forms, they would not seem the same.

The barrier to the creation of Orthodox women rabbis is, in other words, psychological. If one is to find no refuge from change in the synagogue, where else can one find it? There is, however, no such impediment to the appointment of women rabbis (let them assume what title they will) as counsellors, educators, or even judges.

The idea of a woman judge may seem even more revolutionary than that of a woman rabbi, but we had them in Israel in biblical times, so that they would be creating no precedent, and given the sort of wisdom displayed by some of our dayanim, we could do with them on the Beth Din.   *Jewish Chronicle*, 18 July 1986

The Idle Wife

I WAS SURPRISED to read about the Sassover Rebbe's advice on au pairs, not because his remarks were in any way out of character, but because one would have thought that the subject was outside his purview. But clearly the good man is in touch not only with what is happening in the next world, but with what is happening—and could happen—in this one.

Au pairs, he said, should not be allowed to wear dresses without sleeves or of "an insufficient length", nor should they be allowed to wear trousers of any description or of whatever length. He also cautioned about the sort of company which au pairs could be keeping and he is clearly of the opinion that the sort of au pair who might be acceptable in a good Jewish home should not be keeping any company at all.

If one studies his proscriptions in detail, it quickly emerges that the ideal au pair for the ideal Jewish home would be a nun, and there is, in fact, an order called the Little Sisters of Chastity, which might have been expressly established for service in Orthodox Jewish homes.

The problem is not a new one, but it has assumed new forms. In *der heim* (there he goes again!) everyone was pretty poor, but no one was so poor as not to find someone even poorer beneath him, and though my father was but a rabbi in a small shtetl, we even had a maid—but I think that, taken in the round, she would have been passed as kosher by the Sassover Rebbe. Her arms, certainly, were fully covered, and, although she did wear trousers (one could not survive a Russian winter without them), it was only under her long and voluminous skirts, and I would not have known about them at all but for the fact that she smoked a pipe and kept her matches in her trouser pocket and would hitch up her skirts every time she lit up.

Her hair was covered in a black shawl in the style of a Russian babushka and we loved her dearly, but she did not—even to my young (if precocious) eyes—appear as a temptress, and maids in general tended to be grandmotherly figures. Moreover, even when they were young, they belonged to a different social strata and Jewish snobbery was sufficient to limit the sort of hazards they represented.

Au pairs in this respect, as in so many others, are different. They are the social equals of most Jewish families among whom they might find themselves and, in not a few cases, they are the social superiors, so that impressionable children (to say nothing of impressionable adults) might come to emulate their ways. I know of more than one pot-smoker who picked up the habit from his au pair.

And au pairs, whether they be chi-chi French girls, strapping Scandinavian wenches, or exotic little Polynesians—even if clad, Sassover-style, in long sleeves and dresses—can be a good deal more attractive than Russian babushkas. They can, if anything, be too attractive and I know of cases where the head of the household absconded with the au pair, leaving his wife and children, to say nothing of his talit and tefilin, behind. (I also know of wives who absconded with their gardeners, but then, at least, the matter of talit and tefilin didn't arise.)

In the circumstances, the Sassover's apprehensions are not wholly unwarranted, but in all the cautions which he has urged upon his flock—and, indeed, upon the entire community—there is one which does not appear to have come to his mind, and that is the possibility of doing without au pairs altogether. After all, the sort of Jewish home which can afford an au pair is also likely to have every necessary labour-saving gadget, and not a few unnecessary ones, such as meaty *and* milky dishwashers and, in some instances, even meaty *and* milky kitchens, with two of everything else (and perhaps another two for Pesach), and it should not be beyond the energies of a Jewish *baaleboste*, who does not go out to work, and does not have another occupation, to manage without living-in help.

But what of households where they have nine, ten or even twelve children? They can certainly be a handful, and yet, if my own observations are anything to go by, it is precisely those households which somehow manage without au pairs, while it is the smaller families who find them indispensable.

An au pair can bring certain hazards to any household, but they are as nothing compared to the hazards which can be brought by an idle wife.

Jewish Chronicle, 15 November 1985

Wily Women

RABBI ALAN KIMCHE of London recently told a sad story about a girls' seminary in Jerusalem.

These seminaries are a comparatively recent development. They attract thousands of young women from all over the world and give them a sound Jewish education. One graduate—Rabbi Kimche described her as "a star pupil"—complained that the education she had received was perhaps a little too sound, for the boys she went out with were overawed by her, and that her range of knowledge was impairing her marriage prospects.

When the girl's teachers heard of her complaint, they came together in consternation and asked themselves whether she did not have a valid point, and whether as far as girls were concerned, a lot of knowledge was perhaps a dangerous thing.

I was saddened by the story because it concerned not some obscure little hole of a place, but the *Michlala*, perhaps the biggest and almost certainly the best girls' seminary in Israel. It suggests that while education for boys is recommended as a form of godliness, education for girls is seen merely as a holding operation to keep them out of mischief between the time they leave school and the time they set up home as wife and mother. Any knowledge that they may pick up while they are at the seminary should be treated as a bonus.

I must add that this is decidedly not Rabbi Kimche's view, and I may have read far too much into his story. Learning should be worn lightly and it is perfectly possible that the young men (or even the old ones) who went out with the "star pupil" were not so much over-awed, as bored by her.

Imagine the scene. You have been introduced to this charming young woman. You go to the candle-lit room of a Jerusalem restaur-

215

ant (there has probably been a power failure). A violin is playing in your ears. You look into her eyes over the flaming crêpe-suzettes and what does she say? "You know this reminds me of the second chapter of the *Mishna Shabbat*. With what materials may the Shabbat lamp be lit, and with what not? It may not be lit with cedar-bast, or uncombed flax, or floss silk, or willow-fibre, or nettle fibre, or water-weeds, or pitch, or liquid wax, or cotton seed oil, or oil which, having been dedicated as a heave-offering and having become defiled must be destroyed by fire, or with fat from the tails of sheep, or with tallow . . ."

Who would not run a mile from such a woman? I, for one, would have left her to pick up the cheque.

But wait. Supposing it had been the other way round, and the young man had started spouting the second chapter of *Mishna Shabbat*, or the third one, or perhaps even both? The young lady, whether bored or not, would have clasped her hands in ecstasy and, convinced that she was in the presence of a *talmid chacham* ("brilliant scholar") would have rushed home with the sound of wedding-bells in her ears.

Learning among Orthodox Jews is like plumage among birds. It's the males who display their intellectual finery, while the females are supposed only to twitter in awe, so that men will affect a show of learning even if they lack it, while women—in conformity with the Talmudic dictum that they are light-headed—will make a show of frivolity even if they are learned. They only have to keep their heads covered when they are married, but while single they have to keep their very brains under wraps.

No one underestimates the importance of marriage and the family, and for the Orthodox woman, certainly, there is no life outside it, but the prevailing attitudes, and the insistence that almost any marriage is better than none, means that, in intellectual terms, women often marry beneath their level.

There are, of course, no rules to happy marriages or, for that matter, unhappy ones. I once knew a distinguished lady professor who was happily married to a taxi driver, and I know of many couples, intellectually on a par with one another, who have fallen out, but any woman who feels she must curb her intelligence to get her man, cannot have all that much intelligence to curb.

Israel Scene, November 1988

Topless in Nuweiba

THERE'S BEEN A lot of breast-beating in Israel lately about topless bathers. I've always thought the term "topless bather" something of a misnomer, for the young—or, indeed, the middle-aged—ladies involved are anything but topless. If anything, they are over-topped, and they bask rather than bathe. There would be no problem if they actually stayed in the water, where they could at least pass for mermaids. It is their tendency to come (and stay) ashore which has caused many an innocent promenader to stop dead in his tracks. They already have red or black flags out on Israeli shores to indicate swimming hazards. Perhaps they should have blue flags to indicate non-swimming hazards.

The source of the trouble lies with tourists from the frozen north, females from places like Stockholm and Oslo, Helsinki and Manchester who descend on Israel with oceans of lotions, balms and creams, determined to soak up enough sun in two weeks to see them through the cold, darkness and gloom of their endless winters, and who believe that a thick film of Bergasol, or even a thin one, is enough to cover their modesty (and, given the extent of their modesty, it is usually ample).

"The Sea that bares her bosom to the Moon" (to quote Wordsworth) is not quite as brazen as the many who bare their bosoms to the sea. It all smacks of ostentation, but for the pious who may unwittingly stray among them, they do provide an occasion for the benediction, "Blessed art Thou, O Lord . . . who variest the form of Thy creatures."

As a rule, they make for the deep south, where the sunshine is hotter and more prolonged, and the further south they go, the more they discard, so that—in the good old days when Israel ruled

217

Sinai—by the time they got beyond Elat to Rafi Nelson country and Sharm el Sheikh, they were not only topless, but bottomless.

In Nuweiba, Dahab and other points along the coast, anything went, which is to say, everything went. Rafi himself may have kept a blind eye on such things (which is presumably how he acquired the surname of Nelson), but others were disturbed by what they saw, or rather, by what they tried to avoid seeing.

This may well explain why the National Religious Party, while insisting that every inch of territory taken in 1967 should be held, was quite glad to see Sinai go back to Egypt.

With the return of Sinai, the Taba strip is now the southernmost point in Israel, but those who have rushed there believing that the name represents a habit rather than a place have been disappointed. The five-star Sonesta Hotel has cast a chill of respectability over the place, and even Scandinavian visitors are disinclined to let rip in the strip.

Moreover, it is small and cramped and likely to be partitioned, and any well-built lady anxious to bask half-clad will have to be careful about which half she keeps in which territory. Such matters may only excite a titter among Jews, but Muslims view them gravely.

No, the place for sun-worshippers is Elat, which has for some years now functioned as the San Tropez of the Orient. It has always had a slightly extra-territorial feel about it which is likely to become more pronounced now that it is a free port.

The air (by Israeli standards) is relaxed, cares are thrown off; and once cares are thrown off, clothes not infrequently follow, and anyone taking a walk on the shore will be treated to a rich display of natural endowments, or, as one might call them in this context, sun absorbers.

But what is fitting in Elat can cause a fit elsewhere, and friends who keep abreast of such events tell me that the Elat habit (or lack of it) has been spreading northwards; and Tel Aviv, ever-mindful of its status as Israel's premier city and as a family resort, has decided to put its foot down on topless bathers.

This is easier said than done, however, for the Tel Aviv beaches are, in the main, used by natives rather than foreigners, and if one tells Israelis to do one thing, one may be fairly certain that they will do another.

Moreover, swimsuits (if they may be so called) have become so attenuated in recent years that there is a grey area (or, if you prefer, a pink one) between what may be defined as decently covered and indecently exposed, and even those who may fall into the first category may, through the slightest movement, fall into the second (or rather, fall out of the first).

There are also no clear frontiers between titivation and titillation. We are, in other words, on shaky ground.

All that notwithstanding, I am informed (I am not sure on what authority) that the Tel Aviv municipality is to appoint a body of undercover agents who will require topless bathers to keep their bodies under cover.

I have volunteered my services.

Jewish Chronicle, 3 May 1985

Femme Fatale

I DON'T KNOW if you are familiar with the words of the old song, "Im 'Enery the Eighth, I am, I am, I'm 'Enery the Eighth, I am". It continues something like this:

"I've just married the widow next door,
she's been married seven times before.
Every one was an 'Enery . . .
So 'Enery the Eighth I am."

Well, had 'Enery lived in Israel, he would have been discouraged from doing any such thing and I doubt if any rabbi would have consecrated his marriage.

There is a man in Kfar Saba who wants to marry a widow, but the local rabbis have warned him against it because she already has two husbands in the grave, and as such is a super-widow, or, as the French might call her, a *femme fatale*.

There is a presumption in Jewish lore, and perhaps even in Jewish law, that any woman who has more than one husband in the grave has something to answer for, or, as Lady Bracknell might have put it, "To lose one husband may be misfortune, to lose two looks like carelessness."

The Talmud puts it more strongly and calls such a woman a *katlanit*, a slayer. Yet there is no such thing in the Hebrew language (or, indeed, the French) as an *homme fatal* and a man who has had more than one wife is merely a person of more than usual vigour, especially where he has had them concurrently rather than consecutively.

It must be admitted that, in statistical terms, the super-widow is more commonplace than her male equivalent (whatever one might

220

call him), because women generally live longer, and marry younger, than men. They are also more optimistic and are always disposed to give fate a further chance.

The greater longevity of women is a comparatively recent phenomenon. The Patriarchs, for example, all outlived their wives and we have to wait until Jacob's grandchildren before we come upon the actual incidence of a widow in the redoubtable person of Tamar, the daughter-in-law of Judah.

Tamar was, indeed, a *femme fatale* in every sense of the word and I suspect that it was her experience, or rather the experience of her unfortunate menfolk, which gave rise to the idea of the *katlanit*.

In the Pale, to judge from the novels of Sholem Aleichem and others, stepmothers were more common than stepfathers, and even a generation or two ago old men were more numerous (among Jews, at least) than old women.

If things have changed since, it is, I suspect, because in hard times the burdens of life fall mainly upon women, while in times of plenty they fall mainly upon men.

To a poor man, a wife is an asset; to a rich one, she's a liability, which is why one has more rich widows than rich widowers. (It could, of course, be argued conversely, that to a poor wife a husband is a liability, and to a rich one he's an asset.)

The second point, however—that women marry younger than men—has always been true, partly because they mature earlier and partly because changes in male physique are less dramatic, so that men are less aware that they're getting on (or, indeed, that they've got on) and any sign of age, like a receding hair-line or an advancing paunch, is taken as evidence of virility.

Some men regard themselves as ageless, and there is a saying somewhere (not, I believe, in the Talmud) that one is as young as one's next wife. Thus, where a woman is as much as twelve months older than her husband, she will try to keep it as a dark secret (if possible, even from her husband).

But a man of eighty will think nothing of marrying a woman of thirty and will even trumpet the fact with pride. As a result, a woman has an infinitely better chance of going through several husbands than has a husband going through several wives.

But to get back to Kfar Saba: the super-widow, or *katlanit*, is a mere 70, while her suitor is 75, so that the fears of the rabbis that he may go the way of her previous husbands are not wholly unfounded.

221

On the other hand, there is no assurance that he will live forever if he stays single. I would advise him to take the plunge. I'll even dance at his wedding.

Such an event could happen only in Kfar Saba, whose very name (*saba* being Hebrew for grandpa) carries intimations of antiquity. There's obviously life in the old dogs yet.

Jewish Chronicle, 6 February 1987

Second Innings

ACCORDING TO A recent social survey, one Israeli husband in three would, if given the chance to live his life again, take a different wife. The strange thing is that the survey was confined entirely to men, presumably in the belief that women are too glad to be married at all to have any regrets on the matter. What makes it stranger still is that the survey was conducted by a woman, Dr Ninna Zemach.

Dr Zemach has also found that Orthodox men are more content with their spouses than their non-Orthodox brethren, but then they have more to be content with, for the Orthodox housewife is enjoined to be "a woman of valour", to fall in with her husband's wishes and to adapt herself to his needs, while her non-Orthodox sister can be, and often is, rebellious and wayward. To the devout Jew, moreover, the possibility of living his life again is not entirely academic, for if the Messiah should come, he will enjoy a second innings, and better the partner one knows than the partner one doesn't.

I should perhaps add that, according to some authorities, there was a well-known figure in Israel who did live his life again, but he, of course, was a bachelor, and all in all I feel that Dr Zemach's study tells us less about Israeli husbands, or even Israeli wives, than it does about Israeli sociologists.

Sociology, like the fur trade, is almost a Jewish calling. I don't know why it should be because, unlike the fur trade, it's not particularly lucrative. One could, I suppose, ascribe it to Jewish compassion, though given the tendency of sociologists to pry into other people's business, one might ascribe it more to a somewhat morbid curiosity.

But the fact remains that most of the great names in the field, from Durkheim onwards, have been Jewish and it has always attracted more than its share of Jewish students.

Social studies are often spoken of as a "soft option", but the hardest of subjects can be the softest of options if one doesn't care to excel in it, whereas sociology, in fact, calls for a fairly rare combination of talents.

One can be semi-literate and still be a good chemist or physicist, and I have known brilliant mathematicians who were incapable of uttering a grammatical sentence. But one cannot be a good sociologist without being a good writer, and the best of them—the names of Raymond Aron and Seymour Martin Lipset come immediately to mind—may be enjoyed at least as much for the quality of their prose as for the originality of their ideas.

But what can a small country like Israel, with its four million inhabitants and seven universities, do with all the sociologists it produces? Some, of course, are busy producing other sociologists, preparing BAs for their MAs, and MAs for their PhDs. But what of the rest?

I review the occasional book and come into town every two or three weeks to raid the shelves of this or that newsaper, and I am amazed at the welter of sociological works emanating from Israeli academics, volume upon volume of unsung dissertations. And these are, of course, only works available in English. I can imagine the number that must appear in Hebrew, and I am left with the impression that half of Israel is busy studying the ways and the waywardness of the other half.

One sometimes feels that the same is happening in Britain. Wherever one goes these days, one finds people lurking in dark corners with clipboards under their arms, and a wild light in their eyes, waiting to pounce on innocent passers-by with the most improbable list of questions.

Who did you vote for in the last election? Who will you vote for in the next one? When did you last see your father? What did you have for breakfast? What will you have for tea? Do you crack your egg open with a spoon, or do you decapitate if with a knife? Do you believe in hanging? How often do you change your underwear? Have you stopped beating your wife?

I have myself been importuned in this way a number of times over the past few weeks, but no one has, as yet, asked me what I would do if I had my life to live again. Dr Zemach's survey suggests that Israeli sociologists, having exhausted the possibilities of this world, are now turning to the next.   *Jewish Chronicle*, 17 July 1987

Chi Chi Cicciolina

CICCIOLINA! NOW THERE'S a name to conjure with, even if one doesn't know how to pronounce it and, like all great names, it comes sans prefix. It is not Mrs Cicciolina, or Miss Cicciolina, or even Ms Cicciolina, nor is there any whisper of a first name, like, say, Mavis Cicciolina. It is Cicciolina *tout court*, like Melba or Gallicurci or Callas, from which one might conclude that the good lady (or bad, as the case may be) is a celebrated prima donna.

A prima donna she is, and celebrated she certainly is, but not for her voice. At which point I can hear impatient voices muttering: then what the hell is she celebrated for?

I suspect that anyone so unworldly as to ask the question will be too unworldly as to be interested in the answer, but here it is.

Cicciolina is to Italy what Cynthia Payne is to England, except that while Mrs Payne was alleged to have kept a disorderly house in Streatham, Cicciolina is a member of a disorderly house in Rome—namely, the Italian Chamber of Deputies—and has added a colourful strand to the political life of the country. It would not surprise me if they made her Minister of Culture.

Before becoming a politician, however, Cicciolina (hereinafter to be known as C) was an artist, or rather artiste, specialising in exotic entertainments in which she employed, among other things, a boa constrictor, a stuffed dog, a baby doll, a violin, a double bass, a saxophone, five golden rings, four colly birds, three French hens, two turtle doves, and a partridge in a pear tree.

Though now busy with matters of state, C still finds time to give the occasional performance on the side (to mention but one posture), and she was recently invited to perform in Israel, which immediately raises the question of whether she is Jewish.

C, to do her justice, is ready to reveal everything. She not only confesses to being a strumpet, she readily admits to being Hungarian (her actual name is Staller), and if she were Jewish she would have said so; but Jewish or not, Israel was agog with her visit. The peace process (what there is of it), the economic problems, the religious conflicts, the state of the schools—all vanished from conversation and the one word on everyone's lips was Cicciolina. There was, surprisingly, no attempt to impede her arrival, nor did the Israeli Society for the Prevention of Cruelty of Animals try to impound the boa constrictor, but once her presence became known, the Ministry of the Interior (and who better?) ordered the police to make sure that she did not give any live performances (or even dead ones) in Jerusalem. She did, however, stage a performance in Jaffa, where anything goes, and to which everyone went, at a price of 100 shekels a head.

I am not at all sure what she did during the course of the performance, but she assured reporters that, whatever it was, "everyone does it". Which makes one wonder why anyone should have paid so much to see it done.

But perhaps we are seeing lewdness where none existed. Jaffa is, after all, the home of Andromeda, who, according to legend, was chained to a rock in the harbour and threatened by a serpent until rescued by Perseus. It is perfectly possible that C, who likes to introduce an element of local colour into her act, may merely have restaged the story of Andromeda, with the boa constrictor, presumably, in the role of the serpent.

Yet I must confess to reservations about her visit. Had she gone to Israel to offer her devotees a cheap, or, as in this instance, an expensive, thrill (did they pay VAT?), she might have been forgiven; but she arrived in a mini-skirt (with a slit going up to her armpit), bearing a ten-page manifesto calling on the public to "make love, not war" and declaring that erotica "is not shameful". Well, perhaps not, but humbug is. She has been in parliament for only a matter of months, but already shows all the traits of a seasoned politician.

The Chief Rabbis, both Sephardi and Ashkenazi, remained silent on her visit, but a comment of sorts came from on High, for the moment she left, the skies opened, and although it did not rain for forty days and forty nights, it rained sufficiently hard to convert the roads of Jerusalem into rivers. If that was not a warning, what is?

Jewish Chronicle, 6 November 1987

Putting the Boot in—
Kosher Style

WHAT NEXT?

The Jewish Marriage Council is giving Jewish housewives lessons in assertiveness, which is a little like teaching Irishmen how to drink or ducks how to swim.

No two women—Jewish or otherwise—are alike, and while some are over-assertive, others, no doubt, are not nearly assertive enough. But one may safely assume that any woman who actually feels that she needs lessons in assertiveness falls squarely into the first category, and the JMC seems intent on converting decent common or garden shrews into screaming banshees.

It has added, possibly by way of a defence, that it is also prepared to give assertiveness lessons to men, if sufficient interest is shown; but sufficient interest has clearly not been shown, which may mean one of two things.

Either Jewish men are already assertive enough, or they are so unassertive as to be unaware of their unassertiveness, and it seems that, for the time being at least, the put-the-boot-in sessions are for women only.

Which reminds one of the story of the marriage guidance counsellor who was addressing a large meeting on Jewish family life, its joys and its sorrows. When he had finished, he asked all husbands who thought they were henpecked to go to one side of the room.

At first no one stirred. Then one man rose, followed by another, followed by a third, after which there was something like a stampede, until about forty men were lined up on one side of the room.

Only one wispy, forlorn little figure remained in place, and when someone asked him later why he had not lined up with the rest, he looked nervously around him and whispered: "My wife told me to stay put."

I have not been shown the curriculum of the JMC course in higher assertiveness, but it is not very difficult to imagine the form it might take.

"The first thing, my dears, is to buy some cheap crockery in an Oxfam shop—not to eat from, heaven forbid, because it will almost certainly be non-kosher, but to throw about; or you may still have some wedding presents, such as vases or fruit bowls, which you will be only too happy to dispose of.

"Start by throwing a vase or a dish or two on the floor. If that doesn't help, throw them at your husband. And if even that doesn't help, throw a fit, for which purpose it may be necessary to have a rug at hand to chew on, though here one must be careful, because some rugs are made with non-kosher dyes . . .

"Now, don't wait until *he's* in the wrong before you make a scene, for by then it's too late. Do it when *you're* in the wrong, so that he should know what to expect when *he* is . . ."

It could be argued that, in encouraging assertiveness, the JMC is helping Jewish women to conform to an ancient tradition.

All the matriarchs, with the possible exception of Leah, were highly assertive. The same is true of Deborah, Bathsheba and almost every other woman in Scripture.

I dare say that had they been less assertive in what was, after all, a man's world, they would have remained anonymous—which does not mean, however, that assertiveness is an admirable quality, or even a quality at all.

Any partnership, either within marriage or without, calls for a certain amount of give and take, and where the relationship is healthy, there is no need to measure how much is given or taken, any more than a healthy individual needs measurements of his temperature or blood pressure.

To be assertive is to claim rather more than one's due, and to inculcate assertiveness is to inculcate either paranoia or selfishness, and perhaps even both.

All of which may suggest that I am critical of the Jewish Marriage Council. Well, I'm not, or at least I wasn't, for it is a benign institution with an honourable history and worthy aims.

It helps the single to get married, the doubled to stay married, the troubled to get demarried, and the demarried to remarry; but it has grown so far and so fast as to lose sight of its original aims and it has come perilously close to immersion in the murky waters of feminism.

Jewish women may suffer from numerous handicaps in Jewish law, but it cannot be said that they have been nobbled by nature. Yet, instead of tackling the deficiencies of the former, the JMC is attempting to enhance the generosity of the latter.

Jewish Chronicle, 10 November 1989

Shadows

Breslev

ABOUT TWENTY YEARS ago I was involved in a debate on Zionism and someone brought up the question on the number of Jews killed in the Holocaust.

I said I wasn't in a position to speak of exact numbers, but I could speak with certainty of twenty-two members of my own family who were done to death for no better reason than they were Jews.

I then gave their names, which more or less closed the argument. Most of those names now appear in a recently published memorial volume on the Jews of Breslev.

Breslev should not be confused with Breslau. The latter (now called Wroclav) is, of course, a major city in Silesia, while the former was a shtetl in the province of Wilno, in Lithuania.

In 1921 the province was seized by the Poles, so that it was Polish for as long as I knew it, though it is now part of Russia.

I divided my early boyhood between Breslev, where my grandmother lived, and Barovke, over the border in Latvia, where my father was a rabbi and shochet.

There was no Jewish day-school in Barovke and shortly before the war I was sent to live with my grandmother so that I could attend first the Yavne school and then the Etz Chaim Yeshiva.

Breslev was built on an isthmus between two lakes near a bend in the river Dvina and was surrounded by swamps and forests. In the spring, when the snows began to melt and the swamps filled up, it was like an island.

It was ideally situated for fortifications and it was dominated by a castle on a hill, and, as with every hill in Eastern Europe, there were legends of treasures buried in its depths.

Before the war, Breslev had a population of about 4,000, most of

233

which was Jewish, and non-Jews lived either on the outskirts or in the Domkes, a new suburb, with wide, tree-lined streets, brick houses and even electricity.

Jewish Breslev was of timber and consisted largely of one long thoroughfare called Pilsudzki Street and a number of side streets.

There were two churches, one Catholic and the other Greek Orthodox, whose bells still ring in my ears, and four synagogues, three of which were grouped round a courtyard and which formed a sort of sacred enclave.

The yeshiva was in a bleak, tumbledown building and had about sixty boys, none of whom, as far as I could remember, was beyond barmitzvah age. I always had a famished appearance as a child, but I looked well fed compared to most of my contemporaries.

There were, I have since gathered, two Breslevs, the sacred and the profane. I was, of course, part of the former and was completely unaware of the latter, but it had a flourishing Bund organisation, a militantly secular Yiddish Folkshul and a godless intelligentsia. Such differences were soon to become tragically irrelevant.

My mother's family must have belonged to both camps, for if one uncle, Chaim Kasre, was a leader of sacred Breslev, I learnt later that another, Rachmiel, was a Communist; and both, in their different ways, were to have a fatal influence on what was to follow.

I had been happy in Barovke; I was unhappy in Breslev. Barovke was a shtetl with houses scattered here and there among fields and orchards. Breslev, comparatively speaking, was a metropolis, with paved roads and even a railway station.

The word antisemitism was on everyone's lips everywhere, but I had had no personal experience of it in Barovke and I felt free to roam in the nearby forests and splash around in the lakes.

In Breslev I was set upon by young thugs the minute I set foot outside town, and if I was attacked by goyim because I was a Jew, I was attacked by Jews because I was a Latvian; and my worst tormentor was the rabbi's grandson, a brute of a boy called Leibale.

The whole town seemed to be enveloped in anxiety and fear and one rarely saw a smiling face. Poland was going through an economic crisis and, if things were difficult for Poles, they were that much more difficult for Polish Jews, whose enterprises were threatened by boycotts and government-sponsored co-operatives.

But there was a general feeling of unease. Enemies seemed to be closing in on every side, and those not weighed down with possessions made hurried arrangements to leave for the Argentine, Mexico, Brazil, even China, any place which would have them.

My mother's people were corn and flax merchants and comparatively prosperous, which was the source of their misfortune, for they remained behind and a few years later their house was the scene of an unspeakable tragedy.

My father had in the meantime been offered a job in Glasgow. My mother and sisters came over to Breslev for a family reunion and we left Breslev for the last time in the summer of 1938.

Fourteen months later Poland was partitioned between Germany and Russia and although Breslev was in the Russian zone, we lost all further contact with the family. What follows derives from conversations with survivors and from the Breslev memorial volume.

The Russians at first allowed life to continue as normal. Then, in 1940, they began to uproot the more prosperous families and to deport them to Kazakhstan, and the fact that my mother's family was spared was probably due to the influence of Rachmiel, the Communist uncle.

On Sunday, 21 June, 1941, Hitler invaded Russia. The Breslev commissar assembled the community and assured everyone that the Nazi invader would soon be repelled and that there was nothing to fear. But the front had by then already crumbled and the Russians were in full retreat.

Some people began to make for the forests, but my uncle Chaim Kasre, a calm, even phlegmatic figure, said there was no need to panic. "These people are Germans," he said, "not beasts. What can they do to us? We are better off where we are."

He had lived through the First World War, when the area was under German occupation. The Germans had been far more benign than the Russians. The extermination process had not yet been set in full motion, and there was, certainly among the Jews of Eastern Europe, a lingering respect for Germany which somehow transcended the knowledge of Nazism, and, as everyone kept saying, "they can't be worse than the Poles".

The Germans in the meantime hurtled across the great plains of Eastern Europe without hindrance, and four days later they were in Breslev. Poles greeted them with bread and salt, and the Germans found ready collaborators in Kowalski the mayor, Jasinski the police chief, and Szliachczik, superintendent of the local prison.

The terror was at first sporadic. People who ventured out to synagogue or to visit a friend sometimes never returned. Shots rang out over the still waters of the lake on warm summer nights, and in the morning bodies would be found on the shore.

Some Jews, among them a cripple, my mother's cousin Beilka Daets, were seized on suspicion of spying for the Russians, tortured, and hanged. Thirteen Jewish labourers at the railway station were accused of malingering and shot dead.

In April 1942, on the eve of Passover, the terror began in earnest. Pilsudzki Street was cordoned off with barbed wire and formed into a ghetto, and its population doubled and then trebled as Jews were herded in from the surrounding villages and dumped on top of one another. The ghetto was then divided into two, the able-bodied in one part, the old, the lame, the sick in the other.

It was at this point that my mother's family went into hiding. Their house faced on to Pilsudzki Street, but they had warehouses at the back with a cellar extending from the house to underneath the warehouses. They stocked it with what provisions they could and it served as a refuge for several dozen people.

A few days later the Germans came to search the house. Their footsteps could be heard on the floors and the stairs and tension mounted below.

Suddenly, a child began screaming and they expected the Germans to come bursting in, but for a time nothing happened. A few hours later the building was blown up and those not killed instantly suffocated slowly under the debris, among them my grandmother, then aged nearly seventy and half-blind.

The systematic slaughter began on 3 June. Liuba Byk, one of the few survivors, recalls:

"Our house was the first in the ghetto. At about two o'clock past midnight we heard the sound of heavy footsteps, a door wrenched open. Two policemen rushed in, started to beat us and flung us down the stairs.

"They did not let me take my three-year-old daughter with me, but brutally murdered her in her sleep. I was driven out of the house at the end of a rifle butt. I saw them kill my sister Rosa and her two little girls right next to the barbed wire of the cordoned-off ghetto near our house."

Other survivors recall scenes too harrowing to be described. Within the next three days, nearly three thousand Jews perished.

Some Poles, Lithuanians and White Russians joined enthusiastically in the slaughter, to which one must add that others gave refuge to Jews at the risk of their own lives.

The brutes, of course, outnumbered the heroes, but then brutes always do and one has to imagine the atmosphere of terror in which the entire population lived to appreciate the scale of the heroism.

Only forty Jews survived the slaughter, among them a young man called Moshe Milutin, who escaped to the forests, where he joined a group of partisans and later served with the Red Army and was decorated for valour.

Two members of my family survived, Rachmiel the Communist, who joined the Red Army before the German invasion and fell in battle, and a fifteen-year-old second cousin called Malka.

She fled when the Germans first came, hid for a time in the forests and then continued on foot through the Russian lines, across European Russia and over the Urals to Kazakhstan, in central Asia, where she found work and studied and eventually qualified as a doctor.

She returned to Breslev after the war and found a handful of survivors, among them Moshe Milutin, searching amid the ashes of what was once a thriving town. They married and a few years later they moved to Israel.

Ten years ago I attended their daughter's wedding in Tel Aviv. They are now retired, with three children and three grandchildren, and live in Petach Tikva.

Life goes on.

Jewish Chronicle, 15 May 1987

Sombre Reunion

HITLER, ONE FELT, must be laughing. He had not only killed six million Jews, but had apparently so savaged the Jewish psyche that even those who had survived the Holocaust felt compelled to relive something of the torments nearly 40 years after they happened.

How else is one to explain an idea as improbable as the "World Gathering of Jewish Holocaust Survivors" which took place last week, and whose programme included visits to the Chamber of the Holocaust, to the Museum of the Holocaust, to films about the Holocaust and the dedication of a memorial to three men publicly hanged in Auschwitz.

There were, moreover, fears that Mr Begin, who evokes the Holocaust with every second breath, might exploit the occasion in what was already the dirtiest election campaign in Israel's history for his own ends, but his speech at the final rally—which had to compete with the cry of the Muezzin from a nearby mosque—was dignified if sombre.

Jews, he said, always were and always would be alone, but with this difference. He could promise that "Israel will never allow an enemy to develop weapons of mass destruction to be used against the Jewish people—never again."

There were nearly 6,000 participants from 23 countries, including about 80 from Britain. Among them was Rabbi Hugo Gryn, senior minister of the West London Synagogue, Britain's largest Jewish congregation. In 1943, when he was 13, he and his younger brother, with his parents, were taken in cattle trucks to Auschwitz. His brother, then 11, was killed on the day they arrived. His parents perished later; he alone survived.

I asked Rabbi Gryn how, given what he had been through, he

could bring himself to attend such a reunion. "It's because of what I have been through that I am here. The more you've lost, the greater your obligation to remember."

This point, made by everyone spoken to, touches upon a basic element in Jewish belief. The worst curse known to the Hebrew language is *yemach shemo vezicro*—may his name and remembrance be obliterated—and there is the feeling that while someone lingers in the human memory he is not wholly extinct. Which is why, for example, Jews attach such importance to the *Kaddish*, their memorial prayer for the dead.

"But this meeting is more than a *Kaddish*," said Rabbi Gryn. "We had to make some public expression of disgust at the proliferation of books which deny that the Holocaust ever took place. Such books have been growing in number in recent years. They are crudely written and crudely argued and no informed leader could take them seriously, but Jews take them very seriously indeed for they suggest that the Holocaust was a Jewish conspiracy to extract billions of Marks from the Germans in compensation."

One cannot imagine a more wounding insult, especially to those who have survived the hells of Auschwitz and Buchenwald. "We have come together to bear witness," said Rabbi Gryn. "We were *there*." But there were other reasons for the reunion.

"Very few of us," he said, "have brothers or sisters, and almost none has parents. Our children are not like other children, with two sets of grandparents, a ring of uncles and aunts and hordes of cousins. This gathering gives us a sense of family. And finally, there is the hope that one might come upon a familiar face, a cousin, perhaps, whom one thought was dead, or a schoolfriend, someone who might fill in a gap in one's past."

One of the youngest participants in the gathering was Jack Young, a London taxi driver whose past is almost all gaps. He knows that he was born in Vienna. He has been able to discover that his mother, Elsa Spiegel, was deported to the Minsk ghetto shortly after he was born in 1942. He has no idea how he survived his first months or who looked after him. But he knows that he was raised in Theresienstadt and that he was three years old when it was liberated by the allies.

He is now married with two pretty daughters and lives in Hampstead Garden Suburb. He came to the gathering in the hope of finding someone who might know something of his family or what happened to his father and whether he had sisters or brothers. Until one has

239

been at such a gathering one cannot imagine the agony of being without a past. There was also Mira Givon, a young housewife who was thrown from a train when she was two weeks old. A woman found her and looked after her and eventually brought her to her grandmother. She came to the gathering in search of her parents.

All participants wore their names and places of origin on their lapels. Some carried engraved stones, others placards. Beniek Stern of Warsaw wore a T-shirt with a message "129592—Majdanek. Auschwitz. Buchenwald." It was his curriculum vitae.

"You never know," he said. "People might see me and say: 'Are you the Stern who . . . ?'" and as we were speaking several people came up to him and asked: "Are you the Stern who . . . ?" Sadly he wasn't.

Elie Wiesel, the author, met a survivor of Auschwitz who described how he used to watch a Hungarian boy who did not have *tefilin* to wind round his arm with his morning prayers, and used string instead. "Was he a dark-haired little boy?" asked Wiesel.

"Yes."

"I was the boy."

Such dramas were frequently replayed in the course of the four-day meeting and one sometimes overheard snatches of surrealist conversation:

"Where were you?"

"Birkenau, and you?"

"Dachau."

"Hah!"

Birkenau was largely devoted to slaughter and one was left with the impression that Dachau, by comparison, was Butlins.

Prof Shamai Davidson, an Oxford-trained psychiatrist who heads the Shalvata Mental Health Centre near Tel Aviv, and who has made the traumas arising out of the holocaust his special field of study, was convinced that in general terms the effect of the gathering would be benign:

"It gave many survivors an unprecedented chance to re-examine the extreme traumas and loss that they suffered more than a generation ago," he said. "In the past, all their energies and emotional resources were devoted to adapting themselves to their new circumstances and achieving success. Most were probably teenagers at the end of the war, and now, in their 50s, with children grown up, they have the need to reflect on their experience."

Which brings one to the most remarkable fact about the whole gathering. One expected sombre voices and tearful eyes. Instead there were smiling faces on every side and the meeting hall echoed with shrieks of joy as someone alighted upon a familiar face.

The reunion, with all its melancholy moments, was a celebration rather than a requiem. Here were men and women who, in spite of all they had been through, had been able to triumph over adversity and to build new lives, establish thriving businesses, rise in the professions and surround themselves with children and grandchildren.

It was a display of resilience, and the fact that they were meeting in Israel and in Jerusalem enhanced their sense of continuity and resurrection. It was an affirmation that in spite of Hitler, or whoever might seek to emulate him, Jews were here to stay.

Observer, 21 June 1981

Innocent Liar

A TELEVISION INQUIRY, even if staged as a court hearing, is not, of course, a court of law, but I doubt if any fair-minded person who watched the programme on Waldheim on Sunday night would question the verdict that he could not have been tried on the available evidence and, if tried, could not have been convicted.

All of which need not mean that he was completely innocent, but there is not, and never was, sufficient proof to establish his guilt, or, I would say, to justify the vendetta which the World Jewish Congress launched against him.

It all began two or three years ago, when the WJC unearthed documents which, it claimed, implicated Waldheim in war crimes against the Jews. When Simon Wiesenthal and others contested the claims, it changed tack and suggested that Waldheim was involved in atrocities against Yugoslavs and Greeks—though I cannot see why the WJC should have taken up an issue on which the Greeks and Yugoslavs themselves had remained quiescent.

The only thing the WJC has proved beyond all doubt is that Waldheim is shifty, devious and a liar, and unfit to be either secretary-general of the United Nations or President of Austria. But all that is beside the point, for the WJC is not a court of morals and was never formed to pronounce on the fitness or otherwise of this or that individual to hold public office.

The campaign did incalculable harm to the small Austrian Jewish community, and as the general public probably thinks that the WJC is a sort of latter-day Sanhedrin, it made Jews in general seem bloody-minded, shrill and vindictive.

The clamorous fury with which the WJC pursued Waldheim right up to the eve of the Austrian presidential election made him out to be

242

something of a martyr and thus almost ensured his victory, for small nations—especially when they were once great empires—do not care to be told what to do by outsiders.

At which point it may be useful to examine exactly who or what the WJC actually is.

The Congress was formed in 1936, at a time of crisis, to "ensure the survival and foster the unity of the Jewish people"; it was a "voluntary association" of "representative Jewish bodies, communities and organisations" throughout the world.

Its dominant figure, until his death a few years ago, was Nahum Goldmann, a prince among men and a natural diplomat who—even after the emergence of Israel—functioned as a sort of ambassador-at-large for the Jewish people.

To say that his successor, Edgar Bronfman, is not another Goldmann is not to damn him, for he is a vigorous man who has applied himself to his duties with great dedication and has spent vast sums to keep the WJC in being.

But generosity does not amount to acumen, nor dedication to wisdom, and the entire involvement of the WJC in the Waldheim affair, which grew to assume the scale of an obsession, was a blunder of the first magnitude.

First of all, there are sufficient agencies involved in pursuing Nazi war criminals without the WJC getting in on the act. Secondly, once its evidence was questioned, it might have reasonably withdrawn to think again.

Instead, it redoubled its efforts and became more shrill and assertive, as often happens when people become aware of the weakness of their case.

Nazi crimes were uniquely evil, which does not mean that the normal processes of the law can be abandoned in the pursuit of Nazi criminals. On the contrary, the graver the crime, the more carefully one must weigh the evidence; and at no time did the WJC produce evidence to prove beyond all reasonable doubt that Waldheim in person was actively implicated in atrocities.

He may have known about them and, if so, he did nothing to stop them, which merely shows that he was not a hero. But to show that a man is not a hero, and to establish even that he was a liar, is no proof that he was a criminal. In short, nothing adduced by the WJC justified the hue and cry it provoked.

If the WJC had been even remotely as representative as it claims to

243

be, heads would have been rolling by now. It is, however, answerable to no one and accountable to no one, and Mr Bronfman can remain in office for as long as he wants.

It is not a happy arrangement—for the WJC, the Jewish people, or even Mr Bronfman himself.

Jewish Chronicle, 10 June 1988

Zealots Galore

PEOPLE ARE GETTING so worked up over the Carmelite convent at Auschwitz as to lose all sight of the facts.

First of all, the convent, a small, makeshift edifice housing 18 nuns, is not on the site of the death camp. Auschwitz and Birkenau were twin cities of massive extent, with a huge population. The former comprised a forced-labour camp which had more than its share of fatalities; the latter was dedicated to destruction. The convent is not in Birkenau, but is adjacent to Auschwitz.

Secondly, although Auschwitz-Birkenau has become *the* symbol of Jewish martyrdom, it is generally believed that about one-third of the victims were non-Jewish; the actual figure may have been much higher.

According to the *Encyclopaedia Judaica*, estimates of the Jewish dead "vary between 1,000,000 and 2,500,000" and if, as it says, "probably the lower figure comes nearer the truth", then non-Jewish victims may have outnumbered Jewish ones.

But the proportions are immaterial. Every human soul, according to Jewish teaching, comprises a universe, and it is not difficult to understand the emotions of nuns who feel moved to meet for contemplation and prayer near the site of what was the ultimate expression of inhumanity.

And yet the road which led to Auschwitz began with Christian persecution and many Jews are affronted by the sign of the cross so near the site of their martyrdom. So, in 1987, the Catholic Church, which had never formally authorised the convent in the first place and which regards it with embarrassment, agreed that it should be moved.

It has, however, done nothing since, and its tardiness has further

245

exacerbated feelings. But that hardly justifies the escapade of Rabbi Avraham Weiss and his merry men who, a week or so ago, tried to force their way into the convent.

To read some American reports of their foray, one would think that Weiss and company were the innocent victims of a pogrom. Weiss, who may have been a double-glazing salesman in an earlier incarnation, explains that he merely wanted to talk to the nuns, but they didn't want to be talked to—as was their right—nor did they welcome his intrusion. He was forcibly ejected by nearby work-men.

The World Jewish Congress has since declared that it holds the Polish authorities responsible for a "vicious and unprovoked attack". Vicious it may have been; unprovoked it certainly was not. Weiss asked for it, and if he possibly got more than he bargained for, it is hardly proof of Polish Jew-hatred.

Rabbi Weiss, it seems to me, is sadly misguided. He is, one gathers, a rabbi in the Bronx and I suspect he has seen too many bad films about vigilantes. He obviously thought that this was an issue where he could take the law into his own hands.

Moral arguments are never advanced by the use of force, and Weiss' exercise in false heroics may have undone the patient efforts of many men over many years. But he has received no word of reproof from any established authority, and as American society is short of heroes, I half suspect that he may yet receive a medal for gallantry above and beyond the call of duty.

American Jews have a conscience about the Holocaust because they feel they did not do nearly enough to stave it off and they are overreacting now because they feel they underreacted then. But they are, in fact, doing the memory of their parents and grandparents a serious injustice.

The fate of European Jewry was, to a large extent, sealed by the closing of American doors to Jewish immigration. American Jews, though anticipating nothing of the horrors ahead—who did?— fought against the closure with some determination, but they were themselves immigrants and lacked the numbers, the resources, the self-assurance and the influence they have now.

Their present influence is in itself partly an outcome of the Holo-caust, for American gentiles, too, have a conscience about it—as well they might; but one cannot redress the impotence of one age with excessive zeal in another. One has already seen this in American-

Jewish support of Israeli extremists, and now they are beginning to show their hand in Europe.

It seems to me that European Jews may yet have to establish a united authority, if only to curb the excesses of their American colleagues.

Jewish Chronicle, 28 July 1989

Killers at Large

MY FATHER'S FAMILY came from Latvia, my mother's from Poland. Neither of them survived the war.

My father's family was murdered by Germans and Latvians in 1941, my mother's by Germans and Poles in 1942. But for the grace of God, I might have shared their fate, for a day or two separated me from the closing of frontiers.

I therefore have as good reason as anyone for wishing to see Nazi war criminals, no matter how broken or old, hounded to the ends of the earth.

But apart from my own personal feelings, there is an elementary issue at stake. No one should get away with murder—especially mass murder—no matter where or when committed, and yet I remain uneasy at the prospect of further war-crimes trials.

If a Bill enabling the authorities to act against alleged war criminals is tabled at the end of this year, it is unlikely to become law before the end of next year and, given the pace of legal proceedings, the first case will probably not be heard before the end of 1991—or some fifty years after the crimes were committed.

It is not easy to amass reliable evidence after five years, let alone after fifty, but the Government would not even have contemplated legislation unless it was satisfied that it had overwhelming grounds for a successful prosecution, so that any fears one may have about a miscarriage of justice are, I believe, unfounded.

My own fears on that score have certainly been allayed, and the sense of urgency with which the Home Office has approached the matter is commendable.

But what of the trials themselves? Many survivors who might have given evidence are dead, and of the rest, most are old and frail, with

248

unreliable memories.

The prosecution will thus depend mainly on documents supplied by the Soviet authorities, and it would not be difficult for a skilled counsel, or even an unskilled one, to cast doubts on their authenticity.

The cases, moreover, will be heard before a jury, most of whose members may have been born well after the crimes were committed. They will have no personal memories of the war, nor any recollection of the hatreds generated by the Nazis.

In a strange way, the very scale of a crime works in favour of the criminal. Where there are a few victims with known names and known histories, one can identify with them, but where they are numbered in hundreds or thousands, they become nameless and faceless, for the imagination cannot cope with enormities.

Once the trials begin, the jury will see not the innocent victims who were slaughtered in the forests and swamps of Eastern Europe, but the broken old men standing in the dock who were alleged to have slaughtered them.

Juries can be perverse in even the most straightforward cases, and these will be far from straightforward. The British judiciary is also against such trials and, given the prevailing atmosphere, I doubt if any jury will come up with a verdict of guilty.

What, then, will have been achieved? For the Jews, a reopening of wounds. For the Jew-haters, an occasion to inflict wounds, to surface and draw breath and parade their hatreds.

Their campaign has already begun. It will gather volume in the course of the preliminary debate, grow in strength as the Bill goes through the two Houses of Parliament, and rise to a crescendo during the trials themselves.

It is argued that such trials are a necessary deterrent, and certainly punishments can deter, otherwise there would be little point to them; but an armed thug with people at his mercy is conscious only of his power and not of the consequences he may suffer from its abuse.

And in any case, we are dealing not only with unique crimes, but with a unique atmosphere, where every principle of legality and justice was subverted, so that the usual arguments about crime and punishment are irrelevant.

But that is a secondary issue. The primary issue remains, and I believe that an increase in antisemitism, no matter how virulent and sustained, is not too high a price to pay for the assertion of the principle that men should not get away with murder—only, as I have suggested, I do not feel that in this instance the principle will be asserted.

We are, in other words, inviting certain hazards for the sake of uncertain benefits.

Jewish Chronicle, 4 August 1989

Press
and Impress

Ancient Oracle

THE ANGLO-JEWISH COMMUNITY is small, numbering about 410,000 and most of its members belong to an Orthodox congregation or at least are eventually buried in Orthodox cemeteries. There is also a strong Reform movement. At least three major factions divide the Orthodox, and the Reform group is split in two, but all of these elements have this in common: practically everyone "takes" the *Jewish Chronicle*. This is not to say that the *Chronicle* is regarded with universal affection. Hardly a week passes in which it is not denounced from an Orthodox pulpit. Indeed, some ultra-Orthodox rabbis have gone so far as to issue a formal interdict banning it from Jewish homes—but to no avail, for it is too ingrained a habit.

Now 132 years old, the weekly *Chronicle* has become as much a part of the Anglo-Jewish Sabbath as candlelight. While journals once regarded as national institutions have faded away, the J.C. has not only survived but prospered. It is one of the oldest newspapers in Great Britain and the oldest Jewish newspaper in the world.

Among the reasons for J.C.'s longevity are its independence, its adaptability, the essential conservatism of the Anglo-Jewish community (which it has helped keep that way) and the accomplishments of a brilliant editor at a crucial phase of its existence. He was Leopold Greenberg, of whom more later.

Another factor is the growing prosperity of Anglo-Jewry. The economics of newspaper production are such that an increase in circulation can mean a loss of revenue. The nineteen cents which the J.C. costs wouldn't even pay for the newsprint of an average forty-eight page issue. Everything depends on advertising, especially on its quality. Since most J.C. readers are in the sought-after AB (top

253

quality) advertising category, the paper can charge about $1,200 per page. This is extraordinary for a British weekly with a circulation of 70,000—including about 5,000 in the United States—and some 300,000 readers. Also, the J.C. has probably benefited from the common belief that Jews are more prosperous and more numerous than they actually are. (When I told an editor of a national daily that there are less than half a million Jews in Britain, he said: "Come off it ,there's *millions* of you.")

Advertisers of quality goods and services flock to the J.C. like pigeons to their cote. The display ads would lead one to believe that the average British Jew smokes Havana cigars, drinks Moët and Chandon champagne, drives a Daimler, swathes his wife in minks, frequently visits Israel, buys his kosher chickens pre-packaged and frozen, and is chronically short of rabbis.

Actually, the "Classified Announcements" are the *Chronicle*'s major source of revenue. Every Jew in Britain who is Bar Mitzvah or Bat Mitzvah, becomes engaged, gets married, has a child or adopts one, celebrates a silver wedding, dies and acquires a tombstone pays tribute to the J.C.—directly or through his heirs—in the form of an ad. Not unusual are annual insertions on the anniversaries of deaths, in some cases for as long as forty years after the events. A single death can be a gold mine for the J.C., producing columns of paid condolences from relatives, friends and neighbours.

Equally lucrative is the J.C.'s "Social and Personal" column, a monument to Anglo-Jewish snobbery. Usually taking up at least a page, it carries the traditional "hatch, match and dispatch" ads found among the "Classified Announcements", but at more than twice the charge. Yet everyone who wants to be among the elect pays up cheerfully. As one wit put it, if the dead could ever rise again most of them would probably announce their return in the J.C.—and on the "Social and Personal" page rather than the common one.

The *Chronicle* began in 1841 as a four-page paper, price twopence. The Jewish community was tiny, some could not read English, others could not afford twopence and there was already a rival in the field, *The Voice of Jacob*. The two merged to save each other from extinction. When another rival appeared some ten years later, the J.C. merged again. So it struggled along with varying fortunes until the early 1880s, when the first of a series of pogroms occurred in Russia, Poland and Lithuania.

During the previous decades, while the Anglo-Jewish community was waging the battle for emancipation, the J.C. was largely a family news-sheet padded out with theological essays. With the pogroms there came a quickening of Jewish life as English Jews sought to aid their stricken brothers. Soon thereafter mass immigration from Eastern Europe began, and what had been a small, staid, inbred and largely Anglicised community was transformed into a teeming immigrant society.

The old community saw in the new a threat to its Englishness, a reversion to the ghetto. Many established Jews supported the fierce agitation against mass immigration that quickly developed. But the *Chronicle*, which had been regarded as the mouthpiece of the old guard, took an independent stand and championed the cause of the alien. In 1891 it inaugurated a monthly supplement, *In Darkest Russia, A Journal of Persecution*, which helped greatly to open British eyes to tsarist barbarity. In place of foreign news largely lifted with due acknowledgement from other newspapers, it began to print dispatches from J.C. overseas correspondents.

The J.C.'s alertness to happenings abroad was not matched, however, by awareness of the transformation taking place at home. During the last years of the nineteenth century, the paper sometimes read as if it were written for a Kensington dowager with private means, a charitable disposition and an insatiable interest in the life and works of Anglo-Jewry's own royal family, the Rothschilds, or such lesser royals as the Montefiores and the Sassoons. The lives and works of these personages were often, if subliminally, put forth as examples of the heights to which English Jews could aspire. As they began to marry out of the faith, the J.C. reacted with an almost personal sense of betrayal.

When Hannah Rothschild, daughter of Baron Meir and then the wealthiest woman in England, married a Christian, the Earl of Rosebery, the *Chronicle* found no consolation in his being one of the foremost peers of the realm and a rising politician—in fact, a future prime minister. It was convulsed with grief, as witness this excerpt from its comments:

If the flame seized on the cedars, how will fare the hyssop on the wall? If the leviathan is brought up with a hook, how will the minnows escape? . . . was there amongst the millions of brethren-in-faith all over Europe no one of sufficient talent, sufficiently cultured, sufficiently high-minded to be deemed

255

worthy to be received in the family circle, that this honour must be bestowed upon one who must necessarily estrange the partner from her people? . . . A sad example has been set which, we pray God, may not be productive of dreadful consequences.

(The term "leviathan" was particularly unfortunate, for Hannah was a bulky wench, or "heavy baggage", as her husband once described her.)

In 1873 the paper was shaken by the appearance of the *Jewish World*, produced by Lucien Wolf, Laurie Magnus and Meyer Spielman, a trio of journalists well known in the newspaper world and with ready access to the skills of Fleet Street. The newcomer's innovations were quickly imitated by the J.C. The J.W. had lavish illustrations; the J.C. followed suit. The former had a Yiddish page for immigrants; the latter produced a Yiddish supplement. One courted small-town readers with more provincial news; the other issued provincial supplements. One Friday the *World* came out with a "Children's Column". The following week the J.C. appeared with "Aunt Naomi", forerunner of the present "Junior Chronicle".

The pace of the competition was wearying and expensive. The *Chronicle* got into difficulties and was acquired in 1906 for a mere L13,000 by Leopold Greenberg, a journalist who had worked on the liberal *Daily News*.

Greenberg had been a close associate of Theodor Herzl and was a founder and secretary of the English Zionist Federation. He saw the paper mainly as a vehicle for Zionist propaganda. Up to then the J.C. had described Zionist events and reported Zionist polemics, but had seldom expressed its own opinions. In 1896 it had published Herzl's *A Solution of the Jewish Question*, which contained most of the ideas later incorporated in his *Judenstaat*, but this did not reflect any commitment to Zionism by the J.C. Altogether, there was a soggy ambivalence about the paper's attitude.

Greenberg knew where he was going and was determined to take the community with him, to the dismay of the older families. The J.C. had for many years received a monthly subsidy from the Rothschilds and no major matter of policy had been settled without a meeting at New Court, the head office of the Rothschild bank. Greenberg dispensed with the subsidy and the meetings. When Lord Rothschild protested about something in the paper, Greenberg retorted: "I can't call in the edition now, but I'll give you back your twopence if you like."

Greenberg's Zionism brought the immigrant masses into the *Chronicle*'s orbit. There were a number of ephemeral Zionist Yiddish papers, but a well-established "Englischer papier" voicing Zionist sentiments was very reassuring. However, for a time during World War I the J.C. alienated a great many newcomers.

The war was going badly for the Allies; Britain and France were being bled white on the Western Front. In 1916 Britain proposed to augment the size of its armed forces—up to then composed of volunteers—by conscription. Most of the Jewish immigrants were Russian subjects. They were to be given the choice of enlisting in the British army or being deported for service in the Russian army. This was regarded as eminently fair by the general public, which probably was not aware that many had fled from Russia for their lives and were being asked to fight for their persecutors. The J.C., while unhappy about the prospect of deportations, supported conscription. To the embarrassment of the paper, already known as "the voice of Anglo-Jewry", the worried newcomers found a champion in the *Manchester Guardian*, which argued that the proposed act would violate their right of asylum. The J.C. thought it would do nothing of the sort, stating that:

> The Russian Jew may still come here. But in coming he must be prepared to abide by what is on his arrival, or what may subsequently become, the country's law. To ask the privilege of settlement here, and to demand exemption from the burdens that weigh on other residents, is, in our view, to set up an impossible claim and to bring the whole principle of asylum into disrepute.

The resentment against the J.C. on this issue was soon forgotten in the face of a larger one: the Balfour Declaration, which first saw the light of day in the form of a letter from Lord Balfour to Lord Walter Rothschild. The old families feared that the basic premise of Zionism would expose their loyalty to question, and tried to prevent the Declaration from being publicised. Greenberg, who played an important part in the negotiations leading to the Declaration, insisted they were speaking only for themselves. The idea of a Jewish state, he declared, had fired the imagination of world Jewry.

The Rothschilds and others attempted to counter his arguments by publishing an excellently written newspaper, *The Jewish Guardian*, but it petered out, mainly because non-Zionist Jews were not sufficiently interested in Jewish life.

In recent years, the *Chronicle*'s solitary eminence has occasionally tended to limit its freedom of expression. To create the impression that it is not part of the ruling Establishment, the paper often goes out of its way to attack the powers-that-be. But whether it appreciates the honour or not (and one suspects it does), the J.C. is generally considered to be the official voice of Anglo-Jewry. This has made for some delicate situations.

Following World War II, for example, when the Jews of Palestine were in open rebellion against the British, the editor, Ivan Greenberg, son of the great Leopold, ignored the directives of his Board and applauded the rebels in near-Revisionist terms. This produced consternation in the Anglo-Jewish establishment, of which the Zionist Federation was by then an important part. There were threats that another journal would be started (and one almost certainly would, but for paper rationing), and Greenberg was finally dismissed. For the next decade or so the J.C., careful not to offend anybody, took a middle-of-the-road attitude on controversial issues.

During and shortly after the war, paper rationing held the circulation to 15,500. It increased to 22,400 the week that rationing ended in 1947, reached 51,500 by 1949, and thereafter moved steadily to its present level. The Holocaust heightened Jewish consciousness and a series of dramatic events during the second half of the 1940s—the UN debates on the future of Palestine, the massacres in the Jerusalem corridor, the illegal immigration, the War of Liberation—brought a succession of new readers.

Since the time of Leopold Greenberg, the foreign news service has been the heart of the *Chronicle*. Able correspondents report from centres of Jewish population throughout the world and capable analysts in London comment on events abroad. The very quality of the foreign news service highlights the deficiencies in local news coverage, but there is no dichotomy in treatment or approach. Overseas reports deal with "hard" news, while practically all the happenings at home are "soft" news, or no news, or gossip. The farther the J.C. goes from London into the provinces, the more gossipy the items become. No week passes without columns of snippets such as this:

The fourth annual speech day of the Newcastle Jewish day school was held at the Imperial Hotel, Jesmond, with Mr. A. S. Science presiding. Mrs. Ray Guttentag of Sunderland, formerly of Newcastle, distributed the awards.

There is also a restless quest for *naches*, for assurance that Jews are still making it one way or another in the great world. Twice a year, on the Queen's Birthday and the New Year, half the staff is sent searching through the Honours List to try to unearth a new Jewish Baron or Knight, or even a humble MBE. More often than not, those who turn up have no connection with Jewish life. But no matter, their names are blazoned forth.

On the other hand, the arts and culture pages rank with the best in British journalism today. In recent years, the J.C. editor has responded to the tastes of his subscribers by bringing together an outstanding team of theatre, film and music reviewers and critics, among whom are some of England's most gifted writers. A favourable review of a book can have a dramatic effect on its sales.

There was a time when J.C. critics felt impelled to sniff out a "Jewish" angle and to praise any Jew involved at any level in the arts, but today works are approached entirely on their merits. There are still a few weak spots in the J.C.'s coverage, but if the current trend continues many readers who are disinterested in or tired of Jewish affairs may take the paper solely for its pages on the arts.

The main body of the J.C. is a continuing celebration of Jewish tradition. Every event in the Jewish calendar is marked by commemorative and descriptive essays and memories of how *zeide* and *bubbe* did it. "Junior Chronicle", read avidly by the young, is today, as in Aunt Naomi's day, a primer of Jewish religion. The women's pages discuss issues of interest to women generally—and also print recipes which are thoroughly checked so that every ingredient will be acceptable to the most Orthodox housewife. When a steak house advertises in the J.C., it must include the assurance that "omelettes and fish dishes are always available". No advertisement announcing an event on Friday night or a *Yom Tov* is ever accepted.

Actually, the J.C. is both newspaper and parish magazine; this may be another reason for its longevity. It is also a constant challenge to William Frankel, the present editor.

Soon after he took over in 1958, he decided that real news could be found on the home front, but it had to be dug out. Reporters who had been content to accept handouts from communal institutions were sent forth to ask questions. More important, Frankel found a Cause with a capital "c". Before we examine the Cause we had better first examine the proprietorial structure of the J.C., and the not uncomplicated nature of its editor.

When Leopold Greenberg bought the *Chronicle* he was helped by three leading Zionists acting in their private capacity. One was Leopold Kessler, a prosperous mining engineer who had led the El Arish expedition early in the 1900s to investigate the possibility of a Jewish settlement in the Sinai. Kessler eventually became chairman of the company and his shares were inherited by his son David, the present chairman and managing director.

David Kessler, now sixty-six, lives the life of a rather urbane country squire in Buckinghamshire near the Vale of Aylesbury, an area known as Rothschild country because of the numerous residences once occupied by Rothschilds in the surrounding hills. He and his wife, who is a local judge and a social worker, are popular figures in local country society. Their spacious house breathes the spirit of Olde England. It is hard to believe that his forefathers did not land at Hastings with the Conqueror, but came from Silesia. A major in World War II, he has the soldier's staccato manner of speaking and still looks martial, even in mufti. He is a member of the Liberal synagogue, his wife is a convert, and he wears his Judaism lightly. He is intensely interested in Israel, but finds it difficult to discuss events at home without suppressing a yawn. He occupies a different universe from his readers.

William Frankel, on the other hand, is in some ways the J.C. reader writ large. He was born fifty-six years ago in the East End, the son of a *shammos* in a Hasidic *shtieble*, who through great perseverance went from the bar to a highly successful career in journalism and considerable public eminence. His is in many ways a typical East End success story. What is untypical, and endearingly old-fashioned, is his passion for things English—English ways, English mores, English attitudes, English tolerance, the English sense of fair play, and, above all, English cricket. On an ideal Sabbath he will go to *shul* in the morning (possibly officiating as *Baal Tefillah*), then to a quick lunch and finally to Lord's (London's leading cricket ground), with nothing to disturb his rest save the click of bat on ball—truly a Lord's day. At the beginning of his editorial career he was a member of the Reform Club. He has since gravitated to the Athenaeum, a meeting place of bishops, High Court judges and dons. He is a Justice of the Peace and a CBE (Companion of the British Empire) and will one day no doubt became a Knight. But he is shrewd enough to realize that even as Sir William he will never enter Kessler's Olde England, for his past exerts too strong a pull.

He has tried to make the Anglo-Jewish community more attractive, which is to say more English. This was his Cause, and in 1961 he thought he had found his instrument. In that year the Chief Rabbi vetoed the appointment of Louis Jacobs—possibly the ablest rabbi to have served Anglo-Jewry since the war—as Principal of Jews' College of London University, because he thought Rabbi Jacobs' views were not in keeping with traditional Jewish teaching. When Jacobs was invited back to the synagogue he had left to join Jews' College, this appointment was also vetoed and his followers were expelled from the United Synagogue.

Here was a Cause if ever there was one, indeed a whole complex of causes. Involved were the right of free speech, the right of congregations to appoint rabbis of their choice, the question of whether an institution of London University has a right to impose theological norms, and finally the question of whether Rabbi Jacobs' ideas placed him outside the Orthodox pale. In an American context, these ideas would have put him in the right wing of the Conservative movement and possibly even beyond it. They were shaped by a number of distinguished rabbis in the United Synagogue and elsewhere. But the United Synagogue, up to that time a very English institution, had shifted away from the traditions of tolerance. In a campaign that went on for several years, William Frankel set himself to check this. And he lost, for the bulk of the Anglo-Jewish community regarded the conflict as essentially one of Louis Jacobs versus the Chief Rabbi. Anglo-Jewry is not a concourse of theologians, and few of the J.C. readers understood the basic conflict of principles involved. Had Jacobs challenged God in his heavens, they might have been disposed to side with him, but he was challenging the Chief Rabbi and they could not.

The campaign for the Cause was also handicapped by both Anglo-Jewish and J.C. history. The concept of a Chief Rabbi is basically alien to Jewish tradition, but when the United Synagogue was formed by a private Act of Parliament in 1870, it was decided to appoint a dignitary who would bring unity and discipline to all elements in the community—and also perhaps to satisfy the Anglo-Jewish craving for a King of Israel.

So over the years the J.C. built up the Chief Rabbis, printed their speeches, reported their movements, echoed their exhortations, applauded their actions. On the whole, it had good material to work with. What the J.C. had done for almost a century, it could not undo in a relatively short time.

After Rabbi Jacobs was out of the United Synagogue, Frankel (who frequently visits the United States and is an admirer of the Jewish Theological Seminary) hoped to make him the leader of a new English-style Conservative movement. He envisioned a situation in which different rabbis would be free to follow their different ways, with everyone working for a true synthesis of all that is best in English and Jewish life. Again it did not work, and again because of the attitudes instilled over the years by the J.C. itself. For whatever criticisms of the religious leadership are published in the opinion columns, and they are frequent and outspoken, conservatism is still the J.C.'s hallmark.

English conservatism has tended to preserve Jewish conservatism, and the J.C. has helped to preserve both. It gives an occasional frustrated kick against the ghetto walls, but on the whole it has helped to maintain them, and in maintaining the ghetto it has maintained and enlarged its readership.

Present Tense, Vol. 1 No. 1, Autumn 1973

Heaven and Hell

ISRAEL IS A journalist's paradise—or a journalist's hell. It is a paradise because there is always something happening. And it is hell for the very same reason, because as there is always something happening, the conscientious pro feels he should be at the typewriter, or the telex, or on the phone to capture events for eternity.

Even non-events have a way of becoming eventful in Israel. There is, for example, nothing so banal as a strike, for they are so frequent and ubiquitous that they have ceased to be news; but in Israel, even strikes are newsworthy.

Thus, for example, in May the weathermen began to apply sanctions by withholding the weather forecast from the media, with the result that the onset of summer was delayed for a month, and when we should have had blue skies, constant sunshine and temperatures in the 80s, we actually had clouds, and even rain.

More remarkable even than the weathermen's strike was the diplomats' strike. Again, they didn't leave work altogether, but merely applied sanctions. Which is to say, they kept the usual office hours, but refused to attend diplomatic receptions and dinners in the evenings, which seems to me a crazy way of doing things. If I had been a striking diplomat I would have worked it the other way about, and one must take their tactics as a serious reflection on the quality of Israel's catering.

(Incidentally "sanctions" in Israel are what we would call "work-to-rule" in England, but the term would have no meaning here for in Israel people don't work-to-rule even when they're not working. They do sometimes go-slow, but such tactics would pass un-noticed in the public services, which have never been known for going-fast.)

But the strike of strikes is of course the doctor's strike which, at the time of writing, is 14 weeks old, and which seems set to continue for a further 14 years, and everything about it has been newsworthy.

Israel has more doctors per head of population than any other country in the world, but then it has more Jews per head of population than any other country in the world, and the medical brotherhood has a unique and exalted place in Jewish lore. It is not Rabbis who are regarded in the popular imagination as the successors of the Temple priesthood, but doctors, and if the writings of Maimonides enjoy a veneration second only to those of Moses, it is precisely because he was a Rabbi Dr. (It is true that his writings were considered heretical in his lifetime and were publicly burned, but if he had only been a Rabbi and not a Rabbi Dr., he would have been burned with them.) The very fact that such men should go on strike, therefore, is in itself news. It's a little as if the Heavenly Host had applied sanctions. And what a strike it's been. Where strikers elsewhere go on a hunger march to impress their needs upon the public, the doctors booked up in 5-star hotels, had their meals in gourmet restaurants, and spent their time cruising round the Sea of Galilee—all under the eyes of reporters, photographers and television cameras. It may have been bad for the patients, and I shouldn't imagine it was all that good for the doctors' case, but it was splendid for the media.

Every country has, or has had, its economic crisis, and Israel has them all the time; but in spite of their frequency they are always something to write home about. What other modern, developed country can claim to have an inflation rate of 13½% a month? Which other country with a rate of inflation of 13½% a month, and colossal debts, would be offering expensive homes (on the West Bank) at giveaway prices to people who already have them? And what other country could introduce currency reform, allow the old currency to run in tandem with the new, and let prices accelerate at such a pace that one could not tell the one from the other?

Israel does not have elections as often as it used to, and the conflicts between government and opposition are too predictable to be interesting, but by way of compensation one has the fighting within the parties, with factions breaking up into sub-factions, and with sub-factions from different groups coming together to form new ones. The political scene in Israel therefore has the aspect of a cauldron (some would say witches' brew) which is always on the boil.

To be sure, Israel has few of the spy and security scandals which have shaken other countries, and especially England. Some might ascribe it to the fact that certain sexual peccadilloes are comparatively uncommon among Jews, but I would say that the main reason is that Israel has no state secrets to speak of, or rather, it has a great many, but they are spoken of before they can be classified as secret. It's a marvellous place for leaks, inspired and uninspired, official and unofficial. The country is awash with them, and a Cabinet meeting is hardly over before the details of every utterance are on the presses, ready to roll. Everyone in Israel is privy to what is happening; the really privileged journalist is privy to what is happening before it has even happened, and I suspect that some political correspondents are given previews of cabinet meetings.

But apart from the abundance of news, Israel is an extremely pleasant place in which to gather it. There is military censorship even in peacetime, but it functions with a light hand even in war. And the skies are blue, the weather is sunny, the girls are pretty, the wine is good—and the international telephone service works a damned sight better than the local one.

All of which may explain why Israel is so much in the news.

The Israel Economist, July 1983

Prime Time for God

THERE SEEMS TO be a growing belief that there is a conspiracy afoot between the media and the Reform and Liberal synagogues to deny the Orthodox their place in the sun, or rather, their face on the screen. Readers have written to the "JC" about it, rabbis have protested from their pulpits and even I have been berated over the matter, as if it were in some ways my fault.

I think it should be recognised from the outset that the Liberals have the advantage in that they are liberal, which is to say, they're in fashion and are more likely to say the sort of things programme makers like to hear.

Secondly, there is a tacit assumption that the few hours a week devoted to religious or quasi religious topics (some of which are very quasi indeed) should as far as possible have an ecumenical flavour. A programme like "Songs of Praise", filmed a year or so ago in the West London (Reform) Synagogue, with its black hot gospellers and white mixed choir, and preachers from three or four denominations, and its message that we are all children of the one God and brothers under the skin, and cousins to boot, could not have been held in an Orthodox synagogue; and had it even been held in, say, the Festival Hall, Orthodox rabbis would have felt unable to take part.

Thirdly, there is a strong element of professionalism involved. It is not easy to look and sound intelligent on television, even when one has something intelligent to say.

The Reform/Liberal rabbis/rebbetsins to whom so many people seem to take exception have an easy, relaxed manner before both the camera and the microphone and make their viewers and listeners feel at ease.

The most telling point, however, was made to me by Rabbi Cyril Harris, who, but for his Orthodoxy, could, I believe, have emerged as

266

a media person in his own right (the Scottish accent, to say nothing of his membership of the Scottish mafia, is an immense advantage), and he was perfectly honest about it. "They," he said, "can say anything they like, while we've got to watch it. A word out of place and we're hauled over the coals."

I believe (and so does he) that the constraints are self-imposed and that Orthodoxy, for all its restrictions, leaves scope for the independent mind. I go further: Orthodox rabbis are more secure in their jobs than any other and—unless they have ambitions to be a dayan or a Chief Rabbi—they can say anything they like (and do almost anything they like, including nothing) with complete immunity. Few, however, are disposed to make use of that freedom, and the Orthodox rabbinate is like a small political party, with each member acting as his own whip. All of which makes for predictability, and the predictable is anathema to the media.

Which brings me, perhaps inevitably, to Rabbi Julia Neuberger's ham sandwich. I have heard so many versions of her alleged transgression that I am left with the impression that she either celebrates holy communion over bacon and eggs (free range ones, no doubt), or that she passes round ham sandwiches among the faithful as a priest might pass round wafers.

I don't know if the stories are true, but the fact that they have got around can have done her no harm in the media. "Rabbi eats smoked salmon" is not news; "Rabbi eats ham sandwich" is, and any Orthodox rabbi who might care to flourish a pork chop from his pulpit on Kol Nidre night, and then take a bite out of it, would be assured of prime time on every media network in the land, and not a few abroad. Give a rabbi a bad name and he, or she, is made.

I come finally to the Chief Rabbi, who used to be seen and heard fairly frequently on the media until about a year ago, but who has almost been no-personned since. And the reason, I believe, is this. Last year, while prelate after prelate lined up to sanctify the Church of England report on "Faith in the Cities" with incense and oil, Sir Immanuel, to the dismay of onlookers, poured cold water on it; and if he has not, as a result, been blackened by the media, he has been put in the same compartment as mavericks like Enoch Powell.

In other words, while the media abhor orthodoxy in others, they have their own orthodoxies, and, while they like the unpredictable, it has to take predictable forms.

Jewish Chronicle, 8 August 1986

Shooting the Shooters

I SOMETIMES FEEL that it wouldn't be a bad thing if someone hijacked a television crew, dropped the whole jack pack of them down a black hole somewhere, and forgot about them.

It has been the apology of journalism and journalists throughout the ages that they only mirror events. This is not completely true even of us humble vendors in the word trade, but it is largely untrue of the electronics boys, for once the cameras begin to whirr, they, wittingly or unwittingly (and, I often suspect, wittingly), provoke the events they set out to portray.

I remember arriving with a film crew some years ago at a Glasgow shipyard which had been caught up in some sort of sit-in or strike. There were a few pickets by the main gate, but otherwise the street was empty.

As soon as the first tripod was set up, however, the scene changed. People appeared from nowhere; the streets filled and purposeful-looking young men bobbed up in front of the cameras to offer instant opinions on the iniquities of capitalism. We were not, in fact, a news-crew, but had we wanted a news story, we would have brought one into being by our very presence.

I suspect that the football violence on the scale we have witnessed in recent years is largely a product of the television age, and there would be fewer urchins around to throw stones at troops and police in the streets of Belfast if there were no cameras around.

Britain has more video recorders per head of population than any other country in Europe (which tells us something about the state of Britain), and the hooligan can not only attain a passing sense of achievement by seeing himself in action on a news programme, but can replay it on the video for eternity. Violence can make a man

268

—in his own eyes, at least—a celebrity: I am on screen, therefore I am.

When it comes to international hijacking, the scale is different and the risks are greater, but the principle is the same. A successful hijack, or even a semi-successful one, assures one prime television time beamed out by satellite over five continents.

CBS, NBC, ABC, BBC, ITN and the rest may protest that they were only reporting an event of immediate public interest, but one can be absolutely certain that the hijacking of TWA flight 847 would not have taken place if they had not been around to report it.

As it was, from the time the aircraft was seized, the world was treated to a daily airing of real or imagined Arab grievances; and from June 16 one could hardly switch on the television news without receiving a party political broadcast on behalf of Nabih Berri and the Shia Amal.

Mr Berri may not have actually instigated the hijacking (he is, after all, Lebanon's Minister of Justice), but he was clearly in collusion with those who had and, therefore, an accessory after the fact (if not before it). But because he is clean-shaven, looks plausible, speaks English (after a fashion) and was not directly involved in actually killing anyone, he assumed the role not only of a "moderate", but of an arbiter and saviour.

And, in order to keep his face before the cameras, he milked the drama for all it was worth, releasing this hostage one day, and that hostage the next. Most bizarre of all was his parading of Mr Allyn Conwell as "spokesman" on behalf of the hostages.

No one who has not been subjected to the sort of torments suffered by the hostages has a right to comment on their conduct, but I think I may be forgiven for suggesting that Mr Conwell's behaviour was less than heroic. He may, on his first appearance, have been acting under duress, but he must have been aware that a fellow passenger had been bludgeoned into insensitivity and shot dead for the crime of being an American, and if no one expected him to denounce his captors for the murderous thugs they are, he could have used the opportunity to keep his mouth shut and not indulge in an instant appraisal of Middle Eastern problems.

Again it might be argued that he had no such option and that he was being manipulated by Mr Berri, who was exploiting the fears and miseries of innocent men to advance his political aims. But weren't the media doing the same to enlarge their viewing figures?

The newsmen on the spot have their every instinct trained to catch every moment of drama as it takes place, and to get their stories out whatever happens; and they work under such pressure—and, not infrequently, such hazards—that they have no time to reflect on the consequences of their work.

But what of the men who take their editorial decisions in the calmer atmosphere of New York or London, or their overseers in the boardrooms? Can they still be unaware that television has become the handmaid of terror.

Jewish Chronicle, 5 July 1985

What The Papers Say

MOST JOURNALISTS HAVE a manuscript gathering dust in their bottom drawer, and as long as it remains in the drawer they're safe, but if it should ever be published and praised, they become unsettled and edgy and yearn to shrug off the constraints of regular employment for the freedom of full-time authorship.

I shrugged mine off before my first book was even published. I was working for Granada television with little to do and all the time in the world to do it in and I used my enforced leisure to write a novel. A colleague showed the first draft to Tom Maschler, who praised it so lavishly that I immediately gave notice, moved to a cottage in the country, and applied myself in earnest to literature; but when I presented the final draft—all 200,000 words of it—Maschler was rather less enthusiastic. I don't know if he actually read it, perhaps he only weighed it, but in either case he turned it down.

It eventually found its way into print (in attenuated form) but that took another two or three years. In the meantime I had to eat, and the editor of the *Jewish Chronicle*, for whom I wrote a weekly column, kindly gave me a job. I waited till I had four books in print before I took my life in my hands again and left regular employment. That was 20 years ago and I have remained a freelance since.

I live mainly on my books, but my royalties (if any) come twice a year, while my bills keep pouring in all the time. Moreover, while I cannot plead poverty, my debts have increased in proportion to my income, and in recent years I've had to turn increasingly to journalism to make ends meet. Most writers seem to be doing the same so that the field is fairly crowded, but I am nevertheless surprised at the extent to which freelance journalists are exploited by fellow scribes in lucrative, full-time employment.

Few in-house feature-writers earn less than £30,000 a year, and many earn a good deal more. They all, of course, have to be given office space and computers, and all enjoy pensions and other fringe benefits. Given the number of articles they are expected to file in the course of a year, I would say that each article must cost the paper at least £1,500. How does that compare with the crumbs thrown to the freelance?

I have no complaints about the tabloids, bless 'em, which are usually generous and sometimes extravagant, but the heavies are another matter. *The Times* in particular gives the impression that anyone privileged enough to appear in its pages should, if paid at all, be content with a token fee.

About a year ago I was invited, at short notice, to write an obit of a colourful, if controversial figure, with whom I had been on fairly close terms. I was, however, unfamiliar with his early history and I had to make numerous phone-calls to check my facts. The piece was only about 700 words long, but it was a day's work, for which I was eventually paid £45. I wasn't sure whether to cash it or frame it. (That, I must add, was in the Grays Inn Road days. A recent cheque from Wapping was more substantial.)

The *Guardian* has a religious affairs editor—which is rather like the *Methodist Recorder* having a wine editor—in the person of Walter Schwarz. He somehow manages to produce a lively and controversial column, but only offers contributors—and this without blush—£80 per 1,000 words.

Any old hack can cough up 1,000 words in an hour, and I've done it myself in half that time on a bad line with guns pounding in my ears and the ground quaking under my feet, but a cogently argued piece demands time for reflection. It cannot be written in much less than a day and £80 for a day's work is less than generous. (In any case the length of a piece, as far as I'm concerned, is immaterial, for I start with a long article and boil it down to a short one, so that, as a rule, the shorter the piece the longer it takes me.)

The *Observer* is almost as bad. I was recently asked to write an article on Elie Wiesel. Wiesel is a prolific writer and although I was familiar with his early work, some of his later works had escaped my attention, and I had to settle down to some quick reading. The article was only 1,000 words (the magic figure) but it took me two days to complete, for which I was offered £100. I haggled and eventually received £150.

In fairness I must add that the *Observer* has also sent me on exciting assignments to faraway places which I would never have been able to visit at my own expense, but none of the assignments took me less than a week, some took as much as a fortnight, and I cannot recall that I was paid more than £300 for any of them.

The trouble with the *Guardian* and the *Observer* is that they both have a social conscience, and perhaps they keep their fees low to give their contributors first-hand experience of the poverty and hardship on which they dwell at such length.

The weekly reviews are not particularly generous, but their circulation is small, their resources are very small and so, alas, are their cheques. Even so they are, in comparative terms, infinitely more generous than the heavies. *The Spectator* is paying £90 for this article, which will not make me rich, but it is probably more than I would have got from the *Guardian*.

The worst offender, however, is BBC Radio. Local Radio pays nothing at all, while national radio pays next to nothing. I was recently invited to Broadcasting House and spent about half an hour chatting to a charming and attractive young lady from *Woman's Hour*. I don't know what part (if any) of our conversation was actually broadcast, but the excursion more or less killed the afternoon and I was paid £21.95.

The BBC can plead in mitigation that it is almost as mean to its own staff as to freelance contributors, but what can the papers say? Well, I can quote the former editor of one colour magazine verbatim: "We only manage on our budget because we screw the freelance."

The Spectator, 30 January 1988

Of Fish
and Flesh

Liver and Life

THE SAN FRANCISCO Jewish community centre is holding its first annual "Best Chopped Liver Ever" (as distinct from the best ever chopped liver) contest. The idea, I think, is a good one, for chopped liver is about the only Jewish thing one finds in many an American Jewish centre, and its very Jewishness demands that it be the best ever. And there is also something to be said for striving after excellence for its own sake. But how did we become a nation of liver-fanciers? "Tell me where," asked Shakespeare, "is fancy bred? In the heart, or in the head?" I think it's in the liver. So, probably, did Shakespeare, only liver doesn't rhyme with bred.

The English, as we know, are a nation of beef-eaters, the French eat frogs, the Italians veal, the Muslims mutton, the Chinese pork, but we Jews, if one may coin a term, are icthyverous, which is to say, we are fish-eaters, both in this world and, it would seem, the next, for is it not written that at the end of days the righteous shall feast of Leviathan (the unrighteous, I dare say, if they should feast at all, will have to feast of herring). The chicken too can claim a place in Jewish lore, but not so much as a food as a medicine. The body of the bird, it was believed, was designed for people in delicate health, like expectant mothers, while the rest of the family made do with what would nowadays be called the "spin-offs", chicken-soup, chicken-schmaltz and, the most delicious and poisonous Jewish dish of all, *gribnes* (the skin and onions fried in schmaltz). In fact the spin-offs were often better than the spin-ons.

One should perhaps add that the Jewish chicken of lore and yore should not be spoken of in the same breath as the repellent product of the factory farm which look as if they have been made out of papier mâché and, indeed, taste like it. In America they call tuna-fish "sea-chicken", as if this was some sort of recommendation: they would be far wiser to call chicken "land-tuna".

When one comes to meat one comes upon something unhallowed and unsung, and which is just about tolerated, and I daresay Jews would be content to go meatless altogether, but for one thing—the liver. And here too, I suspect there may be a connection with health. The very name, whether in English, Yiddish or German, suggests it. There is almost a tacit belief that where there's liver there's life and that anyone who eats enough is sure of an extended innings.

The Hebrew (and Arabic) for liver, *kaved*, means honour, which suggests that they put it on an even higher plane than life, while the French put it on a higher plane still, for *foi* also means faith, but then to the French eating has always been a quasi-religious activity. To an extent the same is true of the Jews, for are we not told that the Jewish home is a temple (or rather a mini-temple) and that the Jewish table is an altar? And is there one among us who has not sacrificed his digestive system on it?

Liver has all the properties of what is regarded as a delicacy among Jews. It is rich, heavy, nutritious, slightly bitter and almost wholly indigestible. Taken neatly, in fact, the taste is indelicate, and the price even more so, and it is therefore generally served as chopped liver. The components of chopped liver tend to vary with the chopper, what he or she may have to hand which she or he wants to get rid of, and the price of liver, but the usual ingredients, apart that is from the liver itself, are eggs, onion, bread and schmaltz. Chopped anything is a means of making a little go a long way (if caviare were kosher, we would have chopped caviare) and in some cases the liver is made to go so far as to be virtually out of sight (and out of taste), which, I suggest, is how eggs and onions came to be considered a Jewish delicacy in its own right.

It may seem surprising that something so rich and heavy should be served as a starter, which it almost invariably is, but it is offered up as a form of reassurance that whatever else may, or may not, follow no one will leave the table hungry. It is particularly suited for those barmitzvot and weddings where they have a speech or two (or even three) between each course, for it not only sustains one over the hiatus, it dulls one's critical faculties. And finally, it adds weight and sense of occasion to a reception, and in fact *kaved* is also the word for heavy, and liver, honour and weight indeed go together.

What is surprising is that this most traditional of traditional

Jewish foods should be celebrated in San Francisco of all places, the native home of the *avant garde*. When I was there about ten years ago most people seemed to be counting calories as a nun counts her beads, and nearly everyone I met was living on dried sea-weed and matzo.

Now whatever may be said for chopped liver, it is decidedly not a dish for the calorie-conscious, but that, as I said, was ten years ago, which is a long time in the life of San Francisco, and it may be that the slimming craze has given way to the belief that bulk is beautiful.

Better a meal of herbs and love therewith, than a stalled ox and hate therewith, but better still a plate of chopped liver.

Jewish Chronicle, 27 August 1972

A Snorter

YOU WILL NO doubt have read of the kosher pig. Israel was agog with the news and for a time people spoke of nothing else, partly, no doubt, because it made a change from inflation.

I, for my part, have hitherto refrained from comment because I wanted further and better particulars, for even if it is wrong to look a gift-horse in the teeth, one can, I think, be forgiven for probing in the tonsils something which purports to be a kosher pig. In other words, I wanted to see the animal face to face to establish whether it had not only cloven hooves (which all pigs have), but fins and scales (which most pigs haven't), and to date, I confess, I have failed in this endeavour.

My first reaction was to suspect that our friends in the Hebrew University had been up to some new mischief. It was, you will remember, scientists at the Hebrew University who crossed a goat with an IBX to produce something called a yaez. What was to stop them from crossing a sow with some sort of kosher computer to produce a kosher pig? I, however, gather that this particular pig evolved without the benefit of scientists and that it, or rather its forebears, did their own dirty work.

The idea of a kosher pig may, on the face of it, seem a contradiction in terms, but, as I have already pointed out, it has cloven hooves, which suggests that it is already half kosher. Moreover, the Hebrew for pig (*chazir*) can also mean return, and there are eminent sages who have argued that it is so called because one day "the Holy One will return it to Israel", which is to say that it will become as acceptable on Jewish tables as boiled chicken or gefilte fish.

The Talmud, which has something to say on everything, refers to a fish called the *sheebuta*, which sounds like a cross between a sheep and a boot, but which, apart from the grunt, was said to have many of the properties of a pig and which, according to Rashi, tasted exactly like pork. (If you should think I'm making this up, which I suspect you may, you will find it mentioned at the bottom of page 109b of the tractate Chulin.)

My own fishmonger has never heard of it. Harrods, too, confessed that the name didn't ring a bell, though they were prepared to look into it for me; and it is not on the menu of Wheeler's, Manzi's or the Trattoria Del Pescatori, but the Talmud speaks not whereof it knows not, and if one can have sea-lions and dog-fish and cat-fish and wolf-fish, why not pig-fish?

If *sheebuta* tastes exactly like pork, smoked *sheebuta* could make a passing substitute for bacon, and would probably be cheaper than smoked salmon. Think of it, *sheebuta* and eggs! It would revolutionise the Jewish breakfast, though first, of course, you've got to catch your *sheebuta*.

But this is taking us away from our subject, for no one has suggested that the *sheebuta*, for all its porcine properties, is in itself a porker. The kosher pig should offer a taste of the real thing, and I can envisage a time when no barmitzvah celebration will be complete without a boar's head (with apple in mouth) at the top table.

The rabbis, in the meantime, have approached the matter with circumspection, and who can blame them? It's all they need. They have trouble enough establishing that the beef, mutton and poultry we eat is kosher (or not, as the case may be), and to add pork to their burden would test the wisdom and integrity of even a Federation Beth Din.

One rabbi, however, was apparently so bold as to suggest that a pig could be kosher provided it displayed all the characteristics of a kosher animal and provided its mother was of unimpeachably kosher origin—say a cow—which, I think, is asking a lot of a pig, but then Judaism has always demanded more of newcomers to the fold than of those who are, so to speak, born into it.

If the kosher pig should, indeed, prove to be kosher—and it will not only need a cow as a mother, but a fox as a father, to pass the scrutiny to which it will be subjected—it will blunt the edge of many a popular Yiddish expression. *A chazer bleibt a chazer* (a pig remains a pig), for example, is clearly meaningless when some pigs don't, and the even more familiar *treif vi chazer* and other such colourful expressions will become obsolete.

There are, I should imagine, a whole host of people who will relish the thought of going the whole hog—of *lebenlig a chazersher tog* (living a pig's day)—without imperilling their mortal souls, but most Jews I know prefer sea-food to meat of any variety, and they would be much more excited by the prospect of kosher lobster.

No doubt it will come. Lobsters' hooves are even more markedly cloven than those of the pig. Let someone discover a variety which chews the cud and his fortune is made.

Jewish Chronicle, 30 November 1984

The Whole Hog

THE RECENT KNESSET Bill against pig-breeding in Israel occasioned little controversy. There is already such an Act on the statute book, dating from 1962, but hardly anyone has a good word for pigs and it is nice to have a measure before the House on which almost all parties can agree.

I dare say it will now be difficult for anyone to board an El Al plane with a live pig (or even a dead one) in his hand-luggage, but it will otherwise be difficult, and expensive, to enforce and, in lieu of enforcement, I anticipate that we shall eventually have a third anti-pig Bill. It could even become an annual event, like the State opening of Parliament in Britain, and serve as a focus for national unity.

There are obvious reasons why we should be hard on pig-eaters, but why are we so hard on pigs? What have they done to excite such opprobrium?

Among Yiddish-speaking Jews, it was a thing so abhorred that few dared sully their lips with its actual name, and it was referred to by euphemisms like "the other thing", or "the four-footed one". It is still, of course, the ultimate non-kosher article, and the classical means for a Jew to abjure his faith is to eat a ham sandwich on Yom Kippur and invite God to strike him dead. In Israel, presumably, they use crackling in pitta.

(There is the story of the rabbi and Catholic priest who decided to abjure their respective faiths at the same time and embarked immediately upon forbidden pleasures. When they later compared notes, they agreed that, on balance, pork was better, because, as the rabbi put it, "You can always have it with latkes".)

The pig is detested not only among Jews. Muslims, of course, also

283

ban it from their tables, and while Christians eat it with relish, the word for pig—with such variants as swine, hog, boar and sow—is used as a pejorative expression in almost every society one can name.

The only major exception that I've heard of is China, where, I am told, they speak well of pigs not only as food, but as living creatures; and I can only presume that China is an exception because it has been largely untouched by the influence of the Bible.

Yet, if we turn to the relevant passages in Leviticus and Deuteronomy, we find that the pig is but one abomination among many, and they include rabbits, hares, camels, eagles, ospreys, glebes, vultures, kites, ravens, hawks, cuckoos, little owls, great owls, swans, pelicans, cormorants, storks, herons, lapwings and bats, to say nothing of things which creep on the ground, or which live in the waters but have no fins or scales.

Why, then, should the pig have been singled out for special treatment? Why does no one speak of food as being "as trefa as ospreys"?

The devout Jew cannot even keep a pig as a pet, yet there is nothing to prevent him from filling his house with vultures and lapwings, or his belfry with bats. (I have accumulated a few myself.)

And finally, why, if the Knesset has already passed two Bills against pigs, does it not go the whole hog and pass a third against rabbits, hares, camels, little owls, great owls, pelicans, etc?

The pig is not a thing of beauty, but then, neither is the camel. It has unsanitary habits, but, with the exception of cats, no mammals are clean. It may be greedy, but less so that cats.

What is perhaps more to the point, the pig, with its cloven hooves, is halfway to being kosher, and there is even a legend that it is called *chazir* (which is Hebrew for return) because it will one day learn to chew the cud and return to the favours of Israel. (Which brings me to a question for my colleague, the Rabbi. Lobsters have cloven hooves. If they could be trained to chew the cud, would they be kosher?)

For some reason which I have never been able to fathom, numerous Jewish legends associate the pig (or rather the boar) with the Roman legions which conquered Judea, and all the animosity which the Jew felt against Rome descended upon the head of the poor, innocent pig.

What makes it all the more unfair is the fact that the emblem of imperial Rome was, of course, the eagle, yet the eagle, far from being hated or despised, enjoys an exalted place in Jewish lore, though, as I have shown, it isn't even kosher.

Will no good-hearted soul form a society of friends of the pig? In the meantime, I say, hands off the pig: it has been underdog for long enough.

Jewish Chronicle, 20 December 1985

Say Cheese!

HAVE I SAID it before? If so I think I may be forgiven for saying it again, for Shavuot is quite my favourite festival. It only lasts two days (or one if you're in Israel); the services are not unduly prolonged, as on Rosh Hashana; there is no fasting or mortification as on Yom Kippur; no need to perish in the succah as on Succot, and there is no damned nonsense about unleavened bread or unleavened everything else as on Pesach.

One can eat anything one likes and one is particularly encouraged to indulge in dairy foods, which I particularly adore, and especially cheesecake and blintzes. There have been moments in my life when I have had the deepest reservations about Judaism, but I have always come round to the view that a faith which actually requires the faithful to eat cheesecake and blintzes must have something to commend it.

Doctors, who are spoil-sports by training, and sometimes by nature, have in recent years been spreading the belief that dairy foods are poisonous, but then they are inclined to condemn almost everything one enjoys. In that respect they remind me somewhat of the rabbis who think up a new prohibition every week, and any day now some bright young medic will come out with the news (if, indeed, he hasn't done so already) that the milk from one's mother's breasts is likely to damage your health, if it's not downright poisonous.

Doctors are concerned with keeping people alive and not with living, which does not mean that their warnings should be ignored, but they should be kept in perspective. Better a meal of blintzes and joy therewith, than a meal of herbs and old age therewith.

The clinical evidence on the toxicity, or otherwise, of dairy foods is inconclusive. I know men in their eighties who have waxed on a diet of butter and cream, and others in their forties who have waned on a diet of steamed fish and spinach. I once worked for a famous film-director, a Scot, who was upbraided by a health-conscious colleague for smoking and drinking too much, and he retorted: "My father smoked sixty Woodbines and drank a bottle of Glenfiddich a day. He lived to be ninety-five and when he'd been dead for a week he looked better than you do now."

When our children were younger (and less discriminating) we used to take our holidays at a vegetarian hotel on the East Coast. It was full of health cranks and food fadists who would let nothing pass their lips which might have been considered unwholesome even by a doctor, but I've never seen a more unhealthy bunch of people under one roof. Their very company was as good as an illness. A preoccupation with health—which I'm sorry to say is very common among Jews—is in itself unhealthy.

I will admit that the general statistics on the matter do, on balance, support the doctors' view that dairy foods may be harmful, but there is no doubt whatever that they are delicious and where one has to weigh the *possible* dangers in a food against the *certain* pleasures, I am inclined to decide in favour of the pleasures.

All sorts of mystical reasons have been suggested for the tradition of eating dairy foods on Shavuot, and one of the most frequently quoted is that the Torah (which was given on Shavuot) is compared to milk. The similarities between them have always escaped me, but if word of the comparison should reach our doctors they may proscribe the Torah as a health hazard.

For my part, I am perfectly convinced that the tradition has its source in the practical good sense and economic literacy of the Jewish housewife. Shavuot happens to be our one and only summer festival. The weather can get hot even in England and before the advent of fridges and freezers the milk went off in a matter of hours. Nowadays it would be poured down the sink, but in the old days it was made into curds and whey (which makes me suspect that little Miss Muffet was Jewish) and cheese, which in turn was made into cheesecakes and blintzes. We all know that necessity is the mother of invention. In this instance it is the mother of mitzva, and Shavuot is one of the two occasions in the year (the other being Purim) when I live like a *tsadik*.

Damn the doctors, bless the rabbi doctors, and put thy trust in blintzes.

Jewish Chronicle, 29 May 1987

Courses for Horses

WHEN ONE IS young one learns that more than a few things in life one yearns for are not kosher. As one gets older one discovers that even if they are kosher, they're not healthy. The most obvious example of this are dairy foods. When I was a lad, cream, butter and eggs were regarded not merely as food but as elixirs. If someone was run-down one topped him up with all three, while the household remedy for most childhood ailments was *goggl-moggl*, a concoction composed of the yolk of an egg beaten into cream with sugar and then mixed with boiled milk. Even if it did not always cure the ailment, it was a compensation for it. Today all three would be condemned as poison, dairy foods are regarded as a health hazard and friends pull one aside with the warning: "Put not thy trust in blintzes."

The dread word is, of course, cholesterol. I used to think it was an engine oil and wondered what it could have been doing in the blood; now I know. Every time I see my doctor she drains off half a pint of blood to check my cholesterol count (that's her story, though I half suspect she's a closet vampire). My cholesterol count, you may (or may not) be glad to hear, is all right but I'm beginning to suffer from anaemia—and acute cheesecake deficiency.

It used to be said that a little of what you fancy does you good, which was taken by Jews to mean that a lot of what you fancy does you better. That, however, was long before we allowed rabbis and doctors to run our lives, and if the former demand that we forgo the pleasures of this world for the joys of the next, the latter insist that we forgo the pleasures of living for the joys of longevity. If they had their way we would all be subsisting on a diet of distilled water and *matzos*. It doesn't mean that everyone who followed their prescrip-

288

tion to the letter would live to be 120, but they would feel as if they did. Doctors are trained to be kill-joys but British doctors are not half as bad as their American colleagues. In Britain, at least, a food is presumed to be benign until it is shown to be harmful; in America it is taken to be harmful unless it is shown to be benign. I was therefore not entirely surprised to come across an article in the *Journal of the American Medical Association* by a Dr. Chaya Rubin and Dr. Albert Wu which condemned even *chrayn* as poisonous. (I was a little mystified by the involvement of Dr. Wu in the piece and can only conclude that there are now so many kosher Chinese restaurants that they even serve chop suey with chrayn.)

Chrayn, or *armoracia lapathifolia*, is generally known in the English-speaking world by the unflattering name of "horseradish", which suggests that only horses would eat it. As a matter of fact only a horse would touch the sort of bland preparations generally available in English shops. But real five-star, high-octane, *heimishe* chrayn, of the type I normally prepare (there are some things which cannot be trusted to one's womenfolk) is another matter, for even a tiny dollop sends steam hissing out of the ears and down the nostrils, while a large one can induce a sense of levitation.

Dr. Chaya Rubin says she was moved to write the article when her aged father keeled over after swallowing a mouthful of chrayn at a Passover seder. She didn't say how much matzo he had eaten before he ate the chrayn, or how much haroset (almond and wine paste) or, indeed, how aged he was, and in any case the good man soon recovered, which suggests that he may have merely passed out in a fit of ecstasy.

Horseradish is of Iberian origin (hence, no doubt, the saying: "the chrayn in Spain stays mainly in the plain"), but oddly enough it never took root among the Sephardim, and it was Polish and Lithuanian Jews who discovered its unique properties and who still cherish them. Though marvellously piquant, chrayn is not a food as such, nor even a condiment, but rather a local anaesthetic which temporarily deadens the taste buds so as to render almost any food—such as gefilte fish—palatable. No Jewish table should be without it and any attack upon it is an attack on basic Jewish traditions and Jewish life—sheer antisemitism.

But not only that. The pious, as we know, will be rewarded for their self-denial in this world with a feast of leviathan in the next, and whoever feasted on leviathan without chrayn?

Israel Scene, Sep.–Oct. 1988

Hooray for Herrings

DELICATESSEN, AS THE name suggests, means delicate edibles, but delicate these edibles are not. They assault the sense, savage the palate, ravage one's innards and announce themselves in loud, pungent terms so that one gets wind of them long before one catches sight of them. But I love them.

Basically they are titbits and are designed to excite the appetite rather than assuage it. As food they are meant principally for the non-hungry, the non-domesticated, those who can just summon the energies to open a tin of pâté de foie gras or unwind a rollmop.

I was born in what is now Russia, and when I came to Scotland shortly before the war the small Jewish grocery shops in the Gorbals district of Glasgow were my main link with home. I still remember their names: Ixe's, Fogels, Ettingers, Callendars. And their wares: huge, steaming loaves of black Russian bread, glossy bagels, crispy pretzels, cinnamon cakes, long, crudely circumcised phallic rolls of salami, pickled gherkins and—their hallmark—open barrels of salt herrings. I only had to shut my eyes and inhale and I was back in Russia.

To me delicatessen means herring, 1,001 varieties of herring, but I did not always regard them as such if only because I virtually lived on them. The herring was to the Eastern European Jew what potatoes were to the Irish, which is surprising, for the herring is a salt-water fish and in Russia and Poland one rarely got a glimpse of the sea. But Jews know a good thing when they taste it and alighted on the herring because it was inexpensive, piquant, nutritious and versatile.

The herring was never quite considered a member of the fish family. The carp and pike, which were found locally, were kitted out with lavish trimmings and served on the Sabbath and at festivals.

The humble herring was treated as crude workaday fare, and in our household we might have pickled herring on Sunday, soused herring on Monday, herrings in sour cream on Tuesday, schmaltz herring on Wednesday, and herrings fried in matzo meal on Thursday.

When we moved to Scotland I discovered the greatest delicacy of all—the smoked herring, or kipper. I am sure the warm affinities between Scots and Jews arise out of appreciation of herrings.

I also came upon a mysterious animal I had not seen before: much larger than the herring, redder and infinitely more expensive. They called it smoked salmon and I immediately concluded it was some sort of rich man's herring.

The Gorbals is no more and neither are the small Jewish grocery shops. One is hard pressed even to find them in London. Instead one has delicatessens which are more brightly lit and infinitely more hygienic than the small corner shops I have known, but with their fridges and freezers and extraction fans they have tamed their wares and robbed them of their pungency.

One's sense of smell, always deeply involved in the joy of the delicatessen, has been rendered virtually redundant. But more than that, all the goods, and especially the innumerable varieties of herring, have gone upmarket. If salmon is still the rich man's herring, one can no longer think of herrings as the poor man's salmon for they have become so expensive that one buys them by the troy ounce.

All of which shows that one man's staple is another man's delicatessen or, rather, that the necessities of one generation can become the luxuries of the next.

The Independent, 7 October 1989

Smoked Salmonella

I USED TO think that salmonella poisoning was something people caught from a surfeit of smoked salmon (and serves them right, too), but who would have believed that one could catch it from something as innocent as an egg?

I not only go to work on an egg (in so far as I go to work at all), I go to sleep on an egg. Which is to say that I like to whisk up the yellow of an egg with hot milk and a drop (well, maybe two drops) of brandy. An excellent soporific, and it works like a sermon.

The egg is a staple of the Jewish diet and enters in one guise or another into every Jewish dish you could name (and quite a few you couldn't), if only because it's the poor man's protein. Those who couldn't afford fish or flesh usually had a chicken or two scratching around in the back yard so that they could always be sure of an egg.

Thus one finds eggs in chopped herring, and eggs in chopped liver, and in cholent and kugel and borscht and lokshen pudding and latkes and kreplech and kneidlech and kichel and fisnogge (otherwise known as calf's foot jelly or putcha), and, of course, egg and onions, and eingemachts. (I don't know what eingemachts is, but I can't imagine it being made without eggs, because Jewish cooking sans eggs isn't Jewish—which is perhaps why so many Jews are egg-shaped.)

I should imagine that the average Jew consumes at least twenty eggs a week, in one form or another, but when it comes to Pesach, the number must be nearer 100. I know whereof I speak, for I am an expert in, and a devotee of, matzo brei—which should really be called matzo fry. A good brei calls for at least one egg per square foot of edible matzo (and more if one uses shemura matzo); and since a sizeable family can go through about an acre of matzo brei in the course of the festival, it could consume something like 4,840 eggs.

One also uses prodigious quantities of eggs in matzo balls, matzo pudding and a delightfully light soufflé of my wife's making which I call matzo-do-about-nothing. There is also, of course, the egg in salt water which one eats at the seder and which makes a rather delicious hors d'oeuvre. (I have tried eating it at other times and it's quite tasteless. I suspect it seems delicious at the seder because after the long haul through the Hagada almost anything seems delicious.)

I suppose eggs are particularly useful on Pesach because they are about the only food which does not have to be licensed by the Beth Din as *kasher le-Pesach* (though, no doubt, that will come). This does not mean, of course, that all eggs are kosher. One blood-spot renders them unfit for Jewish consumption. We once had a very kosher relative staying with us who thought she saw something which, if examined under an electronic micro scope, might have proved to be a blood-spot, and she threw out half the eggs she cracked. By the time she had finished, I had nearly cracked her.

I understand that the chances of coming down with salmonella poisoning from eating an egg are one in 200 million. If one eats 100 eggs during Pesach, the chances are reduced to one in two million. The chances of coming down with matzo poisoning are, I would say, rather greater than that.

A Pesach without eggs would be inconceivable (no pun intended), and—though strictly speaking that isn't our problem—I find it even more difficult to imagine an eggless Easter. The egg has an established place in Jewish lore and gives its name to an entire volume of the Talmud which is called Egg—not Good Egg, or Bad Egg, but simply Egg, which must be one of the shortest titles in all literature.

A hard-boiled egg is also, traditionally, the first food one eats on returning from a funeral. I am not sure why the egg should have become a symbol of mourning. Perhaps our rabbis knew something about salmonella poisoning that we didn't, hence their insistence on having the eggs hard-boiled.

I am saddened by the doubts cast on this most benign and versatile of foods. When I was a child, eggs were not only considered healthy, but were thought of as an actual health food, and they formed the basis of a whole host of home-brewed medicines. Strange how the elixirs of one generation become the health hazards of another.

Jewish Chronicle, 23 December 1988

O Sole Mio!

GIVE A PLACE a bad name, and it's made. When I was a schoolboy in Glasgow, one could not open a paper without reading about London's "square mile of vice", as Soho was then known, and I could not wait to see it with my own eyes. I did not have to wait long for, by chance, one of the first jobs I got after leaving university was in Golden Square, right in the heart of Soho.

It was all very disappointing. It was bizarre rather than vicious, and where one might have expected the sounds of murder and mayhem, one got the whish and hiss of espresso coffee machines.

All this was about 30 years ago, before the Sixties had got into its swing. There were coffee bars on every corner and, as they all served the same froth from the same Gaggias, they vied with one another in the individuality of their décor.

I particularly remember one coffee bar all in black where one sat on coffin-shaped chairs at coffin-shaped tables, whose waiters—likewise in black—looked as if they were newly risen from their graves and were half-minded to go back to them.

There were also any number of "Peep-aramas" and "Strip-aramas" and occasional tarts who importuned passers-by, as early as 10 in the morning, with offers of "a good time". But these did not give the dominant colour to the place, for the sort of carnal pleasures one sought in Soho were connected with food and drink.

They still are. Many of the restaurants I frequented then—Isow's, Goody's, Kettners, Folemans, Schmidts—are, alas, no more, but I recently paid a return visit to one of my favourites, L'Epicure in Frith Street, and was delighted to find that it is not only still flourishing, but that it is as it was, in almost every detail.

The facia and interior are the same; the fading floral carpet is the

294

same (only more faded); the banquettes and chairs are the same. The same chefs and the same waiters seem to be doing the same jobs, and if the service (of which more later) is not particularly fast now, it was not particularly brisk then.

The menu is much the same but the prices are not, and where a meal for two might have cost a fiver, the shindig I am about to describe cost £84 which, though not extravagant by London standards (for we had drinks before, during and after the meal), is not cheap.

The clientele, as I remember it, used to consist mainly of fat publishers and lean authors and dapper media men with exotic companions. It is now made up largely of suburban couples who seem to enjoy the food rather more than each other's company.

L'Epicure is, of course, a French restaurant and its speciality is flambés. As we approached it on a wet blustery January night, it looked like a flaming soufflé itself, for its facia was lit up by huge gas flambeaux. Inside, the place was loud with the spit and crackle of steaks being put to the torch.

I had better confess here to an aversion of flambés. I am heavily bearded and once, while bent over a pair of flaming crêpe suzettes, I caught fire and my companion did not help things by trying to douse the flames with a Rémy Martin. It is one thing to be barbecued, quite another also to lose a glass of Rémy Martin, and I now prefer my food to be prepared in the kitchen.

Flambéry is a piece of showmanship, for the food itself is not always the better for it although it adds an element of drama to an otherwise mundane dish. A steak is only a steak, but steak flambé is theatre (better theatre in fact than *Jeffrey Bernard is Unwell*, which we saw after the meal).

For my part I find a good meal in a first-class establishment exciting enough in itself and, in any case, I feel that one should judge a restaurant not on its specialities (for which it is, after all, readily geared), but on the dishes it serves almost with reluctance.

My wife began with a meal of herbs, asparagus, mushrooms, artichoke hearts, mange-tout and celery, all selected from a hors-d'oeuvres trolley which had about every edible one could imagine, and a few one could not.

I had a plate of marinated salmon with fennel and mustard sauce which was at once fiery and piquant, over which I enthused so much that my wife, having demolished her plateful, went on to demolish mine.

She then ordered a trout cooked with ginger and spring onions in a soya sauce. I ordered a Sole Colbert. I made the mistake of asking if the fish was fresh and they may have waited for the trawlers to come in, for it was nearly an hour before we were served. But the result was worth waiting for.

This time we both enthused so loudly over our respective dishes that I found myself eating my wife's trout, while she disposed of my sole. The accompanying vegetables—spinach and broccoli—were so tender and crisp, so deliciously underdone, that I suspect they bless them rather than cook them.

We had a chablis '87 with an ashen tang which went perfectly with the sole, though I would have preferred a red wine with the trout.

We did not intend to have a sweet, but once they wheeled the trolley under our noses we were lost. My wife had a strawberry concoction which proved to be too solid, almost cheesy, and too rich. I had a crème caramel, cut a hole in its sugar topping Eskimo-fashion and scooped out the innards. It was a generous helping and I finished the lot.

"You'll be sorry," said my wife. I was.

Coffee is a come-down in most London restaurants, but not in L'Epicure. I had cup after cup and wound up the meal with—what else?—a Rémy Martin.

The food, the wine and the ambience may all be warmly recommended if you are not short of time or money.

The Independent, 10 February 1990

Fat of the Land

SIX HUNDRED DOCTORS have just spent a week in Jerusalem pondering on the problems of obesity, and a fat lot their deliberations will do anyone.

It is strange how what is ideal to one generation becomes a problem to the next. When I was a lad, health used to be measured in bulk. If you were gaining weight, you were healthy, and if you were losing weight, you were sick; and if you were badly run down, you would (if your funds ran to it, or even if they didn't) go away to be filled up.

Indeed, Jewish hotels, and Jewish cuisine, were dedicated to this belief—as they still are—and the most basic of all Jewish culinary ingredients was (and still is) schmaltz. To that extent, I suppose, there is a certain symbolism in the choice of Jerusalem as a venue for the obesity congress. Did they, I wonder, get Arik Sharon to open it?

When we read in the Bible that "Jeshurun waxed fat", it was almost certainly on either chicken or goose fat. The golden colour of chicken soup is merely melted schmaltz, and schmaltz, too, is an essential ingredient in almost every traditional Jewish dish one can name, including chopped liver, egg and onion, and latkes, while a cholent large enough to feed an average family contains enough schmaltz to lubricate a battleship.

As a result, anyone addicted to Jewish food (and who could afford to eat regularly) was likely to put on a bit of weight, and if he did, it was—as I have suggested—a sign of well-being. If you wished somebody that he should be *gezunt und shtark*, you really meant that he should be good and fat.

And bulk was accepted not only as a measure of health, but of

297

social standing and commercial well-being. The man of substance was a substantial man and carried his good fortune before him.

All this was also largely true of women. I still recall a ditty from my childhood which went: *Ite chaya is a mad fun drei hundert funt/nor zi halt in schreyen zi is nisht gezunt*, which, roughly translated, means, "Ite Chaya is a maid, weighs three hundred pound/but even so she keeps screaming that her health ain't sound"—as if to say, a woman of that weight couldn't be anything other than healthy.

In those days, the body beautiful was the body bulky. This was true not only of Jewish women. There is an old Irish song with the refrain, "Fat, fair and forty were all the toasts of the young men".

Girls approaching marriage were fattened up like steers in the plains of Nebraska and I remember brides who seemed a fair representation of Mother Earth and who filled most of the space under the chupa. There was custom in those days—it has since been revived—for the bride to circle the groom seven times: if the groom had had to do the circling, he would have needed a bicycle.

The sort of scraggy, undernourished, skeletal little things without poop or prow which one sees under the chupa these days would never have found a husband in the old days, not unless they were propped up with money bags.

All that has been reversed. I have friends who spend more on starving themselves than I spend on food.

It is, of course, true that excess of anything is harmful and there is, after all, the well-known case of King Henry I, who died of a surfeit of lampreys; but doctors are now putting it about that even a little of what you fancy—presumably even lampreys—does you harm.

Calories have become the new shibboleth, and if you take a young lady out to a meal, she'll start counting her calories as a nun might count her beads.

Doctors have it easy. If a writer wants to make a name for himself, he has to write a masterpiece. All a doctor has to do is to take some established orthodoxy and stand it on its head; and if he makes even a tentative case, colleagues will clamber on to his bandwagon and presto! a new prophet and a new orthodoxy have arisen.

An example. For a time it was thought that men who wanted to save their energies had to rest them. Then exertion became all the rage, and round where I lived one could not venture out of doors in the early hours of the morning without being trampled underfoot by joggers. Now the word has spread that jogging is dangerous and

I anticipate that doctors are about to discover the benefits of sleep.

For the time being the fat is—or rather the fat are—in the fire, but I'm willing to bet that a generation hence there will be a further medical congress in Jerusalem—on the problems of emaciation.

Jewish Chronicle, 19 September 1986

Of This
and That

Is the Queen Jewish?

WHO IS A Jew? Someone who has made it. There is nothing more Jewish than a yearning for *naches* and *yichus*. *Naches* means joy, and *yichus* means connections, but exalted connections, and the highest joy of all, therefore, is the *naches* which is to be had from *yichus*. It is the yearning for both which is at the source of what must be one of the oldest Jewish activities, the quest for Jews.

Nearly every family has relatives, and close ones at that, whom they don't speak about—and others, who may be comparatively remote, of whom they rarely cease speaking, but who make up in distinction what they lack in propinquity as, for example, a second cousin twice removed who has become a millionaire, or a movie star, or perhaps a celebrated athlete, or even a college professor. (One man's *yichus* is another man's embarrassment.)

Any book cataloguing Jewish achievement will cast a very wide net and come up with some curious names. There are, indeed, Jewish writers who will see proof of Jewishness in the very achievements of a man. For example, I have heard it argued (I think seriously) that Abraham Lincoln was Jewish, first, because he looked it, second because his name was Jewish, third, because there was a Scriptural ring to his utterances and finally—and this seemed to clinch the argument—"What *goy* would have had the vision to realize that slavery was finished?"

The late Cecil Roth, doyen of Jewish historians, Reader in Jewish Studies at Oxford University, author of numerous widely regarded and widely read works on Jewish life and Jewish history and, toward the end of this life, editor-in-chief of the *Encyclopaedia Judaica*, was an avid Jew collector and went after Jews as a lepidopterist goes after

303

butterflies though with a much wider net. He seriously suggested that Christopher Columbus was Jewish, mainly on the grounds that some of his best friends were Jews, a criterion which would have made a Jew out of King Edward VII or, for that matter, General Charles de Gaulle. He also added that the name Colon or Colombo was not uncommon among Italian Jews (Columbus was of course born in Genoa), that his signature was mysterious and "susceptible to a Hebraic interpretation" and that "he seems to have deliberately postponed the day of his sailing till August 3rd, while all was ready for the purpose on the previous day, which was the unpropitious fast day of the Ninth of Av". Taken together it was not the sort of evidence on which one could hang a man. Though Dr. Roth admitted that it was "impossible to exclude or confirm the hypothesis that he was descended from a Jewish or ex-Jewish family", he nevertheless found Columbus Jew enough to include in the *Encyclopaedia Judaica*.

He also felt it worthy of note that Rembrandt "lived among Jews, painted Jews and worked frequently under Jewish auspices. In view of all this it has been suggested, without any documentary evidence, that he was himself of Jewish blood." Which suggests Jewishness by contagion and overlooks abundant documentary evidence that Rembrandt was almost certainly not of Jewish blood.

More curious still was Dr. Roth's insistence that Sir William Herschel, the celebrated 18th-century astronomer, was "of Jewish birth". Here too there is no documentary evidence, but "the name is typically Jewish, and he came over from Germany as a musician in a Hanoverian band".

Now it is true that Herschel was a common Jewish name, but it was also a common German name (which is why it was common among Jews), and while many Jewish 18th-century immigrants came from Germany, not every German immigrant was a Jew, and neither, for that matter, was every German musician. (It reminds one of the widely held belief that George Brown, a Cabinet minister in the 1964 Labour government, was a Jew because he had worked in the fur trade, and that Cecil B. de Mille was a Jew because he was a movie mogul. John Strachey, Minister of Food in the 1945 Labour government, was thought to be Jewish because he had a long nose, but not even Roth drew on appearances as proof of Jewishness.)

Roth's Jewish collection is to be found in his *Jewish Contribution to Civilisation*, published in 1938 (though it also spills over into the

Encyclopaedia Judaica), and it inspired a similar work edited by the late Dagobert D. Runes, called *The Hebrew Impact on Civilisation*, published in 1952. The Runes work, which out-Rothed Roth, was disposed to regard everyone who was anyone as Jewish, unless he could prove otherwise.

Thus, for example, Runes lists Karl Landsteiner as a Jew. Landsteiner, a pathologist of international repute, discovered the basic human blood groups and the Rhesus factor (for which he was awarded the Nobel Prize), but he was in fact a Catholic and in the interwar years he sued a Jewish biographical dictionary for suggesting he was a Jew. There are extenuating circumstances, for Landsteiner was at least of Jewish origin, but the book also suggests that the great 19th-century mathematician Ludwig Otto Hesse was likewise Jewish because in spite of his eminence it took him many years to get a professorship—a criterion which would make Jews out of a great many people.

The name of Herschel, not only of Sir William but also of Ferrer Herschel (they were not related), a 19th-century Lord Chancellor of England, also appears in the Runes book. Little is known about the first Herschel, so there is perhaps room for speculation, but a great deal is known about the second. Ferrer's mother was a gentile, and his father was not only a convert to Christianity but a missionary to the Jews. He himself was a member of the Church of England and could not (at least in 19th-century England) have been Lord Chancellor had he been anything else.

The most assiduous Jew-seeker of all—as befits the most widely read Jewish newspaper in the world—is probably the London *Jewish Chronicle*.

"The J.C.", as it is affectionately known, has correspondents in most corners of the globe. It is uncertain whether these journalists are actually paid a bounty for discovering Jews in high places but they sometimes act as if they are. For about thirty years the *Chronicle* employed a film critic whose main joy in life was to find Jews, on screen if possible, but, if not, behind the camera as producers, directors, cameramen, lighting men, stunt men, continuity girls, clapperboard boys. If he failed in those places, he would turn to the distributor or cinema proprietor, who were almost invariably Jewish.

This tradition, though now defunct among *Chronicle* critics, is still extant in other parts of the paper. Thus, for example, after every

305

election there is a count of Jewish M.P.s, with a brief potted history of each. Among those sketched after the last election was Clement Freud, Liberal M.P. of the Ise of Ely (who is perhaps better known for his role—which he shares with a beagle—in a famous dog food advertisement). The J.C. must have felt on safe ground, for Freud is a grandson of Sigmund Freud, but he wrote in to protest that he is not a Jew, and does not care to be described as one. His name has been dropped from further such references, but he is still listed as a Jew in the *Jewish Year Book* (which is published by the J.C.). There seems to be a feeling in the councils of the *Chronicle* (and elsewhere) that the number of Jewish M.P.s is an index of the standing of British Jewry in the wider community.

The role of American Jewry is followed with almost equal assiduity. The following story, which appeared in the *Chronicle* while President Carter was choosing his Cabinet, is typical:

"President-elect Carter's choice of Mr. Theodore C. Sorensen to head the Central Intelligence Agency brings to four the number of Cabinet and Cabinet-level posts held by men of Jewish origin in the incoming administration.

"Mr. Sorensen had a Christian father and a Jewish mother, whose maiden name of Chaiken is Mr. Sorensen's middle name. Although he does not practise Judaism, Mr. Sorensen is reported to have told rabbinical friends: 'Halachically, I am a Jew.' He has not converted to Christianity.

"Nor has Dr. Harold Brown, who will be Defense Secretary, although he is non-practising and has a non-Jewish wife.

"The two other Carter appointees who are of Jewish origin are both converts. They are Mr. Michael Blumenthal, who will take over as Treasury Secretary, and Mr. James Schlesinger, a former Defense Secretary, who will be a special Presidential adviser on energy matters.

"Mr. Schlesinger will be elevated to a Cabinet place if and when Congress grants permission to Mr. Carter to establish a Department of Energy. A convert to Lutheranism, Mr. Schlesinger is considered a Lutheran theologian.

"Mr. Blumenthal, it now appears, converted to Christianity when he married a Presbyterian."

One would have thought that there was not much *naches* there. Of the four, none are practising Jews, and two are practising Christians, but the J.C. nevertheless felt the story to be worthy of front-page treatment on the supposition, presumably, that half a Jew is better than none, and four half-Jews are as good as two full ones.

British papers reporting an overseas story will tend to look for a British angle (which is usually why it is reported in the first place) and Jewish papers may be forgiven for doing the same, but the principle is never applied with consistency. For example, I suspect that at least one of the people involved in the Watergate scandal was "of Jewish origin", but if he was, one saw no mention of him in the Jewish press. Let me give a more concrete example. The nearest thing that Britain has had to Murder Inc. are the Kray Twins (who are both currently behind bars), a pair of gangsters from London's East End, who are half Jewish (and half Irish—an explosive mixture if ever there was one), yet I recall no reference to their activities, or their trial, in the J.C. Clearly Jewish papers are not so much after news as after *naches*, and there is little *naches*, and even less *yichus*, to be had from the career of a professional criminal, however newsworthy. One also senses an inference that positive achievement makes an otherwise tenuous semi-Jew into a full one.

There is of course a tendency for every nationality to claim the great as its own. I recall an article on modern literature in an American magazine which described both T. S. Eliot and W. H. Auden as American—the former, presumably, because he was born in America (though he was domiciled in England), the latter because he was domiciled in America (though he was born in England). Columbus is claimed by Italy and Spain (and half claimed by the Jews, or at least by Dr. Roth). Alexander Graham Bell is claimed by Scotland and America. Handel has been described as German and English, Picasso as Spanish and French.

Jewishness, being based on impalpables, offers wider scope for such claims, but two crucial factors, namely birthplace and domicile, count for nothing among Jews. (They possibly count too much elsewhere. Wellington, who was born in Ireland but did not like to be described as Irish, said the fact that one was born in a stable didn't make one a horse.)

The search of Jews is a search for reassurance, a desire to prove that whatever our detractors say about us, and whatever we've been through, we have not only survived but have triumphed, and wherever one turns in the firmament one can see the glow of Jewish stars. Yet, while searching for reassurance, we often alight on those very Jews who have either renounced their own Jewishness or have taken pains to keep it hidden. Is there not something at once paradoxical and indecent in taking pride in the achievements of Jews who are ashamed to be Jewish?

Roth's *Jewish Contribution to Civilisation* was essentially a public relations work written at a time when Jews were everywhere under attack. In seeking to refute the charge that Jews were *untermenschen* it went far toward suggesting that they were perhaps *ubermenschen*, but if read in the context of events it is a forgivable, perhaps even commendable work. The same is perhaps true of *The Hebrew Impact on Civilisation* (though it lacks Roth's elegance or style). But must we pursue the quest for Jews into our own times? It is one thing to invoke the name of a Disraeli who, though baptised in boyhood, displayed a constant feeling of association with Jewish people, but quite another to reach out for a Ferrer Herschel.

If we need *naches* and *yichus* (and who doesn't?) is there not enough to be found in the achievements of actual Jews? Must we flush out crypto-Jews and drag in ex-Jews? If we must, our opening question should read not, Who is a Jew—but who isn't?

Present Tense, Vol. 4 No. 4, Summer 1977

Beat the Band

JEWISH FUNCTIONS USED to have two major drawbacks, the food and the speeches. (There is a third in the shape of one's machatonim, but there's nothing one can do about them.)

The food, if my experience is anything to go by, has improved and if the inevitable chicken is not always well cooked it is at least well plucked, and one sees less of the ultimate horror of kosher cuisine, the parve ice-cream in the form of a white little mound with a plastic cherry on top, like a chilled breast. Speeches, moreover, have been getting fewer and better or, if not better, then at least shorter, but, as if afraid that a barmitzvah or a wedding might become a positively pleasurable event, we have been overwhelmed by a new affliction—the band.

But what, you may ask, is new about the band? Was not King David himself a musician? He was. Did they not have musicians in the very Temple service? They did. And were not the *Klei Tzemer* (the musical vessels) as they were called in *der heim*, not regarded with more affection (if not more respect) than the *Klei Kodesh* (the holy vessels)? They were and, to an extent, they still are.

Musicians are artists—nay, artistes—and if they have not always thought of the barmitzvah or wedding as the ideal occasion for the display of their art, they have added immeasurably to the gaiety of Jewish life. I have the deepest admiration for them, and can claim a sense of affinity with them, or at least, the trumpeters, saxophonists, clarinettists among them, if only because I used to perform on the shofar (or, to coin an expression, the *cor Juive*) in my youth. Long may they blow their guts out.

If so, what have I got against bands? I have nothing against them as such, but I have everything against one of the least called-for

309

miracles of modern science—the amplifier. It can, I will admit, give rise to important savings so that, with the necessary electronic bric-a-brac, a one-man-band can sound like a thirty-piece orchestra. The trouble is he often does and the resulting noise is insufferable.

You've heard of the Hatikvah or Hope Quarter of Tel Aviv. Well, there's also the Despair Quarter—it's where they have all the weddings. It consists largely of garages and banqueting halls (some of the premises, one suspects, serve as both), and at busy times of the year, with up to a dozen weddings celebrated at the same time, and up to a dozen bands going full blast, the buildings themselves go up and down in time to the music, while the entire area quakes.

A few years ago I encountered the grandfather of the bride rushing from the banqueting hall with his hands to his ears. "I can't stand the noise," he cried, and he was stone-deaf.

I used to think that Israeli musicians measured their effectiveness in decibels, but they have since moved on to the Richter scale, and the same thing is happening here.

Music at a function should form the background to the event and not overwhelm it, and even as accompaniment to dancing it need not pierce one's ear-drums.

Barmitzvahs and weddings are often reunions and one looks forward to seeing old friends, some of whom may have descended from remote corners of the globe, but given the amount of noise generated by the average band it is almost impossible to hear and be heard and one is reduced to semaphore or sign language.

Why all the noise? One reason, I think, is due to economy. As musicians become more expensive, fewer are employed, the few like to give a semblance of many, and the amount of noise is often in inverse ratio to the size of the band.

A second may be due to the fact that the musicians may have been deafened by their own amplifiers and are cheerfully unaware of the noise they're making.

It must be admitted that soft music would be lost at a Jewish function because we are loud eaters, and the musicians may resort to amplification out of the simple desire to be heard.

Musicians are sometimes in league with the caterers and if the music is loud enough people can't be heard complaining about the food.

But at the bottom of it all the loud noise may answer to a puritan streak in the Jewish character. If the English take their pleasures sadly, we take ours exuberantly, but we think we shouldn't, and we engage hands not to add to the gaiety of an occasion but as an atonement.

Jewish Chronicle, 4 August 1979

Kosher Kick-Off

JEWS, IT IS generally agreed, are a competitive race, but though they excel in commerce, science and the arts, they have been rather less accomplished in the field, and there is, I think something symbolic in the fact that Israel's national sport—basketball—is not a field game at all, but an indoor game.

But, then, is it not written that our uncle Esau (whom we have since disowned) was a "man of the field", while our forefather Jacob "was a plain man, dwelling in tents"; and it would seem that we not only dwell in tents, but play in them, and with limited success at that.

Our mental agility has stood in the way of our physical agility, and we comfort ourselves with King Solomon's adage that "the race is not to the swift". As a result, we have left swiftness to horses, and regard the fact that we are less rich in Olympic medallists than Nobel laureates with a certain amount of equanimity. One cannot win all the prizes, and one shouldn't want to.

It is otherwise in Israel. Israelis (to adapt a saying of the first Viscount Samuel) are like other Jews, only more so, and they do not go in for fun and games just for the fun of the game. They are earnest and purposeful and mean to win and, failing to convert Jews into sportsmen, they have taken to converting sportsmen into Jews.

In basketball hardly a season passes without some Black player being put through the hoops, to emerge as a fully blown, or even over-blown, Jew. Tel Aviv Maccabi, in particular, has a larger proportion of new Jews in its team than Mrs Thatcher has of old Jews in hers, and converts like Earl Williams and Aulcie Perry have become national heroes.

Each of them is said to be as good as any two Israeli players, but then they're about the size of any two Israeli players, and while the

312

natives have to hop, skip and jump to score a goal, the newcomers nonchalantly lean over the net and plop the ball in.

The Jew-making policy has clearly paid off, for Israeli basketball has become a force to be reckoned with nationally and internationally, and when Israel beat Russia in basketball last year, no one declared a national holiday; but it was nevertheless treated as one, and people spoke of it as another, and more wondrous, Entebbe.

No such triumphs have been claimed by Israeli football, and none is anticipated, and after the débâcle of the Israeli team in the World Cup there were people who felt that the Government, or at least the Rabbinate, should have proclaimed a fast.

It must be said that Jews are not at their best when it comes to their feet, if only because they are naturally inclined to using their hands. This, added to the traditional antipathy to field games, has formed a handicap which few Israeli footballers have been able to surmount, and Hapoel Haifa has therefore followed the precedent of Maccabi Tel Aviv and has imported a first-class player in the person of Peter Lorimer, of Leeds United.

One has to be Israeli to play in an Israeli team and, since the quickest way to become an Israeli is to become a Jew, Mr Lorimer went to New York and, after going through the usual rituals of immersion and circumcision, he has returned as Alon Ben-Avraham.

As Mr Lorimer is Scots, and as the Scots are widely believed to be the chosen race, I am not sure if the conversion was, strictly speaking, necessary, and, in a sense, he can now claim to be a Jew twice over.

I have often admired his playing over the years. He is a zealous and dedicated sportsman and he will no doubt give his heart and soul to the game, especially as he has already given something of his body. Israeli football will never be the same again.

Mr Lorimer's prompt acceptance as a Jew by the Ministry of the Interior will, I should imagine, be regarded ruefully by Miss Shoshana Miller. She, too, is a convert, but although she has been an earnest student of Judaism for the past twenty years, and went on aliya in fulfilment of her religious beliefs, the Ministry of the Interior has refused to register her as a Jewess, on the grounds that she was not converted by an Orthodox Beth Din.

Neither, of course, was Mr Lorimer, but he, as I said, is Scots, and a football international. Miss Miller may, for all I know, be Scots, but she does not play football, or even basketball. Perhaps she should take up hockey.   *Jewish Chronicle*, 7 February 1986

Laugh? I Nearly Cried

THE HONORARY OFFICERS of the Board of Deputies are usually moved to protest whenever the word "Jew" is uttered in public in other than a flattering context, but now it seems that even the name of Hitler cannot be taken in vain.

On 1 April, BBC-TV screened a harmless little spoof about a secret visit of Hitler to England and—*before either of them had seen it*—both the president and the senior vice-president of the Board fired off protests. "Hitler is no joke and it is in bad taste," thundered the first. "Surely the BBC would realise that there are some things you don't joke about, and this is one of them," fumed the second.

Had they acted in their private capacities they would have merely made fools of themselves, but acting as they did—on dubious grounds, I may add—in the name of the community, they made fools of us all.

Why shouldn't people laugh at Hitler? Jews, especially, have laughed at their adversaries through the ages and across the globe, and Haman, who in a sense embodies them all, is lampooned religiously every year.

Did anyone—even in the Board of Deputies—object when Charlie Chaplin made "The Great Dictator"? Or when Mel Brookes wrote "Springtime With Hitler"? One could argue that the former, though making fun of Hitler and everything he stood for, had serious intentions; but the latter was hilarious both in purpose and in effect.

And what of the recent Woody Allen film where the weedy little hero, Zelik, finds himself right next to the Fuehrer at a Nuremberg rally, and even goes as far as disrupting his speech?

During the war years, when Hitler was, indeed, no laughing matter, no variety turn was complete without some joke about that

314

familiar moustached figure. Three of the most popular characters in my favourite comic were Addy and Hermy and Musso the Wop ("He's a big-a-da flop"). There were even—oh fie for shame—lewd songs about the various Nazi leaders, the lewdest of which, sung to the tune of Colonel Bogey's march, and beginning, "Hitler has only got one . . ." may be heard even now. (I am, as part of my service to readers, prepared to supply the rest of the lines under plain cover to anyone over eighteen enclosing the necessary postage stamps.)

Laughter is an instrument of war. To make fun of someone is to diminish him, and one of the reasons why the Jews have, in the end, always prevailed against their enemies is that they have always been able to laugh at them.

Nothing one knows of either Dr Kopelowitz or Mr Moonman suggests that they are stupid or humourless as private individuals, and one can presume that either their judgement has been buckled by the weight of office, or that they are required by the traditions of their office to discharge a certain quota of protests every few months, and that if the occasions for them do not arise, they have to look for them and, if necessary, invent them.

The gentlemen do protest too much, methinks. It may be useful to keep the machinery of protest ticking over, but if the president and vice-president of the Board make angry representation on a piffling issue—or rather non-issue—of this sort, who will listen to them if they should have something important to complain about?

Having said that, I must add that I was nearly moved to protest to the BBC myself, not because the Hitler spoof was in poor taste, but because it was so unfunny. The actual fusion of real and mock films, in Woody Allen fashion, was brilliantly done, and the idea was a good one; but its comic possibilities were never fully explored, and the result was a good deal less amusing than the almost nightly cock-ups which are the redeeming feature of BBC news.

In mitigation, it must be added that *The Times* diary gave the game away by exposing the hoax before it was broadcast and thus virtually robbed the joke of its point.

Moreover, it is becoming increasingly difficult to concoct spoofs which out-spoof reality, and during a recent illness, when I spent many hours ogling the box, I received the distinct impression that All Fools' Day in Britain is a year-round affair.

Jewish Chronicle, 11 April 1986

Roads Ahead

AT THIS TIME of year when the trees are in bloom and the pavements are pink with cherry blossoms, Hampstead Garden Suburb is like a corner of Merrie England—or it would be but for the torrent of traffic which roars through it at all hours of the day and most hours of the night.

When originally laid out 80 years ago the Suburb, where I have the good fortune to live, was criss-crossed with lanes and footpaths and minor access roads, all of which still remain. Then came the rape. In 1928 a trunk road was pushed right through it to link the A1 to the north with the Archway to the south. The Suburb, which was almost a rural community, has not been quite the same since.

Local residents had protested in their genteel, restrained way and were brushed aside. They have since become more vociferous and less restrained, and when a plan was mooted to widen the trunk road in the early Seventies, they held rallies, protests, demonstrations and a memorable sit-in with infants and toddlers and prams right in the middle of the road, which disrupted traffic for miles around. And they won, or half won, for while the road was widened at some points, it remained narrow at others.

Since then they have become rather obsessed with the matter of traffic. People are courteous, congenial and friendly but mention the word roads and they undergo a transformation. Their eyes redden, their hair bristles, their skin turns scaly, and their voice is reduced to a hoarse croak. And this in broad daylight. I daren't think what could happen when the moon is full.

They believe that there is no such thing as a road improvement, for improvements mean more traffic and more traffic could threaten what is left of the Suburb. They are now bracing themselves to

316

challenge a scheme which would ease the congestion on the nearby North Circular Road.

Now their hostility to traffic would be commendable if they went about their work on foot, horse-back, bicycle, or even on camel, and never made use of a private vehicle; but, in fact, they rarely move 10 yards without a car. And if other parts of London had as many cars per household as the Suburb, all movement in the capital and its surrounding areas would come to a halt.

There are some one-car families in the Suburb. I belong to one myself, except that, given the state of my vehicle, we are more like a half-a-car family. But I know of families with five cars, four are not uncommon, while the norm seems to be three—a Volvo for dad, a Metro for mum, and a banger for the kids. Even the au-pairs have cars and, but for the jogging craze and the fact that most families also have dogs, one would rarely set eyes on anyone actually using his legs. (The dogs, incidentally, also do their bit for pollution, and more than their bit, and if one can hardly use the roads because of the traffic, one can hardly use the pavements because of the dogs.)

In many a street the attractive façades of the houses and the lovely vistas between them are half hidden by a solid and unprepossessing wall of vehicles. They're a nuisance when they're parked and a bigger nuisance when they move. While the zealots have been busy manning the ramparts with the slogan "they shall not pass", the place is slowly being choked by the press of its own cars.

The Suburb, in other words, probably contributes more to traffic congestion than any other district of its size in London, yet it constitutes one of the most effective anti-road lobbies in the country. What they are really saying is: We are not against traffic as such, we are only against it in, or near, our blessed plot.

The car must get through somewhere and if traffic through the Suburb is to be limited while the number of vehicles continues to grow, it means merely that adjoining districts must carry more than their share of the increased flow.

Most of the local residents I know tend to be people with liberal sympathies. Some vote Labour, many vote for the Alliance, and they would be aghast at the suggestion that they are preserving their amenities at the expense of their less fortunate neighbours. They are, however, doing just that.

Everybody wants good roads and everybody needs them, but nobody wants them through their own neighbourhoods, and they are

317

therefore pushed through the area of least resistance. Urban motorways, for example, are generally cut through working-class districts: not only is the land cheaper but the working-classes are less equipped to stop them.

I have alighted on Hampstead Garden Suburb because I've lived there for 20 years and happen to know it well, but I imagine that what I have said is also true of Chigwell, Dulwich, Chiswick, Barnes—and any other attractive area of London. For if I may state Bermant's Law: the determination of any district to limit the flow of vehicles is in exact ratio to the number of vehicles per household. The more cars they have, the more they're against traffic.

One man's amenities are another man's nuisance and conservation has become another word for selfishness.

London Daily News, 16 May 1987

What's in a Name?

WHAT'S IN A name? A lot when it's as long as "The Charles Kalms, Henry Ronson, Immanuel College". A school by any other name would not occupy half as much note-paper. To say this is no reflection on the school itself, which is due to open in September and which, given the care and attention lavished on it, promises to be one of the best in the country. I also appreciate the need to recognise generosity and effort, but a great many people have played a part in bringing the scheme to fruition, including Simon Caplan, Trevor Chinn, Denis Felsenstein, Leo Grahame, Henry Knobil, Ronald Metzger and Fred Worms, to mention a few.

I, too, feel entitled to some recognition, for I have not uttered one word against the scheme, or, what's more important, for it, and if we are to give credit where credit is due, the school should be called "The Chaim Bermant, Simon Caplan, Trevor Chinn, Denis Felsenstein, Leo Grahame, Henry Knobil, Ronald Metzger, Bill Brewer, Jan Stewer, Peter Gurney, Peter Davey, Dan'l Whiddon, Harry Hawk, Charles Kalms, Henry Ronson, Immanuel College. "And if that should be too much of a mouthful, why not simply call it "Old Uncle Tom Cobbleigh's and All"?

Jews are a fairly generous people, but in many instances their generosity is combined with a craving for immortality, if not for themselves, then at least for their loved ones, and I should imagine that when King Solomon built the Temple he was tempted to call it the David and Bathsheba House of God. I once visited an American hospital where every immovable object—other than the long-term patients—had a plaque on it. Similarly the beautiful gardens of the Givath Ram campus of the Hebrew University are strewn with boulders bearing the name of this or that benefactor who paid for the upkeep of this or that flower-bed.

The most favoured form of immortality, however, is the foundation stone which has nothing remotely to do with the actual foundations of a building, which are necessarily deep in the ground, whereas the foundation stones of lore are well, sometimes very well, above it. Legend hath it—and if it hathn't then I'm about to provide it—that the Tower of Babel, as originally designed, was of modest proportions and that it only reached up to the skies because everyone who contributed to the building fund insisted on the laying of a foundation stone in memory of their parents.

About 30 years ago I attended the foundation stone ceremony of a new synagogue and they laid so many stones that by the time the ceremony was over the building was half complete. To which I must add that synagogues are not a good buy when it comes to immortality, if only because they have such a short life, and many a foundation stone laid amid great pomp and ceremony 50 or 60 years ago, now graces a warehouse or mosque.

Maimonides lists different degrees of benevolence in ascending order of merit. Those who give, but give reluctantly. Those who give less than they should, but do so cheerfully. Those who give, but only after they are importuned. Those who give without being importuned. And those who give anonymously. I am not sure if Maimonides had it right. One of the most generous men I knew was also one of the meanest. He parted with considerable sums, but with gritted teeth, as if he was parting with blood, and indeed, he would have parted with blood more cheerfully than with money, but he gave because as a devout Jew he felt obliged to do so. His meanness was the measure of his generosity.

Maimonides, however, was absolutely right in believing that charity at its most sublime is anonymous, but there is nothing ignoble, and much that is praiseworthy, in wishing to perpetuate a name.

Nor is the instinct limited to Jews. In 1349 an East Anglian clergyman, Thomas Gonville, founded a college in Cambridge and named it after himself. Two centuries later it was enlarged by the physician John Caius who added his name to it, and it has since been known as Gonville and Caius. Later benefactors, however, did not follow his example otherwise Gonville and Caius (or "Gon" as it is popularly known among undergraduates) would have an even longer name than The Charles Kalms, Henry Ronson, Immanuel College.

Not that anyone will call it that, and given the tendency to abbreviate everything, it will probably be known as Manny College.

Jewish Chronicle, 23 February 1990

Stolen Kisses

THOU SHALT NOT kiss thy husband, nor thy wife, thy father, nor thy mother, thy sons or daughters, or friends, or menservants, or maidservants, nor the stranger within thy gates—not even the au-pair—at least not while they are "within the sanctuary of the synagogue".

I am not quoting the laws of Moses, but the nearest thing to them—the laws of Rabbi Benjamin Rabinowitz, of the Edgware Synagogue.

I wish someone had pronounced on the matter earlier, for my childhood was blighted by kisses. I would live in fear of marauding aunts who would descend from nowhere, clasp me in a stifling embrace to their ample bosoms and drench me with kisses.

One couldn't fight against such things and one accepted them resignedly, like measles or whooping-cough, as one of the penalties of childhood. And that was in *der heim*.

In Britain, I discovered something worse. When I was a lad, it was mandatory (and in some congregations may still be mandatory) for the barmitzvah boy to go up to the ladies' gallery the minute he had finished the haftara and kiss his female relatives in full view of the congregation.

It was by far the hardest part of his ordeal, and only when it was over could he come downstairs again and declare with conviction: "Today, I am man."

As a result, I approached my own barmitzvah with an apprehension verging on dread, and when the day finally came, I dashed upstairs, closed my eyes, thought of Lithuania, and ran down the line of relatives as one might run one's finger down a piano, until I tumbled at about middle C over an aunt with buck-teeth.

321

In my anxiety to get it over and done with, I even kissed their silver foxes—which should tell you how old I am.

If one is really fond of people, they tend to rouse cannibalistic rather than erotic instincts. One could quite literally eat them, and kissing is about as near as one can get to eating somebody without doing him or her any harm—and as Jews are lavish eaters, they tend to be lavish kissers.

Nor are they always satisfied with a kiss. Small children have to face the hazard of the affectionate pinch on the cheek, which leaves them black and blue and which is really an attempt to tear away whole chunks of flesh.

One must admit that the weight of Jewish tradition is with Rabbi Rabinowitz, but in many Reform and Liberal congregations it is customary for the rabbis to stand by the door after the service and to kiss his female congregants as they emerge. Presumably female rabbis kiss only male congregants (which is possibly why they have female rabbis).

I don't know if it's one of the perks of their calling, or one of the penalties, but I know of one synagogue where the practice was stopped after the rabbi caught herpes. I much prefer rubbing noses as a form of greeting, but there I have a natural advantage.

There isn't much kissing in the Old Testament (as distinct from the New) and what there is of it is mainly a matter of men kissing men, which I would say (though the rabbis don't) is a good deal more reprehensible than men kissing women.

The only exception I know of comes early in Genesis, when Jacob kisses Rachel as soon as he meets her. It is a beautifully impulsive gesture, but Jacob, taken aback by his own action, "lifted up his voice and wept", out of either shock or contrition. Rachel must have been made of sterner stuff, or she was used to the experience, but either way she did not shed a tear.

(J. H. Hertz, in his commentary on the Pentateuch, slightly scandal-ised by the thought that one of our forefathers could have kissed a woman long before she was his wife, argued that he kissed her on the hand, presumably in the manner made fashionable by Menachem Begin—which would suggest that Jacob was a Pole.)

Some rabbis condemn kissing because it could lead to lewdness; others condemn it as a form of lewdness in itself; but there is nothing erotic about a peck on the cheek (especially a hairy cheek), and kissing has lost all significance as a form of intimacy because it has become so indiscriminate.

Rabbi Rabinowitz's strictures may thus do something to rehabilitate the kiss, for no pleasure is really pleasurable until it is forbidden.

Jewish Chronicle, 23 September 1988

Dead of Night

I RECENTLY CAME across a line from Charles Wolfe's poem, "The Burial of Sir John Moore at Corunna"—"We buried him darkly at the dead of night . . ."—and it made me wonder if Sir John had been seen to by the Jerusalem chevra kadisha.

Jewish custom demands prompt burial out of respect for the dead, which seems reasonable enough, but the belief seems to have spread that the prompter the burial, the greater the respect. In Jerusalem, people are snatched from their deathbed the moment the last breath has left their body, if not before, and hurried at the double to their graves.

Hearses do not travel with police outriders and sirens blaring, or at least not yet, but in the meantime they can be a good deal quicker than ambulances, which brings Sir John Moore to mind again:

"Not a drum was heard, not a funeral note,
As his corpse to the rampart we hurried."

There is a custom in Jerusalem—I don't know how it arose or why it hasn't been suppressed—that a cadaver cannot be left in the city overnight, so that if someone dies on Shabbat or yomtov, or towards evening, or even at night, he will be buried, like Sir John Moore, during the hours of darkness.

This may not make much difference to the deceased (provided, of course, he is dead in the first place, which, given the rush, is by no means certain), but it adds greatly to the distress of the bereaved, who have to phone around frantically to let people know of the arrangements—which, with the vagaries of Israel's telephone system, is no small matter.

Many people cannot get to the funeral in time, others cannot get

324

there at all, and it can be a nightmare for all concerned. I know one man who is so disturbed by the local customs that he has solemnly sworn he wouldn't be seen dead anywhere in Jerusalem.

I once had the melancholy duty to attend a funeral near the Jerusalem bus station, and thus near the busiest junction in the city. I rushed there by taxi and, as all the approaches were paralysed by the Saturday-night traffic, I continued the journey on foot. It was one of the most bizarre experiences of my life. The night was dark and blustery. There were no illuminations in the cemetery itself, which is a vast, wind-blown escarpment, but in the distance I could see a shadowy group with torches and candles clustered round an open grave.

I quickly made my way towards it and, to atone for being late, I grabbed a spade and set to briskly to throw earth over the coffin; and it was only when I looked up that I found myself staring into a circle of bewildered eyes blinking in the candlelight, while on all sides there were anxious murmurs of *Ver iz er? Ver iz er?* Who is he? Who is he?

I had come to the wrong funeral and my sudden and unannounced descent, together with my grim visage, may have given the impression that I was the angel of death.

I don't suppose I did any harm, for I have in my time also come to the wrong wedding (it was in the Dorchester, and I was enjoying the reception immensely, until the Sheikh of Dubai entered and I thought that either he was in the wrong place, or I was), but it was still frustrating and, in fact, rather frightening.

I eventually found my way to the right funeral, in another corner of the cemetery. The deceased was by then safely in the ground and the funeral party had left, but there were still stragglers, vague, shadowy figures, stumbling in the darkness amid the stones. One had to step warily, not only because one was on sacred ground, but because there were any number of open graves about, and I could imagine that if one toppled in, the chevra kadisha would get to work with their spades without asking too many questions. But, after what seemed like hours (though in reality they were minutes), I gradually made my way out of the city of the dead and into the city of the living. Never again. I have told my friends (both of them) that if they intend to expire in Jerusalem, they should not expect to find me by their bier.

One hesitates to criticise the chevra kadisha, for they perform their melancholy task with great dedication. But what's the hurry? Should they not give as much thought to the living as they do to the dead?

Jewish Chronicle, 24 July 1987

'Ullo! 'Ullo!

THERE WAS A time when there were two books which could be found in almost every household in Britain—the Bible and Shakespeare. These were ousted long ago by the "London Telephone Directory", whose scholarly S–Z volume had just been revised.

The L.T.D. pioneered the paperback revolution. Its first issue was published in 1880. Skimpy, hardly more than a pamphlet, it ran to 702 copies. Today it is produced in editions of over three million and they are snapped up as soon as they are in print. Not even Bond can claim such popularity.

This spectacular success is well deserved. The Book is clean, wholesome, and one will not find among the 2,500 pages of the entire four volumes a single line unfit for the eyes of one's children, or even one's servants. What the Postmaster-General permits on the BBC he atones for in the L.T.D. One will not find any "Mr" in it, or "Mrs", or "Miss". It has banished sex to the point of banishing genders. It is the sort of book that may be read to the assembled family after dinner on a Sunday. It is ideal for bed-time, for nothing is so conducive to innocent sleep.

There are people who still use the L.T.D. as a guide to telephone numbers. I do myself from time to time. We are all addicted to archaisms. In every modern man there is a John Betjeman trying to get out. Most telephone subscribers, however, have long ago reconciled themselves to the fact that the numbers they have in their directory bear little relation to the numbers they are likely to receive when they actually dial. If the L.T.D. has a function it is surely as literature, and as such it deserves serious attention, for does it not represent the ultimate direction of the novel?

We are all familiar with the novel without a plot. The L.T.D. goes a stage further. It is a novel without a plot and without dialogue. By way of compensation it abounds in characters—nearly one million of them.

And what characters they are, knights, baronets, peers of the realm, bishops and archbishops, C.M.G.s, C.B.E.s, distinguished dons, senior civil servants.

The authorship of the L.T.D., like that of the Authorised Version, is anonymous, but the *dramatis personae* and the general prose style suggest that the author might be the Parliamentary Secretary to the Ministry of Technology, *alias* Lord Snow. Consider some of the names—Crichton-Stewart, Craig-Vettwinkel, Crawley-Boevey, Stott Lane, Stout-Kerr—they evoke the very corridors of power which they must daily tread.

And all this without a baroque flourish, or any concession to the stylists. The names are left to speak for themselves, and they tell us volumes. Adjectives are few, and usually truncated, with upholsterers reduced to "uphols", plumbers to "pbrs" and fruiterers—and only here does the L.T.D. verge upon the *risqué*—to "frtrs".

The L.T.D. though *avant-garde* in some ways, is traditional in others. It begins determinedly at the beginning with the "A.1 Café, 349 Montague rd N9" and continues without deviation to "Zywicki E. M., 47 Argyle rd W13". This is the sort of book which should be dipped in, and in this way one can best sense the dramas throbbing in almost every page. Take the nine Szczpiniskis of Earls Court, for example, and their good neighbour Sczpanski, and Sczpanowski of West Hampstead, and Szczpankowski of Hammersmith and Szczeribiski of Putney, and a hundred like them, whittling their days away in spelling—"No, not Shapinooski. Szczpankowski!—S-Z-C-Z . . . ." How many have wilted under their polysyllabic burden and melted away into Smith?

The unpronounceable can sometimes be less painful than the pronounceable. Consider the daily embarrassments which Aage Thaarup must encounter:

"What did you say your name was?"

"Thaarup."

"Thaarup yourthelf."

One is fascinated by the Frenches, the Ffrenches, and, above all, the ffrenches, to say nothing of the Fords, the Ffords and the ffords.

I have a theory that the first fford was but a Ford with a stutter. But perhaps not—I know several Finkelsteins with a stutter, but not one ffinklestein. What a difference an "F" makes. What distinction it adds to an otherwise common name.

The Saints and the Sts continue to abound, which is rather surprising, because I always thought that the originals were either non-existent, as St George, or celibate.

Not every name that should be in the L.T.D. is in it. There is a great deal of snobbery connected with being ex-directory. It is the "in" thing to be out, like not having a car, and I suspect that most names which are kept out would mean nothing to anyone save their owners. They are like the countless unknowns who try to hide their anonymity behind a pair of sun-glasses.

Readers of the A–D volume will no doubt recall the exhilarating experience of coming suddenly and unexpectedly upon Buckingham Palace, biding its place in the queue between N. S. Buckingham of Deptford and the Buckingham Palace Road Baths. If her Majesty (WHI 4832), the Archbishop of Canterbury (WAT 1313) and Harrods (SLO 1234) are not afraid to stand and be counted, need the L.T.D. pander to the snobbery of the unknown unknown?

I must add that the whole appearance of the L.T.D. is shoddy and drab, and without one illustration to relieve its grey columns of print, which look like rain upon a dirty window. The "Subscriber Trunk Dialling Book", which, one was tempted to hope, might even appear as a coloured supplement, is no improvement. Could the next edition not carry a picture of the new Postmistress-General?

Observer, 26 September 1969

Final Exit

CAN IT REALLY be true that Edmonton is to close? It's the cemetery of cemeteries and is to London what the Mount of Olives is to Jerusalem. There is an old saying (which I've only just made up), if you're not buried in Edmonton, you haven't lived. There is no better place, certainly in Britain, to be gathered unto one's fathers. If Edmonton dies, can the Federation of Synagogues live, for the two were, and are, indissolubly linked in the public imagination? The Federation does, in fact, have another cemetery at Rainham in Essex, but that, to coin an expression, is only for the *nouveau morts*. The older families opt for Edmonton and wouldn't be seen dead in Rainham.

People used to belong to the Federation because its synagogues were more heimisch than those of the United Synagogue, but this is no longer the case, for while US edifices are getting smaller those of the Federation are getting bigger. The Federation also claims to be more Orthodox, but it wasn't even in its hey-day, and it certainly isn't now, though it has always felt compelled to make a greater show of Orthodoxy so that its rabbis still wear black instead of mufti, and its cemeteries are not too well maintained; for a well-maintained cemetery, with carefully-tended footpaths and neatly cropped lawns, is a little like a churchyard and smacks of *chukat hagoy*.

The finances of the Federation are decidedly un-Orthodox, depending as they do on its burial society—if an hon. officer of the Federation wishes you long life, he means it (so, incidentally, do people in the insurance trade)—and it attracts members because it still offers the prospect of a comparatively inexpensive burial.

London Jewry is blessed with many cemeteries, Willesden, Bushey, Waltham Abbey, Hoop Lane, to mention but a few. Willesden, being the last resting place of our Chief Rabbis and the Rothschilds, offers

329

Chaim Bermant

the most select company. Bushey is the most fashionable. Waltham Abbey is the most beautifully landscaped, but it has non-Jewish associations and to say that one's parents are buried in Waltham Abbey can give a misleading impression. The Sephardi cemetery in Hoop Lane is the most accessible, but what with the Reform cemetery on the one side, and the Golders Green crematorium on the other, it has non-kosher associations, and even if one has no fixed ideas about the next world, one would not care to be buried near people who don't think it's there in the first place.

Moreover, with so many termini crammed into one narrow lane, parking is deadly. One must add, in fairness, that one can get to Hoop Lane by Underground, but there is something mildly disrespectful about going to a funeral by public transport, and all things considered one is better off in Edmonton. God knows (and who better) that Edmonton was not, and is not, the poshest cemetery in the country, but it was the best known, and most popular, and the one most immediately associated with expiry. In a sense it was the Upper House of the Federation (and from what one understands it is probably more lively than the lower one), but many an individual who never set foot in a Federation synagogue was eventually to have both feet in Edmonton because, *in extremis*, it was also open to non-members. *Kol dichfin* . . . What will happen when it closes?

However, where there's life there's hope and Mr Leidig Gayer (or should that be Leibush Gayer?) treasurer of the Federation burial society, has promised that funerals will continue for members with reserved plots, "and in special cases". He didn't say what sort of cases he had in mind, but one presumes he meant coffins, though with the Federation of Synagogues one never knows. He also assures us that members had nothing to worry about, for a "part-time grave-digger would be employed", and that burials would be carried out on the same day "if necessary", meaning, I suppose, if one is dead.

The most reassuring part of his statement, however, was that the upkeep of the place would be unaffected, because for those who are fond of small mammals, Edmonton, with its lush vegetation and thick undergrowth, is not only a cemetery but has something of the nature of a safari park.

As William Shakespeare very nearly put it:
"This blessed plot, this earth, this realm, this Edmonton."

Jewish Chronicle, 13 January 1989